Even June Cleaver Would Forget the Juice Box

Cut Yourself Some Slack
(and Still Raise Great Kids) in the
Age of Extreme Parenting

Even June Cleaver Would Forget the Juice Box

Ann Dunnewold, Ph.D.

Foreword by Sandi Kahn Shelton, Author,
A Piece of Normal and *What Comes After Crazy!*

Health Communications, Inc.
Deerfield Beach, Florida

www.hcibooks.com

This publication is designed to provide accurate and authoritative information with regard to the subject matter covered. It is sold with the understanding that the publisher and/or author are not engaged in rendering psychological, medical, or other professional services. If expert assistance or counseling is needed, the services of a competent professional should be sought. The persons described herein are composite examples and represent no real or actual persons.

Permissions

Excerpts from "I Killed June Cleaver," from *I Killed June Cleaver: Modern Moms Shatter the Myth of Perfect Parenting,* edited by Deborah Werksman (Naperville, IL: Sourcebooks, 1999), used with permission of Colleen Kilcoyne.

Margaret Mead quote used courtesy of The Institute for Intercultural Studies, Inc., New York.

Excerpts from "Say You Want a Revolution," *Brain, Child,* Fall 2005, used with permission of Stephanie Wilkinson, editor.

Excerpts from "A Nation of Wimps" by Hara Estroff Marano, reprinted with permission from *Psychology Today* magazine, copyright ©2004 Sussex Publishers, Inc.

Library of Congress Cataloging-in-Publication Data

Dunnewold, Ann.

Even June Cleaver would forget the juice box : cut yourself some slack (and raise great kids) in the age of extreme parenting / Ann Dunnewold.

p.   cm.

Includes bibliographical references and index.

ISBN-13: 978-0-7573-0546-7 (trade paper)

ISBN-10: 0-7573-0546-6 (trade paper)

1. Parenting. 2. Mothers. I. Title.

HQ769.D855 2007

649'.1—dc22   2007001137

Publisher: Health Communications, Inc.
3201 S.W. 15th Street
Deerfield Beach, FL 33442-8190

Cover design by Amy C. King
Interior design and formatting by Lawna Patterson Oldfield

*To all the women
who stumble down this path
of parenting with me*

Contents

Acknowledgments

Thanks to my husband, daughters, sisters, mother, and friends for your patience and help throughout the creation of this work. Maybe I practiced what I preach too much while working on this, for no human being came first for a while. Thanks especially to Shirley Smith Duke, Vivienne McNeny, Kathy Yank, Janet Hilbun, Dianna Hubbard, and Becky McKee for reading, brainstorming, and feedback. Special thanks to Larry McNeny, for the help with connections and the inspiration to follow his lead. To Cynthia Curry, I owe great appreciation for her phrase "little nutty piece." And thanks to Barbara Mandle and Annalisa Pask for cheering me on all the way.

Thanks to Judith Warner, author of *Perfect Madness: Motherhood in the Age of Anxiety,* and Susan Douglas and Meredith Michaels, authors of *The Mommy Myth: The Idealization of Motherhood and How It Has Undermined All Women.* This book could not have been written without the inspiring, entertaining, and lucid explorations of the issues facing mothers that these authors offer. Thanks, also, to Andrea Buchanan, author of *Mother Shock: Loving Every (Other) Minute of It,* and to the contributors and author (again, Andrea Buchanan) of *It's a Boy: Women Writers on Raising Sons; It's a Girl:*

Women Writers on Raising Daughters; and *Literary Mama: Reading for the Maternally Inclined.* Thanks also to Cathi Hanauer, editor, and the contributors of *The Bitch in the House,* and to Camille Peri and Kate Moses, editors, and the contributors of *Mothers Who Think.* By putting together writings about the truth in women's experiences, you have paved the way for more honesty about motherhood. My heartfelt appreciation to you all.

Heartfelt thanks to Sandi Kahn Shelton, author of so much continually hilarious and honest writing about motherhood, for contributing the foreword for this work. Your belief in me and this topic is profoundly appreciated.

And many thanks to Allison Janse and her associates at Health Communications, Inc., for believing in this idea, making it better with such valuable feedback, and making it happen.

Foreword

My mother and I used to have an amusing little game we'd sometimes play in our long-distance telephone calls to each other. We called it "Who Had the Easier Era for Raising Kids?"

My mother, who brought us up in the 1960s, thinks that raising children in my time must have been something akin to heaven on earth, to hear her go on about it. "You gals today have it made: microwaves so you never have to spend any time at all in the kitchen, disposable diapers, cell phones, electronic thermometers that go in kids' ears instead of trying to get them to keep their mouths closed. And you don't have to constantly run in and check on sleeping babies, because the baby monitor lets you hear every sound. And, besides that, you can talk on the phone to your friends in peace because your kids have entire television networks devoted to entertaining them. And now there are good daycare centers and after-school programs and organized sports teams, even for little ones . . ."

I let her go on for quite a while, knowing I can always stop her with two words anytime I choose: Mommy Guilt.

They didn't have so much of that in her day, you see.

Don't get me wrong. I'm the first to admit that being a mom

without disposable diapers, cell phones, and a baby monitor would be tough beyond belief, but I also believe something else even more strongly—that my mother and her generation were blissfully ignorant of all the ways that mothers could be blamed for all that goes wrong.

Oh, sure, they may have had to hang out longer in the kitchen (no microwave to "nuke" the frozen dinner, after all), but they certainly didn't get the heat that modern mothers get. Hard as it is to believe, moms back then *didn't* spend twenty-six hours a week in the car either, driving us to soccer practice, religious education classes, art and music programs, gymnastics lessons, and then off to tutors who would help us score higher on achievement tests. They didn't wring their hands over the fact that we might be bored or "not living up to our potential." In fact, heaven help you if you complained to your mother that you were bored; you'd find yourself cleaning out your closet so fast your head would spin.

I'm not trying to make it sound like everything was all peaches and cream for women in that 1960's world of parenthood; far from it. Not only did they have to wear high heels on most occasions—even in their own homes, if the sitcoms are to be believed—but husbands in those days were no help at all. Men were allowed to come home and slouch off to their easy chairs, never being expected to cook dinner or change the baby. But what I have come to realize—and what Ann Dunnewold has touched on so beautifully in her interviews and anecdotes with real moms in this book—is that somehow making things Absolutely Perfect for children just wasn't part of the job description of parenting back then.

In fact, come to think of it, there wasn't even any such word as "parenting." It wasn't a verb yet. "To parent" wasn't something you *did*. A parent was something you were—just the way you might also simultaneously be considered a wife, a sister, a daughter, a good swimmer, a voracious reader, or . . . a person.

Maybe that's the difference. Mothers were allowed to be just people in June Cleaver's day—imperfect, busy, preoccupied, loving, frazzled sometimes, but human above all. They nagged, they cajoled, they yelled, they threatened us to get us to do our homework, and then they confidently stood by their decisions to withhold dessert and TV time when we didn't. And just forget about trying to make them feel guilty by crying or telling them they were too mean and that you were going to grow up to hate them. Saying those things didn't win you much sympathy or even an appointment with a child psychologist; chances are your mom said, "Oh, well, too bad. Sorry you feel that way. Maybe you'll change your mind."

I don't think that, until the last few decades, mothers even had the idea that parenthood was something they could get *wrong*. It was just part of life. When we threw tantrums in public, our mothers might have been embarrassed or even angry with us, but the whole world didn't turn and point a finger at *them* over it. It was just the way children behaved at a certain age, and the mother's job was to nip that behavior in the bud, but not to hate herself for being unable to prevent it in the first place. Chances are, she got sympathetic smiles and nods of recognition from other moms. Certainly nobody in the immediate area said to her what a woman said to *me* when my three-year-old had a meltdown in the grocery store

because I wouldn't let her go behind the meat counter and disman-
tle the chopping machine: "Why don't you just buy the poor little
darling some candy? You moms today just don't mind if your children act like brats, not thinking how hard it is on the rest of us!"

Tell the truth now. How many of us knew that the day would
come when we would be so frazzled with trying to make life perfect
that we can't think straight anymore? For years I wrote a humor column about family life for *Working Mother* magazine. I wrote about
the time my daughter tried to get me to pour out the soy sauce so
she could drink her apple juice in that bottle instead of her own (I
didn't do it), and the times my youngest, at two, insisted that I push
two rubber bands in her doll stroller around and around the dining
room table while she critiqued my gait (I did do that), and about the
thousands of moments when I thought we were the only family who
couldn't get through a family dinner without at least two glasses of
milk spilling, several people crying, and one major dispute about
whether children should be expected to eat foods that were not
technically noodles.

The odd thing is, I didn't intend to be writing a humor column. I
honestly didn't think it was all that funny that I had a three-year-old
who came into my bed every night, dragging along her stuffed
bunny, a piece of chalk, and an old broken toaster she'd hauled out of
the trash. I was bothered by the fact that I couldn't even take a bath
without being interrupted at least five times by people needing me to
find their orthodontic rubber bands or their lost homework assignments or a clean pair of underwear. ("Sorry—none of that is here
with me in the tub!" I'd call out.) Here I had always thought I'd be

a relaxed, loving mom, always available, always engaged—after all, I dearly adored my children—and yet, more often than I had ever thought possible, I was feeling overwhelmed. One day, at work, I looked down at my feet and discovered I had on two completely different shoes—shoes that didn't even resemble each other. Where had my mind been while I was getting dressed that morning?

The dirty little secret of motherhood is that taking care of children *is* at times exhausting, it's boring, and, outside of a few sterling moments, it *never* feels like something that is going Just Right. What I heard back from other mothers who read my column surprised me: they, too, were out of their minds. It turned out that *nobody* was coping very well, and yet we all felt the need to pretend that things were just going along swimmingly at all times. We all think we're the only ones whose shoes don't match and whose kids don't sleep in their own beds, or who demand to wear their Darth Vader costume to preschool day after day after day and cry when you say no.

The women in this book—none of them June Cleavers, just everyday frazzled and stressed-out moms—give quite a different picture of parenthood from that of our mothers' era, one that I, sadly, recognize from my own experience and those of my friends: a push to be always on top of things, always in control, always with our finger on the alarm button—ready to jump in at a moment's notice and redefine life for our kids. Arrange a teacher conference over the "C" grade on the history paper; drive across town at dinnertime to purchase the fabric for the medieval costume for the clothespins; hire the clown and the pony *and* the professional birthday party manager for our six-year-old's party; call all ten references for the new babysitter *because better safe than sorry.*

The moms who have told their stories to Dunnewold are struggling mightily with society's message that they can, and *must*, control all aspects of their children's lives in order to make sure that they are perfectly efficient, functioning, happy, and fulfilled individuals—a flawless product. Deep down, of course, we all know there's no such thing as a flawless *anything*, much less a human—but when society is whispering in your ear, "Just try harder, give more of your time and attention, do more projects, bake fancier cupcakes, throw more lavish birthday parties, sign them up for more enrichment classes,"—well, would it *kill* you to work harder and give more and do more planning? After all, this is for the sake of your *child*.

Fortunately, this book doesn't just lay the problem out. Instead, Dunnewold shows us how to let ourselves return to that blessed state of being "just people"—not superwomen, nor extreme mothers training for the Olympics of Parenthood. In her delightful, conversational, comforting style, she tells us just how to go about lightening up our lives, how to haul our standards back to the realm of realism, and how to use self-talk to help us judge ourselves less harshly.

The good news is that, by realizing the pressures we have unknowingly submitted to, we can redefine what kind of mothers we want to be. Every mother will recognize herself and her friends here. Even if you wouldn't dream of doing your child's homework assignments or spending all your downtime driving your kids from one activity to another, you still get bombarded by the messages of perfectionism that are pervasive in our culture. Even when we know better, we all get sucked in by that haunting feeling that we alone are the imperfect ones, just barely trudging through the mud of everyday life while in all the other households on the block, other families—those with the beautiful homemade cupcakes and the perfect test scores—are soaring to the heights of familial love and bliss.

Perhaps the best gift in Dunnewold's book is the knowledge that when we relax our own standards and embrace a less pressured life, we become even better at helping our children find their own happiness. When you let your children in on the secret that it's okay to be wrong sometimes, and that the "perfectly good life," with all its maddening imperfection, can be fun, can be surprising, can ultimately be more joyful and real, you are providing them with a blueprint for life that will bring them satisfaction and happiness they can actually attain.

And that's worth a lot more than never ever forgetting the juice boxes, in my opinion.

Sandi Kahn Shelton

Author of *What Comes After Crazy* and *A Piece of Normal*

www.sandishelton.com

Part One

The Problem

"Help! I Can't Keep Up with the Mommy Olympics!"

The Collective Call for a New Paradigm of "Perfectly Good Mothers"

Julia woke up with a start at 5:00 AM the morning of her three-year-old's Easter party at preschool. She had promised to bake bunny cookies! Bleary-eyed and exhausted, Julia rooted in the fridge until she found the slice-and-bake cookie package. She slapped a few jelly beans around the preformed bunny design on each cookie and tossed them in the oven. Carrying the cookie plate into school hours later, Julia met up with Kristy, flaunting a beribboned basket of adorable bunny cookies—peanut-shaped sandwich cookies, chocolate sprinkles mounted with icing for the little beady eyes, mini marshmallows for tails, even tiny slivers of licorice for the whiskers. Amelia clearly had spent hours. Julia's stomach sank; she never measured up in this mother business.

Annette drives twenty-six hours a week, shuttling her three children to and from private school, soccer, fencing lessons, voice lessons, orthodontist appointments, and church activities. Dinner is consumed so often in the car that, on a rare weekend evening when she was able to get all three children and her husband seated for dinner at the same time, five-year-old Corey would not stop swaying in his chair at the table. "I'm just pretending I'm in the car, Mom!" he protested when she told him to sit still.

Karen has two children in college. When Heather and Sam are home, Karen stays up until all hours, waiting for her kids—even to 3:00 or 4:00 AM. It doesn't seem to matter that she has to work the next day at 9:00 AM. When the kids are at school, Karen talks to each at least five times daily, fielding calls such as "Can you send me quarters so I can do my laundry?" "This French professor really is a jerk," and "The chili was really bad in the caf tonight." "I got this bill from *Us Weekly* magazine—what do I do with it?" "Listen to this final paragraph for my psych paper, Mom—please help me with it. Can I e-mail it to you and you can rewrite it and send it back?"

For more than twenty-five years, I have worked as a psychologist specializing in women's issues, particularly postpartum depression and the transition to parenting. Every day in my office and my life as a mom, I hear outrageous stories like these. Women struggle with increasing pressure to do the right thing as parents, and they get sucked up into extreme parenting: Allowing a child to sleep in the parents' bed until she is nearly as tall as they are. "Touching up" the display board for the science fair, to make it a "bit neater." An eight-month-old baby who won't play on his own, not even for ten minutes, because Mom, Dad, or Nanny is always bouncing him, tickling him, reading him books, to the point of everyone's exhaustion. Something is wrong with this picture of American parenting.

What do we all strive for? Achievement. Happiness. Smart kids. Healthy families. Social and financial advancement. Question any parent today, and you will get a similar answer that sounds like the Declaration of Independence: life, liberty, and the pursuit of happiness. When was the last time you heard a friend or neighbor say that what he or she really wanted out of life was *less?* "Oh, yes, as long as they are not in jail I will have done a good job as a mom." That's about as common a sentiment as admiring the parenting techniques of Norman Bates's mom. We all want more for our children: a Ph.D., a hefty 401K, a McMansion, the CEO job, a twenty-five-hour work week. Only the best for our kids. Who ever heard of wanting the worst?

Perfection Parenting 101

The general wisdom says work harder to get what you want. There is certainly nothing wrong with hard work. It is what makes ourselves, our families, and our country strong. In the last decade or two in my practice, the "work harder" part began to apply to parenting. If our goal is the ultimate adult, then it is our job to get our children there: we need to execute the parenting perfectly. We need to control it all. You had better provide the perfect childhood, or your child will be writing a tell-all best seller à la *Mommy Dearest.* What would that ideal childhood entail? Organic snacks and meals, the latest wardrobe necessities, attendance at all the top schools. Enrollment in the trendiest lessons. The latest Harry Potter book or *Star Wars* film at the midnight release. The envied sports car on the sixteenth birthday; camping out to score the latest video game system the day it appears in stores. The right number of politically correct bedtime stories. Sacrificing your rare spare moments for your child's whims. Always reasoning calmly with your child, even when you just discovered the walls are covered with crayon art. No sugar or red dye number two. The list is endless.

Parents aren't simply driving themselves in the parental role for their own amusement. All this pursuit of perfection is not just for the parents' sake, so parents can pat themselves on the back. The need for total control by the parent is to turn out a flawless product: the happy, successful child. This child will sleep through the night by six weeks; speak in full sentences by one year. This is the child who will play select soccer by age five, or Tchaikovsky on the violin by age six. The sweet, loving child who has never uttered "I hate you—you are ruining my life," whether at four or fourteen. The angelic child who is friends with everyone, even if that means you have three birthday parties to attend each and every weekend. The child who will never be in the headlines for some heinous deed, where the sidebar quotes neighbors: "He was always the quietest, nicest boy," while speculating about his dysfunctional home life.

Extreme Parenting Is Born

Today, only extreme is worth watching or doing: extreme sports, extreme makeovers. *Extreme* meaning over-the-top, challenging, with mind-boggling achievement the result. If ultimate success is the goal for our kids, extreme parenting must be the road to get there. Extreme sports or makeovers require giving something your all, pushing the envelope, striving for that adrenaline-inducing action. Every ounce of your being must be poured into an extreme endeavor to succeed. Only when you are lying in the gravel, sweating and spent, will you have done it. Sounds like some moms I know, on the playground after a busy playdate.

Yet throughout this extreme pursuit of perfection and total control there's one complicating fallacy: As a parent striving to give one's child a perfect childhood, messy human emotion tends to get in the way. A crying child is hardly the picture of perfection. The children we want are smiling, content, sleeping. As a model parent, the charge is to protect your child from all the woes of life. Parents believe if only they are attentive and protective enough they truly can shield their children from the pain and suffering of childhood. Years ago, addressing mothers of four- and five-year-olds at a top Dallas private school, my insistence that children could not be protected from all the woes in the world outraged those moms. How dare I suggest that they could not provide a perfectly managed environment, where little Emma and Ben did not have to experience frustration, rejection, or sadness? Of course they could—and planned to do so, putting all of their collective resources of education, financial security, and social status toward the task! These moms insisted, "Why should my daughter ever be sad?" or "I am a good mom only if I can make everything right in my son's world." These assumptions are rampant in current expectations of parenting, quoted often by parents who have sought out the discipline training of TV's *Supernanny*, as they explain their child's out-of-control behavior: "I just don't want him to be unhappy."

Popular parenting advice for infancy offers more fodder for extreme parenting. Heavens—you let your baby cry it out, teaching her self-sufficiency and that you are the boss of the household, à la the book *On Becoming Babywise?* How could you, you heartless beast?! Certainly you don't pick her up every moment, keep her close through the day (and night), so she has less need to cry, à la attachment parenting. How can you let her rule your household? Both camps imply that you have ultimate control over your baby's crying. Our culture pretty much agrees. Think about the looks aimed at parents of crying babies in grocery stores, restaurants, and airplanes. All those glaring onlookers imply that it is Mom's or Dad's job to silence that baby—at least, if Mom is a good mom.

Regardless of the parenting camp you've pitched your tent in, the expectations of control spread from crying in infancy to the rest of your child's world: that you can protect and make everything right for your child, make him happy at all times. Babies can be soothed—you need not simply puncture your eardrums and wait for premature deafness. With an infant, you want to respond to your child's cries as quickly as you can. Every parenting philosophy agrees on that. When you meet children's needs, they learn to trust and enjoy the world. In extreme parenting, we fail to distinguish needs from wants. And parents stay focused on what worked when baby was first born, applying this strategy into his third, fourth, or fifteenth year. Extend this philosophy with age, as your child grows. You don't want Emma to cry, so you pick her up at three months. As part of your eternal quest to control her world so she'll be happy, at three years you don't want Emma to cry, so she only has gummi worms for dinner. At seven, you don't want Emma to cry, so you lurk on the edge of the playground during recess, rushing out to scold that mean boy every time he sticks his tongue out at your little princess. At seventeen, you don't want Emma to cry, so what do you do, arrange her date to the prom?

Somewhere deep within the psyches of today's parents is simply an older version of the imprint that a crying baby is mom's fault. The adage has not evolved as the child ages. The quest to protect the child, engineer her world, spreads like chickenpox in a hot bath to all her childhood. As the big bad world becomes more complex, calling for more parental control, the stakes are higher, too. You must go beyond supermom to protect your child and ensure he has what he needs for a happy, successful life.

The Three Os of Extreme Parenting

You might be saying "I know I'm not perfect" or maybe "My kids aren't perfect." I've found that women in my practice and my social circles usually overdo parenting in one of three primary ways:

overperfecting, overprotecting, or *overproducing.* Overperfecting can apply in any area: pantries are alphabetized and dishes never left in the sink overnight. Children dare not venture from home without matching socks and outfits; harsh words are never uttered. Even when houses aren't spotless and kids aren't impeccably dressed, moms feel pressed into overprotecting their children: from the wrong friends, lack of sleep, or germs. Finally, some families zero in on overproducing: toddler tutoring, Suzuki lessons, German summer camp instead of lazy afternoons swimming. Every mom seems to have her overdoing—her "little nutty piece"—or three, or four. The problem comes when the pressure in any arena stresses you beyond a healthy level.

Much as in the days of Donna Reed and June Cleaver, we cling to our belief that we can totally control what happens to our children, that we can make our kids' lives ideal. Unfortunately, it works both ways. If something goes wrong (or right) with our children, it's our fault (or credit) as mothers. Judith Warner, author of *Perfect Madness: Motherhood in the Age of Anxiety,* states that the real reason we practice extreme parenting is because it gives us a feeling of control. Total control is comforting. It relieves our anxiety, which is really at the base of the problem of overparenting. For lurking underneath that drive to perfection, littered with trivialities, are what Warner dubs "unsayable" thoughts about our mothering: *Am I good enough? Are we rich enough? Can we compete?*

Day in and day out in my work as a psychologist with women, I encourage clients to begin to speak up about the impossibility of this quest for perfection, total control, and protection. Susan Douglas and

Meredith Michaels in *The Mommy Myth: The Idealization of Motherhood and How It Has Undermined All*, do just that, calling these unrealistic standards the "new momism." The new momism raises the ideal requirements for being a mom to a new high. Nothing seems as important, or as central to defining who you are as a person, as being a mom. Not your work demands, nor your sex life, nor your commitments to your aging parents. In fact, in the current culture, time spent on self is seen as subtracting from what you give your children. Read a book or negotiate a million-dollar deal in your non-mom time. You are still off-duty on the kid front—out of control—something bad could happen! Forget the fact that these activities may enrich you or feed your soul.

The new momism calls for women to adhere to the Madonna model of motherhood. No, not the pop culture icon, but the religious icon with the radiant gold halo in fifteenth-century art. Moms must be always loving, patient, kind, groomed, soft-spoken, and happy. The list goes on ad nauseam. Surely any woman who can uphold these ideals brings glory, if not sanctity, upon herself. At the same time, these are rules that no human can really uphold all the time. Judith Warner in *Perfect Madness* calls this crazy pursuit of perfection, for both our children and our parenting, the "mommy mystique." The mommy mystique elevates children to the central point in a woman's life, the apex of her fulfillment as a woman. This is much as the feminine mystique decreed in the 1950s that true fulfillment for women lay in their pursuit of the homemaker/wife roles. The mommy mystique eclipses progress in attitudes about women's work. Today's mothers seem to need to prove that they are good mothers before they can justify their willingness to work, or their existence as human beings. As Harriet said in my office, "It doesn't seem to matter what else I do. I sold five houses this month and won agent of the month, but if my daughter is in tears because she missed a party, I'm a bad mom. No, it's beyond 'bad mom.' If my kids aren't happy and succeeding, I'm a bad person!"

Whether we call it momism, the mommy mystique, or "the mess," as the women who Warner interviewed for her book sum it up, the buzz about "mommy madness" fills the pages, airwaves, and playgroups. This new honesty in the media is enabling women to finally articulate the toll on their lives. After endless rounds of baby swim classes, French for four-year-olds, and all-night campouts for preschool sign-up followed by a full day at work, women are tired—tired of pretending that they are as happy and carefree as June Cleaver as they make their endless carpool rounds. (June, by the way, never had to make carpool rounds—Wally and the Beaver walked everywhere on their own.)

Women are able finally to admit it: mothering is hard, they're riddled with anxiety, and they're running on empty. Rates of depression and anxiety among mothers are highest during the child-bearing years. Mothers are drowning in trivia, in lists like this from Kate Reddy in *I Don't Know How She Does It*:

MUST REMEMBER: Angel wings. Quote for new stair carpet. Take lasagna out of freezer for Saturday lunch. Buy kitchen roll, stainless steel special polish thingy, present and card for Harry's party. . . . Must get organized with well-stocked present drawer like proper mother. . . .

Nanny's Christmas bribe/present (Eurostar ticket? Cash? DKNY?). Emily wants Baby Wee-Wee doll (over my dead body). Present for Richard (Wine-tasting? Arsenal? Pajamas?). In-laws' book: The Lost Gardens of Somewhere? Ask Richard to collect dry cleaning. Office party what to wear? Black velvet too small now. Stop eating now. Fishnets lilac. Leg wax not time, shave instead. Book stress-busting massage.

To quote one mother in my practice: "I am always doing all this stuff—and I never have time to do what I really enjoy. Then give me a spare moment, and I can't even remember what I want to do!"

The good news is we've made great strides in honesty about parenting. Mothers finally seem willing to speak up, uniting in their concerns about these unrealistic, unachievable standards and endless, trivial to-do lists. Women are beginning to be honest, to admit the endless, futile struggle within themselves to meet these impossible standards. I hear this lament daily in my office: "I feel like such a failure because I don't do any of this well—not work, not parenting, not being a wife. Is something really the matter with me?"

While recognizing this craziness is the first step toward a more workable model for our parenting, it also helps to put it in historical perspective. Mothers of previous generations didn't drive themselves to extremes. June Cleaver never played reasoning games with Wally to increase his problem-solving skills or arranged playdates for Beaver, suffering through competition disguised as small talk with Lumpy's mom. Baby boomer parents skipped much that we see as essential to parenting today, such as classes, sports teams, and enrichment tutoring, and their kids turned out just fine.

To really see how crazy it is, play out the assumptions of extreme parenting. Follow all those prescriptions about ideal parenting to their logical conclusion. Is there such a beast as the perfect birthday party? Is it really possible to have twenty children in the room and have everyone happy? Does skill at gymnastics at age four translate into knowing the secret of life? Should your child excel and win a gold medal at the 2016 Summer Olympic games, what does that mean for the kind of life you really want her to have? Indeed, do you want her to appear on a cereal box when she is fifteen, making that the pinnacle of her life's success? You may wish to discipline perfectly and never raise your voice, always interacting in a loving, straightforward manner peppered with "I" messages. Imagine you accomplish that goal: your son has never heard a harsh word in your home. When your child gets to kindergarten, and the teacher has PMS, do you want him to feel like his teacher hates him because she is the first person who ever yelled at him? Look at the push you make in your life, for yourself and your child, expecting perfection from either of you. What is the natural extension at an older age? Sit down and think it through. Is that truly what you want for your child?

I learned what I share here and with women in my practice by being a parent myself. Before I had children, I was virtually never late. Always the first guest at a party, walked into work right after the person with the key. Bound and determined to have my life unchanged by becoming a parent, I was certain I would still be my timely self. Succeed I did—until my daughter learned to talk. As we packed for a daily outing when she was two, she admonished me in her best imitation of my scolding voice, "Hurry, Mommy, hurry,

hurry. It is bad to be late." Our children are little mirrors, reflecting our best and worst traits, and at that moment I realized that my push to be timely was not a burden I wanted to place on my daughter—particularly at the tender age of two! Over the years, she mirrored more of my perfectionistic strivings, and each time it was painful. At four years, I recall her suddenly scribbling all over and then crumpling and hurling a picture that she painstakingly had drawn. She burst into tears, yelling at herself, "Stupid Abby, stupid Abby!" No one had ever spoken to her in that manner, I am certain. She had copied the self-critical style in which her father and I both mutter (or sometimes curse) at ourselves in moments of frustration. While I had always been an admitted perfectionist, the toll it could take on others was not clear until then. Then it clicked, and I saw that I needed to be easier on myself if I was to help my children be realistic about their own abilities and expectations. I did not need to be perfect; I just had to do well. Abby did not need to be perfect; she just had to do her best. And not even that all the time, just the majority. With that realization, I could cut myself some slack—and help my clients do the same.

You may have heard the droves of mothers speaking up on TV or in the papers. You are finally giving that voice within a chance to be heard, the voice that rebels at all those dictates about "the Right Way." Hopefully you see that this is not a parenting model that you dreamed up in a competitive moment with the bragging mom down the street. Perhaps you are beginning to accept that it might be okay to question these cultural dictates or talk back to those television news reports on parenting. You know the ones: they explore the problem of the day, whether shyness, autism, or acting-out teens, and usually feature a parent or two asking, "What did I do wrong?" They include a mental-health expert reinforcing parental over-responsibility by telling what parents can do better. Maybe you can name your own "click moment" when you realized the pursuit of perfection and control for yourself, your kids, and your life had gone far enough. A click moment is the exact second you comprehend that the way you feel is not your fault—and not due to your failures. Rather, those feelings of anxiety and frustration are perfectly valid reactions to cultural expectations that simply cannot be met, at least by actual human beings.

Recognizing the issue is not enough, however. Naming the problem, calling it momism or madness or the mess, is a great first step. But how do we really get to a healthier place with our actions and definitions of ourselves as mothers? Rather than run screaming into the streets with placards that say "No More Baby Mozart," we need to adopt a new definition of motherhood. To do this, we need to understand the underlying fallacies in thinking that reinforce extreme parenting. Mom after mom who enters my office views parenting as black or white, all or nothing. Kelly's son didn't make the soccer select team, so that meant he'd never be good at soccer and should try fencing. Jennifer's daughter wasn't invited to all the best parties, so she must be a social leper. Paul didn't get straight As and a perfect SAT score. His mom obsessed that he'd not get into Harvard and would never get a job. Either your child (or you) is a success all the time, around the clock, or must be a dismal failure. This is a fallacy, whether you are judging child or parent. But that is how we drive ourselves; that is what the choices look like to us. Absolutes: black and white, all or nothing, success or failure.

In line with human nature's propensity to think in absolutes, the tendency is to swing the pendulum to the other extreme to find an alternative. The backlash against intensive mothering has created rebellious mothering. This is not extreme, overinvolved mothering. Rebellious mothering is realistic mothering. It is rebellious in a good sense, challenging the status quo in the same way that the Boston Tea Party was valuable anarchy. You can still be a loving, effective mother even if you don't share meaningful conversations about the gross national product during breakfast or hand embroider your child's nap mat. Mothers who personify this model may be right next door, or you can find them in *Roseanne, Malcolm in the Middle,* and *Everybody Loves Raymond.* If you look past the pearls and fresh-baked cookies persona, you even find real mom moments in June Cleaver. In one episode, Eddie Haskell irks her so much that she spitefully puts mayonnaise on his sandwich, even though he's told her it upsets his stomach.

The rebellious mom image has spilled over from television into parenting books, with *Confessions of a Slacker Mom* by Muffy Mead-Ferro, *The Three-Martini Playdate: A Practical Guide to Happy Parenting* by Christie Mellor, and *Sippy Cups Are Not for Chardonnay: A Practical Guide to Things I Had to Learn as a New Mom* by Stefanie Wilder-Taylor. These writers present their rebellious mom dictates with wit and wisdom, knowing that they are challenging the status quo. To really change anything, it often takes an extreme shift to the other end of the spectrum.

Since we think in black/white, good/bad, all-or-nothing terms, many of us stand back cautiously, admiring moms willing to reject this extreme model of mothering, though not quite convinced that rebellious mothering is truly a good thing. It's extremely tempting to recline on the couch as illustrated on the cover of *Confessions of a Slacker Mom*. It's attractive, downright seductive, to think about imbibing martinis during afternoon playdates. But can it really work? Will our kids really turn out okay if we give up super control? As Yvette said in my office, "If I am not right on top of them, they may as well be raising themselves. What good am I?" If we swing the pendulum to the other end of involvement with our kids, will they turn into fodder for an after-school TV special, to paraphrase Elissa Schappell in *The Bitch in the House?*

What is a mother to do? The pursuit of perfection is making you crazy. You are drowning in the trivia that is aimed at controlling the job of parenting. When women feel out of control of their lives, they fixate on details they *can* manipulate. This is a daily refrain I hear in my work, as young women bemoan the failure they feel in their jobs as mothers. "I am such a terrible mother," they lament, "I am the worst mother ever."

You are so invested in doing it all that you are absolutely running on empty, exhausting yourself with the trivia. You want to do well by your children. You love them; you want what is best for them. The alternatives are kind of scary. Because control is the underlying issue, you fear losing control. Being a slacker mom sounds a little too hands-off, revving up your anxiety about the outcome a teensy bit too much. And won't they call Child Protective Services if you have your four-year-old mix your martinis for the playdate? Where is the middle ground?

A New Motherhood Paradigm: The Perfectly Good Mother

Enter the perfectly good mother. "Perfectly good" is an old-fashioned phrase that merits revival, especially when applied to parenting. *Perfectly,* by definition, means "without qualification; clearly." So perfectly good would mean "clearly good" or "good without qualification." In other words, as good as is necessary. When I was a girl, my grandmother used this phrase liberally. "Those shoes are still perfectly good—you don't need new ones," even when the toes were scuffed. "We had a perfectly good trip" in spite of getting lost three times. The phrases gave me the impression that the matters in question were just fine, regardless of flaws. Workable, wonderful, completely acceptable were all implied—but not perfect.

When I first began working with mothers, a theme of perfectionism repeatedly emerged. Everyone wanted to have the perfect life. Rather than accepting the hard, challenging work of parenting, a "mothering as nirvana" attitude prevailed. As I saw how the mismatch between this attitude and the realities of life with small children drove women to disappointment, I offered them a replacement, the popular concept of the "good enough" mother. Women rejected it outright—good enough was not up to their standards. "Good enough" sounded like "not good." That's when I recalled my grandmother's sensible phrase and began to apply it to parenting.

The perfectly good mother is not a model of perfectly perfect. Perfect is impossible. Perfect implies A++, 110 percent of the time. "Perfectly good" as an adjective keeps the standards high, but achievable. It means clearly good, without qualification. Perfectly good is a solid A- or B+. Compare that to "good enough," or even "slacker." Sounds like barely passing to me. Perfectly good is admirable, but you don't have to "kill" yourself, and it by no means creeps into the realm of failure.

Let's define this new model of parenting. The perfectly good mother is available to her children. She is loving, interested, involved. She knows that she cannot give her all to her kids without some cost to herself, to her relationship with her partner, to her extra-family commitments. She is human. She gets tired, she makes mistakes, sometimes she yells. Small explosions are like the controlled release of steam from a pressure cooker, preventing bigger, more damaging explosions. While not ideal, these small eruptions teach her kids that people have feelings and limits, and neither is too scary to survive. The perfectly good mother looks at her life and knows she has to make choices. Something has to give, but at day's end she is able to look back and say, "I can live with this." The perfectly good mom recognizes there is a difference between losing control and letting go. In losing control, there is an implicit loss. You did not win; chaos or failure may be the result. Letting go, however, is a choice. Letting go, in appropriate increments as your child grows, is win/win. It is making choices about having power over what you can control, and letting go of what you never did control. It is all a matter of perspective, which is all you have: the lens through which you view your life.

The perfectly good mom is able to say wholeheartedly that she is doing a perfectly acceptable job. Her kids may or may not win an Olympic gold medal, Pulitzer Prize, or Rhodes scholarship. But they will have perfectly satisfying lives, full of what matters to them. The children of a perfectly good mom are perfectly good kids— even great kids. Sure, they have moments of self-centeredness and age-appropriate tantrums. Sometimes they mouth off, get bad grades, scribble on the walls, or get into the liquor cabinet. With guidance, modeling of appropriate adult responsibility, and balanced self-care, they will grow up and lead lives as useful, satisfied citizens.

The perfectly good mom has moments of anxiety. She worries whether she is on the right track. She stops and questions her actions, brings herself or her kids or her relationship back in line. Maybe she engineers a house and kids; maybe she also manages an investment fund or the library or a classroom full of six-year-olds. Sometimes she has guilt, too. She missteps, then apologizes to the people in her life. The perfectly good mom is not magically freed from negative emotions like guilt, doubt, and anxiety. Like Kristin van Ogtrop in *The Bitch in the House,* the perfectly good mom loves her children, but knows her love is imperfect, colored by her personality quirks and extra-family demands. Imperfect love is all there is, for all us lowly humans. The overall outcome, however, is perfectly workable. The perfectly good mom knows she has bad days, but the good days outweigh them. The perfectly good mom feels good about herself, her life, and the way she lives it. She has learned to pay attention to the talk in her head and in society around her and the directives about how she should behave, and to sort it out. She knows when her two-year-old scribbles on the wall, that is bad behavior—but does not make her two-year-old a demon child. She applies this same adage to her own behavior—she might have a few temper tantrums herself, but these slip-ups make her human, not a bad mother. She has rejected black/white, all-or-nothing thinking, in favor of the healthy middle ground.

Sound too good to be true? You *can* be a perfectly good mom. Every mother can. It is a simple process of paying attention to the forces in you and in those around you that govern your expectations for your parenting, your children, and your life. While not complex, it takes some steady work to revise those expectations, speak kindly to yourself, and ingrain new habits of thinking. For most women, changes in thinking are the key—their parenting behavior is already perfectly good. Just because you have become comfortable with extreme mothering, so that it now feels normal or right, does not mean that it is natural, necessary, or effective. We need to change the way we think about motherhood, individually and collectively.

Perfectly Good Mantras

Throughout this book, there are "Perfectly Good Mantras" to guide you along. How you think keeps your guilt and anxiety about parenting revved up. Repeating perfectly good mantras such as "Control what you can, let go of the rest" leads you to talk to yourself differently and thereby change your thinking.

The remaining chapters of this book guide you through the necessary changes in thinking, step by step, so you can feel like a perfectly good mother. Chapter 2 explores the societal influences that drive today's parents to extremes of overperfecting, overproducing, and overprotecting. Chapter 3 looks at what we think: the mommy traps that keep us stuck in overparenting. Chapter 4 details the irrational thinking underlying what we think, or the how of our thinking about parenting, and offers strategies to adopt rational thinking. Chapter 5 spells out a healthier paradigm for parenting, how to live as your own version of a perfectly good mother. In Chapter 6, how mothers actually apply the new model to their lives and parenting is discussed, along with advice on stumbling blocks that interfere with living as a perfectly good mother. Chapter 7 offers ideas on connecting with other mothers, for when you have a solid support system of like-minded souls you can better resist the cultural push to extreme parenting. Chapter 8 is specifically for dads with an overview of the problem of extreme parenting and the solution: perfectly good parenting. Chapter 9 concludes with a look at spreading this more reasonable, rational paradigm to your world, for everyone's benefit.

"There Must Be Something the Matter with Me"

The Causes and Consequences of Extreme Parenting

Michelle grew up as a latchkey kid. Her attorney mom was working when she came home from school, so Michelle turned on the TV to keep her company through the afternoon. Fresh-baked cookies did not exist at her house, like they do in those families on sitcoms. Michelle was certain she would be the quintessential model of perfect motherhood when she grew up: immaculately groomed, homestyle cooking, always soothing things to say to her children. When her children were born, she was bored to tears. Michelle couldn't keep up with the house, let alone throw a meatloaf and cookies into the oven before her husband came home. Certainly she was a loser, failing to master such a mundane role. She was a Phi Beta Kappa, after all!

Perhaps just like Michelle, the awareness has been sneaking into you slowly, like a tipped, barely closed syrup bottle hiding on the bottom shelf of your fridge: something is not right with this mother business. You wanted it, you had a sneaking suspicion you would even be good at it. That is not how you feel now at all. Instead, you are mired in a sticky mess: you have these kids, you have ideas in your head about what it should be like, and none of those dreams match up with the reality of your day-to-day life. You feel inadequate, or worse, with your kids, your work, the management of your home. You worry you are messing up your kids. You are miserable and exhausted. Since every other mom you know in the universe appears to be June Cleaver reincarnated, at the end of the day you are left with only one conclusion: there must be something the matter with you.

Take heart. Repeat after me: "There is nothing the matter with me." To begin to let go of this horrible mantra that you are deficient, you have to first admit that the problem does not lie within you. You

Perfectly Good Mantra:
"There is nothing the matter with me."

Recognize that society puts these unrealistic expectations for mothers out there—all you do is buy into them. You can choose not to—and that begins with refusing to blame yourself when you don't measure up.

are not a failure. You are not feeling this way because you are intellectually inferior, or hopelessly disorganized, or just not cut from the right mother cloth. You are feeling this way because you pay attention to the messages our culture imposes upon moms. You read magazines, newspapers, and watch television. You listen to other mothers define success. And you are like a super-absorbent sponge. You take those ideas about how mothers should be, and you suck them right into your own head in defining your motherhood self.

To begin to let go of the idea that something is the matter with you, you have to accept that *it is not you.* Something is the matter with the current messages our culture sends about mothering. You are bombarded with unrealistic ideas about mothers, day in and day out, if you live in the twenty-first century. The problem is not within you. Rather it reflects the current cultural environment. You need to embrace that this is true. This chapter gives a brief overview of the origin of these "perfect mom" dictates. If you know where these ideas come from, you are more likely to catch them, recognize them, and decide if you want to adopt them, rather than accept them as truth with a capital T.

Historical Forces That Have Shaped Extreme Parenting

The current drive to extreme parenting has its basis in the ideals behind this country's founding. Immigrants to the United States, whether in 1756 or 2006, arrive on U.S. shores seeking a better life, with more control over religious, political, and economic aspects of their lives. My grandmother told me a slogan, popular in the forties and fifties, that went like this: "Every day, in every way, I am getting better and better." She, like many of her generation, repeated it five times each morning—the affirmation was born. That ideal is deeply ingrained in the fabric of this country and spills over to our expectations about life in general, even if our forebears weren't on the *Mayflower*.

We all want a better life—and we transfer this desire to our children. Every generation judges success by how much improvement is made in financial, educational, and social standing compared to their parents' lives. If your grandparents were thrilled to have one car, your parents soon became accustomed to two. As standards for having "made it" continue to rise, the work needed to reach those goals seems to double. "Gone are the days of the forty-hour work week. My company expects all managers to put in fifty to sixty hours a week as the average," said one survey respondent in a *Chief Learning Officer* magazine report. Parents work harder, and expect their offspring to do so too—studying, training, perfecting themselves and their skills to advance. This overdoing seems essential to success. (If you enjoy history and want to know more about historical influences that have lead us to extreme parenting, see the expanded discussion in Appendix One.)

It is simply un-American to reject this cultural bias toward betterment. Therefore, parents feel trapped. But this push to always be better is not the sole factor fueling extreme parenting. The current generation of parents has been shaped by research on child development, media pressures that reflect cultural biases, and the expectations of the women's movement. All mix into the recipe for extreme parenting.

Did Freud Start the Funk?

The current focus on children as "center of the universe" grew out of the work of psychiatrist John Bowlby, author of the *Attachment and Loss* series. Bowlby's research, which underlies attachment parenting philosophies, was based on orphans subjected to horrific neglect. Good old Sigmund Freud made his mark on expectations about parenting too. Combine Freud's emphasis on trauma in the first few years of life with Bowlby's work on neglect, and mothers were singled out as potentially powerful. Mothers could make or break the child's victorious arrival at adulthood. Responding in a loving, constant, consistent way meant your child would be fulfilled, confident, and successful. Ignore your child, even for an instant, and she might become Lizzie Borden, or at the very least, the human counterpart of one of those sad-eyed monkeys clinging to the wire mother in a psych textbook.

> "Sure his mom is a piece of work—only a mother can do that much damage." *This line from an episode of* House M.D. *shows how widespread mother-blaming is in our culture.*

As children's development was studied, awareness of the importance of the ages of zero to three as a critical period increased even more. With the advent of the computer and medical technology such as MRI and PET scans, scientists had ever more sophisticated means to study early infancy, gaining critical knowledge about how and when children's brains develop. We used to know less about how to turn kids into geniuses—so we had fewer expectations about being able to sway young Joey in that direction. Once the factors that could actually stimulate brain development were understood, this knowledge could be applied to make kids smarter, brighter, faster. Responsibility for a child's intellectual growth crashed like an asteroid into the parents. If every waking moment of a child's life could have this effect, boosting brain power (and ultimately earning or social power), how dare a parent even stop to breathe? Many parents, like Judith Warner admits in *Perfect Madness*, became a "human TV set," reading, talking, teaching all the livelong day to develop all those tiny offspring brain cells. With each tick of the clock of the child's life suddenly so critical, so influential, mothers had no choice. For example, since the birth of her first child, Jennifer has not stopped narrating each time she loads her kids in the car. During her pregnancy, she read about the importance of verbal stimulation for her children's developing brains. Every time she has to take Bret, four years, Paige, two years, or Connor, four months, anywhere, she becomes a tour guide: singing, telling jokes, pointing out the pretty blooming tree or the fast red car. If she dares to take a breath, Connor cries while Bret and Paige belt each other with stuffed animals.

The Making of Supermom

"Intensive mothering" is the term coined by sociologist Sharon Hays in her book *The Cultural Contradictions of Motherhood* to describe extreme mothering. She asserts that this intensive mothering requires mothers to take on the skills and persona of a teacher, therapist, and pediatrician, acting as the doting, self-sacrificing mother at all times, putting the kids' needs above their own. Intensive mothers compete with other mothers in the ultimate contest of being the best mother, never tiring, never frowning, never yelling or berating children. The one exception is the proper scolding scripted from the latest *Supernanny* episode. Intensive mothers are always on duty, and appear happily so, excelling in each and every moment of parental bliss.

In *The Motherhood Club: Help, Hope, and Inspiration for New Mothers from New Mothers,* Shirley Washington and I challenged some of the myths of motherhood. These myths say that motherhood is endlessly fulfilling, joyful, and rewarding and is best done in one prescribed "right" way, at least if you are a good mother. In *The Mommy Myth: The Idealization of Motherhood and How It Has Undermined All Women,* Susan Douglas and Meredith Michaels call myths like these "the new momism."

Historically, say these authors, having a uterus meant you loved scrubbing toilet bowls and having a scrotum meant blindness to dirt. The image of the fifties housewife vacuuming in pearls is now laughable, but in the 1950s and 1960s, all women were supposed to live this life. The new momism is not about serving men and their needs, but rather about serving children and their needs. As a culture, Douglas and Michaels state, we now declare that the only enlightened, decent, worthy choice to make as a woman is to be a mom. Young women have replaced romanticized daydreams about weddings and marriage with fantasies about becoming a mother, according to the women interviewed by Peggy Orenstein for her book *Flux: Women on Sex, Work, Love, Kids, and Life in a Half-Changed World*. As Lisa Belkin suggested in *O: The Oprah Magazine*, motherhood has become "the brass ring of womanhood." The basic expectation in society today is you are nothing if not a mother. But I think it goes beyond the idea that you just have to achieve motherhood to be a success. Even more damaging to moms is the fiercely held idea that you must deeply love each back-wrenching, hair-pulling, brain-boosting moment in order to show your true colors as a mother. None of it matters if it is not done with absolute joy 100 percent of the time.

Momism is a set of ideals that allegedly celebrate motherhood, but in reality pushes standards of performance beyond human reach. Douglas and Michaels say "by insisting that being a mother—and perfect at that—is the most important thing a woman can do . . . the new momism insists that if you want to do anything else, you had better prove first that you are a doting, totally involved mother. . . . . That is not a requirement for men."

Real-Life Models of Motherhood

What raised these standards of motherhood so over the top? First of all, current mothers represent a generation of overachievers. Many moms I see in my office report hearing in childhood, as women worked to break down barriers, that they could "have it all." Sometimes this message was explicit, like a teacher or aunt giving them a pep talk about women's opportunities. Even if Aunt Jody presented the opportunities as a gift, the underlying message was that the listener betrayed the efforts of those valiant women who had fought (hear the suffragettes singing in the background?) if she did not go for it all. Maybe the message was implicit as teen girls watched mom or the neighbor whose kids they babysat struggle to climb the corporate ladder while balancing parenting. Just as often, women cite that silly seventies commercial, where the perky actor sings to a bump-and-grind medley about bringing home the bacon, frying it up in the pan, and never letting her man forget that she is a woman. Women who struggled for equal rights in the workplace wanted to reap what the women's movement had sown. They wanted the next generation of girls to know how the road had been paved, just for them. Supermom was born.

Today's mothers expect to fulfill this Supermom ideal—to the hilt of their swashbuckling swords. Doors are open—you certainly should take advantage of them. But how? Since the current generation of mothers had few role models for living this mother pattern, confusion reigns. Do you do it all at once? Sequentially? Since mentors who have found a sane balance are scarce, mothers struggle to define their own equilibrium. The hype that "You can do it all" includes no fine print about how hard that actually is.

Many women becoming mothers today have teetered near "doing it all." Andrea J. Buchanan, author of *Mother Shock: Loving Every (Other) Minute of It,* points out that women who have been in the workforce know the kind of competitiveness that exists in, and is even fostered by, that world. When they become mothers, they may put their careers on hold. But old work habits are insidious. The offspring become their work. As Victoria Clayton said in a 2004 MSNBC article, these parents "bring the same work ethic to parenting as they once did to their careers: they're willing to work hard, they're ambitious and competitive, and they have a desire for accomplishment, control and results."

The next factor that led to extreme parenting is that often these women (and men) suffered a "toughen up" style of parenting in the sixties and seventies. It was not uncommon for children to be berated and chastised about stupidity or laziness or have some sense slapped into them. Moms are ultimately responsible for how little Ava turns out. Peter Stearns, author of *Anxious Parents: A History of Modern Childrearing in America,* says our culture accepts that "life's difficulties can be traced back to parental inadequacies." Today's parents follow this trend, blaming their parents for their flaws. How can they change the rules midstream, denying they're culpable for their children's anguish? Determined to do better with their kids, parents who were treated like this have flocked to parenting with the goal of building self-esteem in children. True to our American way, however, this has been taken to extremes. Douglas and

Michaels state that children are viewed as intrinsically unique and precious, "each child as the Hope diamond." These authors point out that claiming each child as more special than others has backlash, requiring your child to become a star, far outshining everyone else's children. Back to the need for extreme parenting.

Then there is total control of your castle that Douglas and Michaels dubbed the "Martha Stewartization of America." How can you "have it all" if your chair cushions don't match your hand-stitched table covers? Won't your child be at a disadvantage if you don't hand decorate his Easter basket for the egg hunt? This focus on domestic diva-hood stresses crafty and klutzy moms alike with its emphasis on time-gobbling, overly ambitious projects. How can you consider yourself a proper mother if you never pack radish roses in your child's lunch, to accompany the smiley-face grilled cheese, or arrange the daffodils for her birthday party (organically fertilized with the bones you adeptly removed from last Labor Day's salmon) in an aged galvanized bucket? This approach is popular given the anxiety and lack of control many mothers feel. At least they can engineer their surroundings, if not admission to the top schools.

Even if you aren't aiming for perfection in raising your children, you have few chances for corrective feedback in the parenting process. How do you know if you are actually producing a worthwhile human being? The results will not be in for twenty-five years or so. Better to invest your energy in the perfect holiday table settings or hand-stenciled pots for your houseplants; at least you can see the fruits of your labor! Nearly every magazine cover you scrutinize as you stand exhausted in the grocery store checkout line seduces you into this demon world of beads and paint, at least if you are a woman of substance. Douglas and Michaels claim the bar of worthy womanhood has been lofted to "an even more ridiculous level than in the June Cleaver era."

Media Moms—from June to Roseanne

Psychologists and child development specialists, armed with alleged scientific knowledge about producing superkids, coupled with our national urge to betterment, have been the source of mothering madness. But what continues to fuel the madness? Why do women continue to strive for perfection in all things home and family? Look no further than that supermarket checkout magazine line-up. Douglas and Michaels maintain that the popularization of these pie in the sky (homemade, of course) standards is due to the media—from advertising to popular television to women's magazines. A 2006 survey indicated that the best TV mother was Claire Huxtable of *The Cosby Show*. Claire was an attorney raising four children—sometimes five. Always fashionably dressed, humor and common sense intact, Claire made it look easy. Tune in to *Cosby* reruns and watch what Claire really did. She breezed in at day's end looking as impeccable as when she left in the morning. She was always loving, smiling, and calmly effective with her children, even when they had pot stashed in their textbooks. Any normal mother would be ranting or crying. Her discipline skills were admirable; she simply tossed out clever one-liners. The errant kid was magically contrite and cooperative. Like all television moms, she only had to parent twenty minutes a week. And Bill Cosby, with his doctorate in psychology, was helping write her lines. Every mother can execute twenty minutes of perfect parenting a week. It is the other 167 hours and forty minutes that trip us all up.

Television characters are not the only template moms have in their heads for the kind of mother they should be. It's a frosty day on the River Styx when a woman isn't taunted by media stories such as "keeping your kids off drugs," "picking the perfect preschool," or "raising strong girls" that prompt the quintessential question: are you a good mother or a bad mother? Women need caution about these media influences, especially if the prescriptions seem natural and the very core of common sense. The ideas touted by the media are usually sound, issuing from the mouth of some expert like me with a Ph.D. or M.D. behind their names. But everything you read or hear need not be immediately and perfectly incorporated into your parenting or disaster will result.

Women need to learn to filter, to take in and file information away for later use, rather than scrambling to upgrade their parenting strategies. Your computer runs just fine with the latest operating system—do you really need to fork over hundreds of dollars just because an upgrade exists? And sometimes, the best course is simply to not listen, or to reject directives outright.

Women must conquer the fear of rejecting these standards, if the ideas seem "out there" or ill fitting or just plain too stressful. What usually happens, however, is women fear they'll be judged harshly— by their peers, their husbands, their own mothers, or their own internal comparisons to other moms—for not abiding by these cultural expectations, no matter how ridiculous and unattainable.

The Toll of Extreme Mothering on Mothers, Marriages, Children

The generation of mothers that walks into my office simply is driven by anxiety: anxiety about parenting perfectly, worry about others' judgments if they don't "do it right," angst about screwing up their kids. Anxiety has always been an inevitable part of motherhood. According to Ann Hulbert in *Raising America: Experts, Parents, and a Century of Advice About Children,* an essay on "The Anxious Mother" was written way back in 1927. When a woman first becomes a mother, she's keenly aware of how fragile and precious children are. Her job is to protect them. Having the full weight of a young life totally in your hands does seem a wee bit important. Among current parents, however, the anxiety and self-blame have mushroomed.

When I first began counseling, women seemed to have a greater comfort level with balancing work and family. Now, most women seem to feel that home and family must take priority—just as in June Cleaver's world. In 1963, Betty Friedan in *The Feminine Mystique* wrote that women succumb to a false belief system. This set of ideas, the Feminine Mystique, required women to link all meaning and self-definition in their lives to their husbands and children. The result, agreed Friedan and many women who lived it, was an emptiness and dissatisfaction rivaled in the present age by what Judith Warner has dubbed the "Mommy Mystique." The Mommy Mystique simply transfers a woman's concern and self-definition from her house and husband, as in the fifties, to her children. Too many women have moved from being husband or home centered, as their grandmothers had no choice but to be, to being totally child centered, even obsessed. The woman is rare who does not feel pulled nearly to pieces, between work, children, husband. "Everyone wants a piece of me," lamented Gillian in my office one day. "If I could clone me, maybe there would be enough to go around."

Since so much of the "outcome" of parenting falls on the mothers, many mothers fear some horrible life-altering error in raising their children. Rebecca complained about too much information, leaving her constantly second-guessing: too many books, Web sites, pediatricians, family members, parenting classes. Inquiring moms solve their dilemmas by looking things up. With the vast universe of information ever expanding, you can never look it all up. The "right" answer is simply unattainable. Google "infant sleep schedules," for instance, and you get 11 million hits. Not even the computer can slog through that much information in a reasonable amount of time. If you are searching for the Answer, it is easier to find the lost pacifier you dropped in your day of sixteen errands.

Warner's interviewees suggested that today's mothers are control freaks, having been raised to believe they could have and do it all. The term *control freak* is not used in a pejorative way, like your partner might do in the midst of a messy argument. Rather, it refers to being tyrannical, almost obsessive. I confess, I get sucked up in it too. I still obsess about whether my kids get enough sleep. My seventeen-year-old was ranting last week about how "No one else has a bedtime!" When my children were small, getting them to nap—on schedule—seemed like the pinnacle of success as a mom. If they would nap, not only would they be more pleasant, but I'd get "me" time. I once left a cart full of groceries with the clerk as my child began to melt down. The line was too long. We weren't going to buy the groceries and get her home on time. Another day I burst into tears when my husband was sucked into the vortex of the home superstore. I could not find him—it was nearing nap time. If I had been in possession of the car keys, I probably would have left him there!

In the words of Muffy Mead-Ferro in *Confessions of a Slacker Mom,* talking about the glut of child-rearing news articles, books, Web sites, and so on: "It is truly dizzying, even for the most clear-headed of us. The biggest problem isn't the confusion, though, it is the seduction. We would just love to believe that someone's discovered a secret formula that will give our children and us a guarantee of success."

Anna Quindlen, in a 2005 *Newsweek* article, asserted that "We live in a perfection society now, in which it is possible to make our bodies last longer, to manipulate our faces so the lines of laughter and distress are wiped out. We believe in the illusion of control, and nowhere has that become more powerful—and more pernicious—than in the phenomenon of manic motherhood." Supermom rears her cloaked head again, ready to control and create all-encompassing perfection.

Today's mothers have lived their lives in the "right" order: finishing education, finding a partner, launching a career and a relationship, creating a home, all before launching into parenthood. When you master each step to adulthood, you feel in control of your life. Pregnancy (sometimes infertility), childbirth, and lactation may be the first experiences of loss of control—of your life, your body, your career. You can't make yourself conceive with the perfect maternity leave schedule in mind. You can't will yourself out of morning sickness or into labor at a convenient time, at least not without a cooperative doctor and scheduled C-section. First strike to the myth of control. The second blow arrives home with the small bundle from the hospital. You discover that control over baby's schedule of eating, sleeping, or pooping is as real as pain-free childbirth. Most moms, facing this temporary loss of control, go full throttle to regain mastery over their lives. Magical thinking sets in. The more we can focus on the tiny details, and feel we are in control of them, the more we think we're in charge of our lives. Remember Kate Reddy, the heroine in Allison Pearson's novel *I Don't Know How She Does It*, smashing store-bought pies at

2:00 AM in order to make them look homemade? Most of us have our Kate Reddy moments.

Just like the character Kate, most women in my psychology practice, frustrated with their inability to be June, don't blame someone else. They blame themselves: their inability to bake perfect pies or find the green sippy cup. Blinded by the mommy mystique, they have embraced this overinvolved style of parenting as their own. If calls for perfection in parenting are everywhere you turn, whether in a magazine or your circle of friends, it is an endless task to evaluate them rationally. Our brains simply get overloaded with these messages, and the messages become the truth. Many women I talk to insist, "I am no perfectionist. You should see my house." The traditional view of a perfectionist is a spotless home, impeccably groomed, and a chicken pot pie baking in the oven. The house is not the only clue. Perfection can be about the kids, not you. You might be endlessly self-sacrificing for your kids. You might feel the need to give them a flawless childhood. You might be overmanaging, in order to keep them safe. In a 2004 *Psychology Today* article, Hara Estroff Marano called this "parental protectionism." Repeatedly in my practice and in my own life as a mother, I have found that the overdoing can be in terms of perfection, protection, or production— that is, producing the superstar kid. Women get sucked into one arena, or all three, depending on their individual anxiety and guilt patterns.

The great Dr. Spock, the parenting guru for baby-boomer parents, made a contribution to this call for mothering that produces perfect children. In the baby boom years, one copy of Dr. Spock's

Baby and Child Care was purchased for nearly every firstborn child in this country. In his efforts to increase mom's confidence, with encouragement to mother to trust her instincts and be realistic about expert advice, he may have fueled maternal anxiety. He preached that child rearing is easy and babies are naturally pleasant beings. What if a mom's perception of her life as a parent did not fit this prediction? What if this was not easy, and this screaming, red-faced urchin was definitely not what one would call pleasant? Many mothers again were left wondering *What is the matter with me?*

How the Need for Perfection Harms Your Health

As anxiety about parenting rises, it takes its toll on women's mental health. In *Redbook* magazine's 2006 motherhood survey of 1,100 women, 58 percent reported feeling guilty "sometimes or very often." One-third feel pressed to be a better, or perfect, mom—and 20 percent feel that every day. In a 1997 survey, 81 percent of women polled said it is harder to be a mom today than thirty years ago. And 56 percent said they're doing a poorer job as mothers than their counterparts twenty years earlier. This guilt and doubt are just the beginning. Married women with children have a higher risk for depression than married childless women, single women, or single or married men. Most women have their first contact with the mental-health system after the birth of their first child. Even if they experienced worry and low moods previously, the birth of a baby tips the scales, steering them toward medication or counseling. The incidence of depression peaks between the ages of twenty-five to forty-four years, just when a woman is most likely to have kids. This makes sense, according to a study published in December 2005 in the *Journal of Health and Social Behavior*. Parents were more likely to feel depressed compared to childless adults.

Perfection and Happily Ever After?

Depression, anger, and anxiety are not the only results of the unrealistic standards we set for mothers, or even for parents. Stearns points out that, in the late 1930s, married couples with children were as happy as childless couples. Every poll of marital satisfaction and the relationship to children since 1950 shows this trend has reversed. The couples without children are happier than couples with children, again and again. Polls show that every parent group except divorced fathers report an increase in ambivalence, negative mood, and feelings of inadequacy. These feelings were tied directly to the emotional aspects of parenting and the intensity of the job. As we've continued to expect more of parents, both men and women have been frustrated and overwhelmed by what they had to do.

Not only do parents feel more dissatisfied, depressed, or anxious with their lives compared to adults without children, but parents enjoy their activities less, day in and day out. A 2004 *Science* study gave scores to daily tasks based on how enjoyable they were. Taking care of children was one of the least enjoyable activities, ranking low with commuting, working, and housework. The 909 women in this poll, at least, were honest about the daily grind of being parents. Thank goodness it is an increasingly accepted fact that changing dirty diapers, wrangling screaming toddlers, and juggling piano lessons and soccer practice from your BlackBerry on the sidelines is not quality time.

Perfection's Toll on Your Children

The toll of extreme parenting on children isn't clear in the research—yet. But it is generating concern among child-development experts. Over the past twelve years in the United States, rates of depression in children and adolescents have skyrocketed. Rates of prescribing antidepressant medications for children with depression have jumped as well, according to researchers at Washington State University. Extreme parenting's insistence on complete and utter happiness for each child creates a backlash, particularly in adolescence. The tendency of teens to do the opposite of what parents want is legendary. When parents are invested in their teen being happy, the only way for teens to rebel is to be dreadfully unhappy. Given the hormonal influences on moodiness for this group, it is not a big leap. Our cultural requirement for happiness all the time, for every child, may reach out to bite us with younger kids, too. If Mom (or Dad) has always been "the family happiness manager," in the words of Susan Bolotin in a *New York Times Magazine* article, then when kids are left to their own devices, even if that device is the latest iPod or Game Boy, they have no clue about how to feel happy without adult intervention.

Extreme parenting doesn't affect just our kids' moods. It takes a toll on the freedom and independence that children have too. When parents worry excessively, kids' actions are restricted in the name of protection. Gone are the carefree days when kids could play outside from dawn to dusk, or take their bikes to the local swimming hole for a long, lazy summer float. When mom structures every minute of a child's life, children can't amuse themselves or make good choices. They can't learn from mistakes they're prevented from making. These problems plague kids when they get to college. The number and severity of mental-health problems among college students have been climbing since 1988. While relationship problems used to be the top issue, anxiety is now the major concern. Anxiety shows up not just in worried students but in increasing problems such as "obsessive pursuit," or stalking, and in self-destructive behaviors such as anorexia or bulimia. Nearly 40 percent of college women report having eating disorders, which have their origin in control issues.

Perhaps the rise in boomerang kids, bouncing home after college or when a job fails, is directly linked to extreme parenting. Adulthood

> **"We have raised a generation of young people who believe they're the center of the universe . . . has led to the so-called boomerang generation. . . . This is just WRONG. This is AGAINST nature. This is like a fully grown 200-pound adult kangaroo climbing back into its mother's pouch."**
>
> —*Dave Barry,* Dave Barry's Money Secrets *(Crown, 2006)*

no longer follows adolescence, according to a recent report. Instead, a period dubbed "early adulthood" spans the ages from twenty to thirty. Using classic benchmarks of adulthood, such as finishing education, beginning a career path, marrying and starting a family, 65 percent of males had reached adulthood by the age of thirty in 1960. By contrast, in 2000, only 31 percent had. Among women, 77 percent met the benchmarks by age thirty in 1960. By 2000, the number had fallen to 46 percent. When mom has been controlling the minutiae of a child's daily life for nearly two decades, organizing study sessions, notebook folders, and social climbing, how can a child orchestrate all this on her own?

Women Really Need a New Parenting Paradigm

The idea that we can ensure success and protect our children from negative feelings begins in infancy, with societal expectations about babies, sleep, and crying. The baby is new to the world, and mom is new to the job. She looks for answers in the form of procedures and guidelines, like she has in her work setting. Where is the definitive how-to manual, anyway? They must have run out right before I got to the hospital to give birth, because I never got my copy.

Nearly every current parenting manual for infancy implies that parents can control their babies' sleep and crying, if they will just choose the right path. Friends, family, and even health professionals try to sway the confused new parents on this basic issue. "Attachment parenting saved our lives," friends proselytize. "*Babywise* was the answer to my prayers," says your sister. To the confused parent, one extreme or the other seems the way to go, with no middle ground on the issue of crying and sleep. The salient issue is not which method is the magic bullet. The issue is two-fold. First is the underlying assumption most parenting paradigms share: that the child can be controlled and molded by the right methods. That you can, as a parent, make your child into a good sleeper, an independent being, a star athlete—and that this is your job, which is yours to pass or fail. Second, that whatever worked in infancy will work *throughout* a child's life. Parents get stuck, and continue to believe that jumping when the baby says jump is a good idea—at any age. Let it begin to sink in, like that syrup oozing around the back shelves of your fridge will do when it hits the cardboard egg box, that you are not a failure because you cannot perfectly manage your crying baby's (or sulking teen's) mood—or world.

Hidden expectations of parents are likely to be unrealistic. Recognize them, listen to the alarm bells that sound in the reasoning part of your brain. Put them in historical perspective. Parenting styles swing with the times and run in cycles, permissive versus strict, evolving as quickly as fashion and hemlines. In the colonial era, our culture viewed children as adults in training. The job of parents was to teach a job or trade, while guarding against immorality. Children were considered evil by nature, easily corrupted. In the mid-eighteenth century, children were seen as innocent rather than evil, and fragile rather than sturdy. The parental role became to protect children. If children needed protection, then there had to be a correct manner of raising them. Experts on the topic, mostly men, were then needed—so much was at stake! Someone had to step forward and define this "right way." But the answers vary by expert and era. Even the most famous parenting expert of modern times, Benjamin Spock, flip-flopped his ideas about doting on children in the manner that we do today. Early in the fifties, he advised mothers to entertain, enrich, and enable their offspring. By the late sixties, Spock and other experts cautioned against overinvolvement by mothers in their children's lives.

Concern about overparenting seems to have been lost in today's extreme parenting. This loss of perspective comes at a considerable cost to women, children, and families: less freedom, more anxiety, less enjoyment and satisfaction from the job of mothering. It's time to rethink current extreme parenting ideals. You will keep blaming yourself for failing to achieve the June Cleaver ideal if you do not keep parenting in perspective. This chapter has laid out the first step toward building a healthier, less anxious life as a parent: seeing how we got here. Television, magazines, historical but insidious social pressures all lead you to internalize the mommy mystique. Tuning in to how attitudes and standards swing with the times can help you let go. Remember, there is nothing the matter with you. It is the cultural push to be a perfect parent, to protect and produce a perfect child, that needs to be replaced. The next chapter explores the ways in which you, personally, have been sucked into unrealistic expectations for the role of mother, and how to begin to beat them in your head.

"I Have Everything I've Ever Wanted, So Why Am I So Miserable?"

Recognizing Mommy Thinking Traps: *What* We Think

The lament rings out every day in therapists' offices everywhere, morning until night:

* "All I ever wanted was to be a mommy and stay home with my kids."

* "I worked hard on my education, getting my career off the ground, even trained to be an occupational therapist so I'd have a flexible work schedule for my children."

* "Ever since I was a little girl, what was most important to me was having a family."

✳ "We spent thousands of dollars for fertility treatments, to have a baby. And now that I have these twins I wonder: What was I thinking?"

✳ "Wiping snotty noses and poopy bottoms as a higher calling? Could we have some honesty, please?"

Statements like these are routinely followed by some version of "and now I am miserable." Along with their misery, these women are riddled with guilt and anxiety, explosive with irritability or outright anger. This is not what they expected motherhood to be—and they're ready to trade it in.

Chapter 2 explored the external pressures that bring women to this hair-pulling, teeth-grinding spot of disillusionment. By now, you are beginning to identify your personal influences that led to your quirky "sucked up in the myth" moment. This chapter examines some universal values and beliefs that fuel the glow around motherhood. The mommy traps in this chapter impinge upon you from every magazine cover and TV news headline; they surround you whenever women talk about parenting. When I ask women about high standards for their behavior as mothers, they deny across the board that someone else is doing this to them. "Oh, no," they say. "My husband (mother/child) doesn't expect that of me. I expect that of myself." And they do. They have bought into unrealistic ideas about how their lives must proceed. These ideas are making them miserable. The more they muck along in their daily lives, trying to be June Cleaver or Claire Huxtable, with a sprinkling of Martha

Stewart, the more they get frustrated, irritable, and worry obsessively. When you set your vision for your life on an impossible ideal, you can't help but feel like a failure.

Take Liz, for example. Liz had a mom who raged. It was not quite to the level of wire hangers, but her mom seemed to think that a bellow at 40 decibels was the most effective strategy for corralling Liz and her two sisters, all two years apart. Throughout her childhood, this mantra ran through Liz's head: "When I am a mom, I will never raise my voice." To Liz, this was the perfect mother standard: show no harmful emotion, be always loving even when provoked.

After she married, Liz gave birth to twins. She managed to make it through the first two years of her sons' lives speaking in the calm, quiet tones she equated with being a loving mother. Then husband Joe took a new job, travelling away from home several nights a week. Her desperately needed break at the end of each day evaporated. She had to bathe, feed, and soothe both boys to sleep—alone! Trevor and Travis were barreling into the terrible twos, and with hurricane force adopted the time-honored goal of testing parents. At times, they could work each other into a frenzy, moving from giggling to hysteria and tears with lightning speed. Then Liz unexpectedly became pregnant again. She was instantly laid out with nausea from dawn to dusk.

One particularly trying day, Trevor had awakened Travis and Liz from their nap about forty minutes earlier than usual. Crankiness ensued. It was time to begin the evening bath, stories, and bed routine, and Liz felt like she had stepped off the Tilt-a-Whirl. Her stomach swam while Trevor chased Travis in circles, shrieking and giggling. Liz could hear the rising crescendo of Travis's laughter. After calmly chastising the boys twenty-two times to "Calm down, time for bed," Liz snapped. She bellowed, "Cut it out! Stop now!" The twins stopped. They stared at Liz for a beat, then promptly burst into tears. "No, no," shouted Trevor. "I want my daddy!" He ran off to their room, with Travis wailing behind him. Liz sank to the couch in tears, certain she had emotionally scarred her sweet boys. How could she have failed so miserably?

Mommy Thinking Traps

Travel inside your own head to look at the mommy beliefs that plague you, like that milk dust collecting on your shiny glass refrigerator shelves. A drop of milk spills down the edge of the bottle, you set the bottle in the fridge, the milk dries: *voilà*, milk dust. This happens a couple times. (No one in your house actually wipes the bottom of the milk jug, do they? If they do, I want to come live at your house.) Soon there is a crusty white layer all over the shelves. It spreads mysteriously from shelf to shelf, even when the milk is returned to the same place.

This is just like the mommy assumptions running through your head. You think you are dismissing all those TV headlines about how to be a better mom. You never actually tune in to ads that promote mothers and children happily lounging in a bed with pristine white sheets, right? At the softball sidelines, you ignore the conversation about who has a pitching coach, or which third-grade teacher's students achieve the best test scores, or what is the latest trendy birthday party. You want to rise above that. Like Kate Reddy discussing her friend Angela in *I Don't Know How She Does It,* "I can feel Angela's maternal ambition getting into me like a flu bug. You try to fight it, you try to stick with your hunch that your child will be perfectly okay without being force fed facts like some poor little *foie gras* gosling." In the end those influences seep into every waking moment.

Mommy thinking traps come in two varieties. The first is *what* we think about parenthood. Current societal beliefs are full of mandates about how to be good mothers, guaranteeing success for our children. Simply living in society, rather than on a deserted island with no magazines, TV headlines, or mothers-in-law, means you are exposed to them—ad nauseam. The first step in letting go of these perfect motherhood or childhood mandates means acknowledging them. Call them as you see them. "Oh, wait," Liz said. "Do I really think a constantly calm mother is essential, or is that society's idea?" You reject these unrealistic beliefs when thinking straight. You realize that moms yell, kids provoke, and children still turn out great. But these beliefs fan the flames of your guilt and anxiety when you're stressed. You react on a gut level under stress, and parenting of infants, small children, or teens is stressful. These rampant beliefs about parenting and children seem to offer The Answer for the perfect childhood. They are littered with implied shoulds about how perfect parents behave.

The second type of mommy thinking trap zeros in on *how* we think, not *what* we think. This trap comes from what cognitive therapists call *irrational thinking:* absolutes, black-or-white thinking, awfulizing. These are described in detail in the next chapter, along with guidelines on catching yourself on the verge of these traps. Even if you can let go of the content of beliefs outlined in this chapter, you still need to defeat the thinking patterns, or the process that leads to guilt and anxiety. It is not just how we process but what we believe that makes us feel "not good enough." Both steps are key to feeling better.

Which Mommy Traps Grab You?

Mommy thinking traps perpetuate the three types of over-parenting: overperfecting, overprotecting, and overproducing. You're more vulnerable to some beliefs than others, depending on your tendency to perfect your life with your children, protect your children from the realities of life, or focus on producing a super child. You know you'll never be perfect, but you throw all your energy and income into producing a child genius through learning experiences, tutors or coaches, and structured playtime: that is overproducing. You may succumb to perfect mother mandates, making sure your child's outfits, your home, or the birthday parties you throw are magazine perfect: that is overperfecting. Or the idea of harm that can come to your child drives most of your life, whether that is emotional harm from your own moods and missteps, a harsh teacher, physical playground dangers, or additives in food: that is overprotection. These are just examples of overparenting, and each mom has her own recipe for anxiety and guilt. You might have a sprinkling of overperfecting, overprotecting, and overproducing, or your over-parenting may fall into just one category.

OVERPERFECTING:

Mothers should be _____
(all-loving, patient, kind—you fill in the blank).
Children should always come first.
Parenting is fun, natural, and joyous.

OVERPROTECTING:

Children are fragile.
Childhood is dangerous.
You should protect your child from all negative feelings.

OVERPRODUCING:

Mothers are solely responsible for children's development.
Every moment is intrinsically precious for a child's growth.
More, better, all is essential for my child's success.

Taking these beliefs to heart inevitably makes you feel bad. When you can't act as a good mom would, you feel like you do not measure up. You feel "Something is the matter with me," or like the worst mother ever. Those mommy traps don't hold up to scrutiny. They are what Stephen Colbert of Comedy Central's *The Colbert Report* calls "truthiness." Colbert defines *truthiness* as "what you want the facts to be, versus what the facts are." Parents want these beliefs to be true. First of all, if these beliefs were true, parents would have total control. Who doesn't want total control? Imagine everything great for your child—no rejection, no failure, no disappointment. If only you had that power! Experts, media, society at large reinforce the truthiness. These beliefs feel like the right answer about parenting, and so it does not matter what the facts support. Truthiness is comforting—it justifies parents' efforts, especially excessive efforts. Parents want to believe they can protect and perfect their children, that their parenting energy is not wasted. Finally, these beliefs provide a template to follow. "Be this way," society promises, "and your child will be a success." This is as close to The Answer as it gets.

When total belief in dogma like this rules your life, guilt and anxiety are as present as head lice in preschool. Disputing these beliefs is critical to moving beyond extreme parenting. As you read the descriptions of the mommy traps, assess which ring true for you—this makes it easier to stop their influence in your day-to-day life.

Reasoning About Mommy Thinking Traps

PERFECTION BELIEFS:

1. Mothers should be _____.

All around you—on TV, in magazines and newspapers, on the Internet, wherever mothers talk—are assumptions about how mothers should be, at least if they want to be good mothers. To get a clear view of these beliefs, fill in the blank. Moms are: _____
_____.

Pick your favorites. Moms are loving, giving, ever-present, constantly self-sacrificing, organized, energetic, joyful. Moms are teachers, coaches, and therapists to their kids. Moms are responsible for their children's educations, social lives, manners, laundry, diets, health, entertainment, moods, creativity, accomplishments on every level—moms put their children first, forsaking their own lives. We are defining good moms—the kind of mommy you want to be—at every breathing moment. The June Cleaver paragon of motherhood.

Think carefully about the good moms you know. Are they all the same? Is there really one researched, tested model of how mothers can create successful adults? Public selves are only seen in public. Rare is the mother who acts according to these cultural shoulds at every waking moment. Equally uncommon is the mother who openly admits she can't be—maybe doesn't want to be—the teacher, therapist, or cruise director.

Moms Should . . .

Ask yourself: what requirements for motherhood do I hold in my head? To evaluate how the societal milk dust sneaks into your own personal "shoulds," use the space below to record any of the mom dictates that govern your life that we may have missed in our all-encompassing definition.

_____

_____

_____

_____

Elly believed that her neighbor Tara was the perfect mother. Always immaculately groomed, patient and loving with her kids, interested in their every peep. Elly envied how Tara did it. She wasn't fazed even when her children were tired, cranky hellions. Elly's temper was short—her kids had memorized her tight-lipped phrase "You are on my last nerve." Tara appeared to have a bottomless pit of nerves—never reaching her last one. Elly walked out of my office into the waiting room one day, and there sat Tara. After that, Elly found it easier to cut herself some slack. If Tara was not perfect, then perfection was simply not possible.

Even that epitome of perfect motherhood, June Cleaver, was an illusion. In an interview, Barbara Billingsley, the actress who played June, remarked on the irony of the role and all it has come to represent: she was portraying a perfect suburban housewife and mother—while leaving her own two children daily to do so. The business of acting competed with the frequency of fresh-baked cookies and pies in her own home. Colleen Kilcoyne, in *I Killed June Cleaver: Modern Moms Shatter the Myth of Perfect Parenting*, reminds mothers that "I have not been a bad mother; I have been a bad June."

One powerful variation of the "Moms should be" trap is "Moms are loved when they are cool." In 2005, the Web site Overflow addressed how "every parent of teens, in their heart of hearts, wants to be" a cool parent. Not just parents of teens, either. In a 2004 *Dallas Morning News* column, Jacquielynn Floyd reported on a survey of 4,000 parents by the marketing firm Synovate. A solid 50 percent of parents, in the United States, Canada, and Great Britain, would rather be their kids' friend first and parent second. Watch the movie *Mean Girls* if you need to understand what is wrong with this picture. The "cool" mom provides alcoholic beverages and condoms but is mocked by the understandably bratty daughter and her friends, not raised to the level of confidante.

When parents are so focused on being a buddy, they forget that their job is to produce a responsible, thinking adult. They never say no. In Floyd's column, the Synovate vice president gives this quote from one of the children interviewed: "My mom is lovely; she lets me do anything I want. But I don't want to be like that with my kids. It's made me lazy." Better to endure a few years of being uncool than to produce spoiled Peter Pan children. Embrace Overflow's first rule about being a cool parent: "You are not cool. Remember that." You are not meant to be.

Challenge This Thinking Trap:
Can mothers really fit any "shoulds" all the time?

Try this Perfectly Good Mantra:
"There are no perfect mothers."

2. *Children should always come first. And so follow the corollaries:*

Every moment I give to my needs detracts from meeting my child's needs.

A mother's work/day care is detrimental to her kids.

In May 2005, Dallas/Fort Worth radio station KERA aired a panel of women discussing the extreme mom trend: "normal moms versus crazy moms." One conclusion was that because women choose to be moms they are dedicated to making the child's life perfect. The underlying reasoning was "Why choose motherhood if you are not going to give your all?" This is reflected in the women I see in my practice, who say, "I could have thrown myself into my career, but I wanted to be a mother. Nobody made me have a baby—I wanted it. So I have to make it my life. Why would I have picked it if I wasn't ready to sacrifice all for them?" The downside of this belief is that, with only twenty-four hours in the day, after the kids' needs there is no place else for your needs but last on the list. One day in my office, Laila summed it up: "I was getting ready to go to lunch with a friend, and my three-year-old was hanging on my leg crying, and I thought 'I am such a bad mommy, such a bad mommy—a good mommy would stay.'" A good mommy puts her kids first, even if the end result is that she never does anything for herself. The majority of women I have seen in my practice agree: time spent on self unquestionably detracts from time available for kids. The end result is the ultimate sacrifice: yourself.

Turn up the volume on that logic, and the reasoning sounds hollow. The more a mother gives to her kids without replenishing herself, the more she is running on empty. If you are empty, by definition you have nothing left to give. Troll mommy* makes fewer appearances at my house when I have adequate sleep, meals, exercise, and a bit of fun in my life. *Definition of Troll mommy: Trolls live under bridges. They charge out at you cranky, loud, and ready to bite your head off. Shorthand at my house for my less than perfectly good days has become "troll mommy."

Extend this "kids first" argument to the workplace, and women quickly feel guilty about time spent on work, too. If one evening playing bunco takes away from what you give your kids, then working eight or more hours per day must be devastating to your child. Penny voiced this in my office: "How can I allow any time for me? I can't stop and work out before I get home—I have already been gone nine hours! I cannot be gone forty-five minutes more." Why not, if you will come home happier? Given good-quality child care, experience shows that if mama is happy, everybody is happy. In other words, if a woman is working because she wants to be working outside the home, or home because she wants to stay at home, the children are fine. If a woman is working or at home against her wishes, for financial reasons or otherwise, children are affected. Add a little perspective when you feel the need to be driven by what kids want. They are kids—they don't want to be told "no"—ever! But "no" is often in their best interests, if you want to raise great kids. If you never tell them no, you'll raise a troll child: a sleep-deprived, overweight, teeth-decay ridden, uneducated brat.

Challenge This Thinking Trap:
Can children realistically always come first?

Try this Perfectly Good Mantra:
"Taking care of me means more to give to my kids."

3. Parenting is joyous, fun, and natural.

This is a common misperception of mothers in my office: to be good mothers, they need to love the job of motherhood wholeheartedly. Anne Lamott, in *Mothers Who Think,* describes mothers who look "as if they're sailing through motherhood, entranced." One client, Carrie, mentioned her friend Rachel. "She never has any angry spells, unlike me—my anger bubbles over, if not outright explodes, every single day. Rachel loves being a mom. She says it's the best thing she's ever done." People with grown children are particularly adept at spreading this misconception. "Oh, isn't it fun!" they gush. "We had so many great times when our children were small—enjoy every minute, because before you know it, they will be gone!" Some months or years after childbirth, did you forget how bad it was? You were ready to do it again? Remembering childhood with this rosy glow is the same process of selective memory. Everyone would be an only child if facts about childbirth and infancy stayed firmly etched in women's brains. Grandparents look forward to time with grandchildren because the havoc and exhaustion that small children wreak

Perfectly Good Mantra:
"Love the kid, hate the job."

If the day-to-day drudgery of parenting drives you mad, remember this important distinction: you can love the kid, and still hate the job. They're not synonymous.

are faded memories. Some forgetting is good. But don't get sucked into "bad mother" thoughts because you don't intrinsically enjoy every bit of parenting.

It helps to be realistic: parenting is boring, repetitive, hard work. It involves lifting, toting, and chasing. It is mind numbing and menial. Anne Lamott, in that same *Mothers Who Think* essay, says "not only do moms get very mad, they also get bored. This is a closely-guarded secret, as if the myth of maternal bliss is so sacrosanct that we can't even admit these feelings to ourselves." Children want the same story read eighty-seven times, and they'll cut you no slack for missing a page. They want macaroni and cheese—for breakfast, lunch, and dinner. They demand to stop at the park after the library—just like last time. You drive the same route for their activities and wash their jerseys on the same day, ad infinitum.

While some times with children are fun and joyous, the backbreaking drudgery and endless responsibility can feel overwhelming. Parenting involves endless self-sacrifice, herding small beings who simply can't fathom that other people, that is, *you,* have whims and needs too. Children are much better than adults at demanding that their needs are met. Most mothers are shocked at how hard it is to constantly put the needs of another human being first, 24/7. Parents end up exhausted. Your perfect self thinks you need to take your children to the park, while the self-preservation voice in your head wants you to collapse in front of *Oprah.* As you go the distance, balance between these two is required.

You drag yourself out of bed to feed these hungry baby birds— after battling a stomach virus all night—and no one thanks you.

The immediate rewards and feedback in the job of parenting are nonexistent. When was the last time one of your small children— or even one of the other adults in your life—looked you in the eye and said, "Good job, Mom!"? This is complicated by the misconception that parenting is natural, or second nature. You've heard the adage aimed at new parents, in particular: "Just relax. You'll know what to do." Without prior experience with children? Herding a screaming two-year-old through the toy aisle doesn't trigger a genuine, expert response the first time—in anyone. As children grow, the challenges do too—and the second-guessing barely ends.

Not knowing if you are on the right track, versus mirroring Norman Bates's mother, makes parenting hard. There will be a reckoning, in about twenty-five years, when you see the fruits of your parenting labors. But not anytime soon. In a world that judges worth by what people do, parenting is hard to quantify and of variable value, depending on who you ask. If care of children fills your days, you ask yourself *What did I do all day?* after an endless loop of soothing, driving, feeding, and mopping. When someone asks, "What do you do?" you may shrug and mumble, "I'm a full-time mom," demeaning your worth. If you juggle work outside the home with your children's needs, all around you it seems like the experts and headlines imply you're sacrificing the best interests of your children. Looks like a lose/lose situation for women, with either choice.

To relish your life as a parent, quit hoping for perpetual fun, joy, and ease. You won't like your child all the time. There are ages that are tolerable, and ages that are abysmal. Some parents love infancy. Others can't wait until their child is three and can converse. Give yourself room to like a certain stage or aspect of the job and to hate others. Hating the job can coexist with loving the child. Making the distinction is critical at times—like the years of three-and-a-half or fourteen. This is the hardest work you will ever do. It is important, life-altering work. If you expect it to always be natural and fun, you may feel like a failure. And it certainly can be peppered with joyous moments: giggles and hugs, hilarious tantrums, and sweet nothings whispered at bedtime as your child strokes your cheek. Peter Stearns, in *Anxious Parents,* says, "Maybe fun is not the best measure of a reason to be a parent." Fun is just the bonus.

Challenge This Thinking Trap:
Can I really expect life with small children to be a constant Disney theme-park experience?

Parenting is like Dickens's opening line in *A Tale of Two Cities*: the best of times, and the worst of times. You are drained and give endlessly—and reap rewards you never imagined.

Try this Perfectly Good Mantra:
"Parenting is the hardest job I'll ever do—but the rewards will come."

PROTECTION BELIEFS:

4. Children are fragile.

Corollary: Constant praise is the route to build self-esteem in children.

Most parents start out fearing their fragile infant. There is a litany of absolute terror in your head. You could drop him. He could roll up in his covers and smother. He could choke when you feed him. You might slip and squash that frightening soft spot. By the third or fourth month, certainly by the time he is walking and definitely when a second child arrives, you see the reality. Children are much sturdier than new parents fear. Sure, they get bumped and bruised. But they survive.

Kent tells of he and his wife having their newborn daughter in their bed. The new mother was so tired when she finally fell asleep that several times the baby rolled out of bed. *Whump,* the dad heard as the baby hit the floor. Kent would elbow his wife, "Honey, she fell out again." That child is in college, an honor student and accomplished pianist, none the worse for wear. Jane tells about the very first "crash." In her baby walker, her daughter rolled out the back door, and down four steps. It was the first time the baby ever bled. Jane said, "You still believe it is a fluke you can prevent next time, rather than an everyday experience. That's the mother's mantra, isn't it? 'If only I could change it, fix it, take away the hurt, make it right.'" Her daughter went on to be a top-scoring basketball player and graduated near the top of her class. Accidents happen; we cannot perfectly protect our children. They survive most everything they encounter, in spite of us.

Perhaps emotional fragility is your biggest fear. Given the cultural emphasis on children's self-esteem, many parents most fear their children turning into drug addicts, ax murderers, child molesters. No one wants to warp a child's little psyche. Judsen Culbreth, in a 2005 *Reader's Digest* article, points out how parents have "bought into the myth that a child's self-esteem depends on never having even the slightest adversity, upset, or setback." Parents want to protect their little darlings to the ultimate degree.

Schools and teachers buy into the same irrational idea. Extreme examples offered by Culbreth include teachers using a black or blue pen to grade papers because those colors are "less harsh" than red, or responding, "That is the right answer to another question," when a student gives a wrong answer. In teacher training in London, Julia was taught that "the child was always right." Teachers were to find another way to say that the child was wrong. A T-shirt in the juniors' department of a local store brags, "My parents have never told me 'no.'"

Not only are we protecting kids from the reality of being wrong. We pour on the praise. Every child gets a trophy. Every drawing deserves framing. With my preschool daughter, we well-meaning parents piled on the praise. One day she was drawing as her dad worked nearby. She handed him a page; he exclaimed, "Good job." She whipped out a few more. Dad offered an enthusiastic compliment for each one. She got faster, drawing a single line on several pages and presenting it to him for praise before he caught on. Too much empty praise had led not to creativity but to meaningless repetition for praise's sake. In an interview on *The Today Show* in 2006,

Jean Twenge, author of *Generation Me,* said that building self-esteem in this way puts the cart before the horse. Rather than psychologically sturdy individuals, this approach creates narcissists. Kids praised for empty accomplishments will think they are wonderful without facts to back up the belief. According to Alfie Kohn, author of *Punished by Rewards: The Trouble with Gold Stars, Incentive Plans, A's, Praise, and Other Bribes,* perpetual praise sets up a vicious circle. Praise makes kids feel less secure, not more, so the more we praise, the more children need it—so we follow up with ever more praise. Kris Bordessa in a 2004 *Brain, Child* article states that "Self-esteem grows from the inside out; praise acts from the outside in." Bordessa adds that "These enthusiastic responses to average performances are setting our children up for disappointment down the road. After years of hearing how fantastic they are, over-praised kids go out in the real world only to discover that they are simply on par with the rest of their peers." Tell the truth.

Challenge This Thinking Trap:
Are children that fragile?

Try this quote by Steven Mintz, author of *Huck's Raft: A History of American Childhood,* as your
Perfectly Good Mantra:

"Children are more resilient, adaptable, and capable than society assumes."

Children are sturdy and can take it. Help children accurately assess their strengths and weaknesses. Give praise based on authentic performance, not random scribbles on the page. Provide opportunities for developing true mastery, in an independent manner. Take to heart Anna Quindlen's perspective from a 2005 *Newsweek* column: "If your mother has been micromanaging your homework since you were six, it's hard to feel any pride of ownership when you do well. You can't learn from mistakes and disappointments if your childhood is engineered so there aren't any."

5. Childhood is dangerous.

In an August 2006 article for the *Palm Beach Post*, Nicole Neal says childhood is far less dangerous now than at any other time in history. In 1930, says Neal, about 11 percent of children died before reaching adulthood. For children born in 2000, 1.3 percent will die before age twenty. Today's news reports lead parents to fear such horrors as child abduction, sexual molestation, terrorism, and disease. Calling child abduction the "airplane crash of parental fears," Neal cites the facts. The odds of your child being abducted and killed by a stranger are roughly one in a million. Compare this to other activities kids readily participate in. Odds in one year for dying—riding horses: one in 297,000; playing football: one in 78,260; riding in a car: one in 228. Extreme tunnel vision is at work. Parents oversupervise their children, drive them to school, have schools ban the game of tag to prevent playground injuries, and prohibit door-to-door trick or treating. Neal interviewed Peter Stearns, author of *Anxious Parents,* on razor blades in Halloween candy: "As far as we can determine this never happened. But it changed the whole pattern of Halloween." Neal concludes that it is not the dangers of childhood that parents should fear but the culture of fear created for our children.

Comic Alonzo Bodden poked fun at this culture of fear on the TV show *Last Comic Standing* in August 2006: "How big does an SUV have to be to carry one kid? . . . Navigators, Suburbans—and way in the back, one little kid strapped into his special little seat, surrounded by air bags and wearing his helmet. These kids are wearing helmets at all times—we are raising a generation of punk kids: ride a bike, wear a helmet; skateboard, wear a helmet. You walking upright?—PUT THAT HELMET ON! When I was a kid . . . we had no safety equipment, and the truth is your mother didn't really worry about you too much. . . . Mother just got tired of looking at you . . . she didn't arrange a playdate, she just said 'Get out of the house.' 'He'll get hungry, he'll be back.' . . . You went outside and EVERYTHING you played with was dangerous. . . . The swing was a big piece of metal . . . and you learned what 'heads up' means!"

6. You should protect your child from all negative feelings.

Two corollaries: A parent's anger is damaging for a child.

Mothers are exclusively responsible for children's entertainment.

It is a psychological truth: no human being can control the feelings of another. You cannot make infants sleep or eat or stop crying when they're not ready to—that's one of the first lessons of parenthood. That wisdom vaporizes as kids grow. The commonplace—but illogical—extension of the attachment parenting philosophy of "Don't let babies cry" becomes "Never allow your child to be unhappy—ever." You can no more engineer your child's constant happiness than you can make a wound-up, nap-fighting toddler sleep. If your child goes into the world, he will encounter difficult situations. And I think you want your child growing up, since the alternative is hiring the counterpart of Sarah Jessica Parker in *Failure to Launch* to lure them to move out when they are thirty-five.

Challenge This Thinking Trap:
Is childhood in fact that dangerous?

Adopt the Perfectly Good Mantra:
"What are the odds?"

Provide health care, car safety seats, clean hands, healthy food, hands to hold in parking lots or streets, appropriate supervision. And let go of worry about minute possibilities of harm.

To be successful adults, they must learn to address these challenges. In Nancy Gibbs's February 2005 *Time* article, a college professor reports that students have called parents in the midst of class to complain about a grade, handing the phone over so the parent can lobby the professor! Tales like this are rampant among high school and college teachers too: a student's schedule change when the high school teacher refused to delete a deserved bad grade; a father who called to challenge an allegation of cheating on his college daughter's behalf. What is the next step—good old mom calling the boss to defend the adult child?

At times, your child won't like a deserved outcome. Just as often, your child will run into mean, rude, selfish people who ignore your child's needs. It is another psychological truth that all human beings are out to defend their own feelings—not your child's. You cannot make everyone your child encounters act decently and treat them well. Teaching your children to deal with disappointment, unhappiness, even anxiety and depression, is essential to their health and happiness.

It is taboo in this culture for mothers to show anger. Did your mother squelch her anger with the cliché "I'm not angry—I'm disappointed"? We fear that losing rationality and yelling at one's kid is guaranteed to scar the child for life. Another call for perspective. In a March 2005 article in the *Dallas Morning News*, Mary Jacobs recalled the laid-back moms of the fifties and sixties: "Cocktail Mom." Jacobs said that "Once in awhile, a Cocktail Mom might yell. She knew that mom's anger is God's way of giving children helpful feedback when they are being obnoxious." Truly, exaggeration about the effect of a parent's normal anger on children is rampant. If you never show anger to your child, whether about their behavior or about the realities of your life, the child is ill-equipped to deal with feelings in the rest of the world. The coach rear-ends another driver on the way to soccer practice and yells at Geoffrey and a buddy who are drawing in the dirt on the sidelines. He blames himself, as children will do—he must be a bad player. A mean boy pushes Geoffrey on the playground and yells, "I will dump you in the trash can." If he has never encountered anger at home, Geoffrey is befuddled about how to cope. Natural human anger in a family, whether from parents or children, offers kids a safe laboratory to learn about feelings. An essential lesson for a functional adulthood is learning that people can be mad at you and still love you—a lesson best learned at home. To protect your children from every negative feeling is not only humanly impossible, but it also doesn't prepare them for the stresses of the world. I am not advocating troll mommy behavior; simple balance is required.

If parents accept total responsibility for their offspring's feelings, guarding against all emotional pain, then it's a short hop to full-fledged liability for children's happiness. Translated: kids' entertainment is mom's job. At all times! Just as parents believe they can control their child's crying from infancy on, parents buy into the flip side: that they are the happiness managers. Sing, dance, point out the big yellow truck—it really does not matter if the entertainment goal is developing your child's brain or keeping her happy. The onus still falls on life's cruise director: mom. Your worth as a mom is judged based on your child's mood nearly as often as on your child's sleep habits. Happy child equals good mommy; cranky child implies bad mommy. Odds of achieving "total happiness"? Equal to those of a termite surviving at the home of the Orkin man. Encourage your children to entertain themselves and handle their feelings. When you always step in to manage feelings or play-time, you send the message that your children are incompetent to do this on their own.

For instance, Julia worried about how much to "play" with her newborn son. Trained as a teacher, she knew the importance of parental stimulation in child development. Reading a child-care manual by Penelope Leach, she stumbled upon a passage that said parents need not involve themselves with the infant every waking moment. Baby could sit and look at the lights, or the fan, and be perfectly fine for a few minutes. This let her relax about it.

Challenge This Thinking Trap:
Is it even possible to protect a child from all negative feelings?

Try this Perfectly Good Mantra:
"Learning to handle (insert feeling: for example, boredom, anger, disappointment) is an important life lesson for my child."

PRODUCTION BELIEFS:

7. Mothers are solely responsible for children's development/ behavior.

A poll by etiquette expert Letitia Baldridge showed that 93 percent of people blame parents for their rude children. Warranted or not, mothers buy into this cultural mandate. Believing they are solely responsible for all aspects of children's lives, mothers hang on to control of their children as if they were hanging from the edge of the Eiffel Tower by their fingernails. Horror stories of extreme, over-responsible parents are everywhere: the teen boy whose mother styled his hair daily; the ten-year-old who was only allowed organic food, reaching the age of eleven without tasting a French fry; the teen beauty queen whose mother did her high school homework. In *I Don't Know How She Does It*, Allison Pearson's heroine Kate Reddy says, "Nature gives mother an advance-warning system, and mother is convinced that no minder or man can match her for speed or anticipation." Mothers appear to be "The One"—and only—who

Challenge This Thinking Trap:
Can mothers even be solely responsible for children's development?

Use the Perfectly Good Mantra:
"Many factors affect my child—I don't have to blame myself."

can do it right. And so they overcontrol, the surefire way to ensure success. Decades of research shows that mothers are extremely important. Mothers can guide, teach, and inspire. But so can fathers, teachers, grandparents, peers, and close family friends. Recent research has shown that the amount that dads talk to their two-year-olds has a greater influence on language development than moms. No reason to be blind to how the rest of the world affects kids.

8. Every moment is intrinsically precious for a child's growth.

Life with children seems to be all about teachable moments. Focus on "the moment" traces back to the revolution in birthing practices launched by two pediatricians, Marshall Klaus and John Kennell. In *Parent-Infant Bonding,* first published in 1976, Klaus and Kennell described the existence of a "sensitive period" immediately after birth. During this time, maternal–infant attachment occurs more readily than if mother and child are separated after birth. Women were no longer drugged into "twilight sleep" for delivery. Mothers and babies needed to be awake to bond in the birthing bed, or the moment could pass by. Exaggeration of the facts set up the idea that there was only one brief time for attachment to occur, like the critical period for bonding that exists in the animal world. Unlike animals, human beings do not have only a small window to connect with newborns. The bonding is enhanced by exposure immediately after birth, but it is not pass or fail.

The child development movement of the 1980s, with educational campaigns such as "I am your child," targeted learning in the years from infancy to three. Widely publicized on television, distribution of "Ten simple things that can boost your child's brain power" flyers reinforced the idea that each minute in a child's life had impact. In the words of Anna Quindlen in *Newsweek*: "Every moment for children was a teachable moment—and every teachable moment missed was a measure of a lousy mom." Once again, ideas that make sense with infants totally out-stayed their welcome, misapplied to older children. Each and every moment became an opportunity to teach, stimulate, socialize. In that 2005 KERA panel, one participant told of a mother giving her preschool child workbook pages to do for every mile spent in the car.

In fact, every moment *is* a chance for a child to learn. Must parents continually make that *their* job? Babies and young children are little scientists. They are busy watching, absorbing, and manipulating their worlds to figure things out. That is why they drop food off high chairs, stick screwdrivers in light sockets, and put on pouty faces as they craftily watch Mom's face from the corner of adorable eyes. Parents can foster children's learning in balanced ways—but

Challenge This Thinking Trap:
Is every moment critically important for a child's growth?

Try this Perfectly Good Mantra:
"In the big picture, my child has plenty of learning opportunities."

it's time to draw the line at the requirement that mothers devote themselves to teaching every waking second.

9. *More, better, all is essential for my child's success.*

Three corollaries: The right toys/tools are essential for my child's development.

Financial investment—toys, lessons, clothing—translates into other kinds of success for my child.

My child will miss out if we don't do what everybody is doing.

If you're going to be a mom, it is expected you will give your all. This includes your financial all and your minute-to-minute all. Why bother to have a child if you are going to deprive him or her materially? Can't give your child the latest miniature Dooney and Bourke bag? Social failure is inevitable. Birthday parties that pull out all the stops seem to be required, as Melinda Fulmer writes in her MSN.com Money Central article. Parents spend $6,000 on parties like this for a five-year-old who loves horses: two live ponies, a magician, a merry-go-round, and a horse-theme bounce house. To think you were worried about keeping up by not having the Cheerio-shaped snack holder!

Don't want to invest in a massive SUV? Then don't expect your child to be respected on the playground. At least that's what a recent Hummer advertisement wants you to believe. In the ad, one boy jumps in front of another for the slide. The nearby mom intervenes, "I'm sorry, Jake was next." The mother of the pushy child looks at the assertive mom and lets her bully proceed up the slide, saying, "Yeah, well, we're next now." The ad ends with the bullied mom trading in her minivan for a Hummer—she will no longer be pushed around!

Thinking parents know the right brand of jeans won't ensure acceptance at either the Ivy League or the seventh-grade dance. Too many parents, as good consumers, have become product focused—only on the child as the product, not the product as a tool. They are sucked in by the same marketing hype applied to vehicles and clothing, but with learning aides. Michelle Cottle addresses this in a September 2006 *Time* essay. Her child's sponge-painting set came with the promise to provide "an opportunity to do original planning and thinking while creating expressive art." Cottle claims that "today's overachieving superparents can't bear the thought of their obviously exceptional offspring wasting breath on any activity that won't help them win early acceptance to Princeton." This is a combination of "every moment is precious to a child's development" married to the necessity of teaching tools and aides. Holly Smith spoofed this parental extremism in a 2003 *Brain, Child* article. At the Apgar Preparation Seminar offered by Infant Learning Centers, your child can learn how to achieve an eight, nine, or ten on this most important test. "Remember" says Smith, "on the Apgar—as in life—there is no curve."

Forget the fancy developmental toys, prenatal education, and Baby Mozart DVDs. A 2006 online study concluded that regular conversation and balanced play with adults is what stimulates brain development. Talking to your kids is perfectly good and fiscally better than buying some learning tool—and you need not play or talk every waking moment. Alissa Quart, author of *Hothouse Kids: The Dilemma of the Gifted Child,* argues that our obsession with "creating" or "nurturing" giftedness has led to a "full-blown transformation of middle-class childhood into aggressive skill-set pageantry." Quart asserts that "enrichment" not only doesn't necessarily work, it can be harmful. The American Academy of Pediatrics has said that children under two should view *no* television, given concerns that it rewires kids' brains in a way that creates attention deficit disorder. Yet Baby Mozart videos continue to fly off the shelves. Perhaps parents are secretly watching them for their own enjoyment.

Another extreme parenting horror story from the KERA panel portrayed a mom worried that her child was not proficient at the monkey bars. She was working with him to "increase his skill set." The number of parents not enrolling children in lessons, coaching, and sports is miniscule. Jeanne Marie Laskas points out how this happens in an August 2006 column in the *Dallas Morning News.* She bemoans the hectic run from rained-out, make-up softball games to soccer practice: "So, on this ridiculous schedule, after we finish here they'll change in the car out of their softball cleats and into their soccer cleats and put on shin guards and new shirts. I swore up and down I would never do this. I would never be a parent who overscheduled her kids. My only excuse is: Everyone is doing it. Softball, then soccer, and then swim team if you can stand to get up early enough for practice. Everyone is doing it! Everyone is signing up for everything, and you get swept away." Remember your own parents' response to that argument "but everyone is doing it!"? It usually went something like this: "If everyone is jumping off a bridge, are you going to jump too?" The underlying fear that keeps parents from saying no is that their children will be left behind. As other parents push the bar higher and higher, you must keep up. If the child on the competing softball team has a private pitching coach, how can you deny your child the same opportunity? That would certainly make you a terrible mother, to deprive your child of training that everyone else has. So goes the thinking trap. This logic, taken to the extreme, leads to what an April 2006 CBS News report called "outsourcing the messier parts of parenting." Coaching for toilet training? Just check out www.bootycampmom.com if you are worried that the question "Age at which potty training completed?" will soon show up on college applications.

Challenge This Thinking Trap:
Is more, better, all truly essential for my
child's success?

Practice this Perfectly Good Mantra:
"Less is more."

When battling the "more, better, all" mentality, parents can use tried and true adages like "Less is more" and "Too much of a good thing." Eating all your Halloween candy at once? Endless pieces of cake served up? You know these excesses are bad for your child. How can other excesses be any better?

These mommy traps are not the sum total of societal misperceptions about mothers and children. They simply represent the more common views. You likely have a few of your own. You may want to jot them here:

WARNING:
My own
mommy traps

_____

_____

_____

_____

_____

_____

_____

_____

_____

_____

Recognizing these traps is the first step to freeing yourself from their snare. When caught up in thinking traps, step back and check facts. Call on your best critical thinking skills. Adjust your perspective. Are you facing truth or Colbert's truthiness? Identify your own top triggers of anxiety and guilt; turn them into a list of questions and keep them in your wallet. In a moment of extremism, you can pull them out and read them to untangle their hold on your brain.

Talking Back to Your Mommy Traps

Wendy was devoted to her daughters. Everything these darling girls wanted, they got. Wendy had stayed home, even though she had dearly loved her work as a radiology technician. She truly believed "children come first," and that meant putting her own satisfaction from work aside to devote herself, body and soul, to her children. She needed to be there each day to pick them up, because "good mothers should," in spite of growing resentment about sacrificing her career. There was a healthy dose of "more, better, all" peer pressure in her community, so Wendy and her husband scrimped and saved to keep up with the other families. Limousine rides home from the last day of school were not uncommon—how could she deprive her daughters? So what if she and her husband had not had a vacation in ten years? Wendy's top triggers of "children come first," "good mothers should," and "more, better, all" were bankrupting Wendy and her husband, emotionally and fiscally. With my help, she wrote out a three-by-five card to "talk back" to these mommy traps, and she kept several copies around—in her purse, by the phone, as a bookmark in the pages of the book she managed to read a few minutes each day. Her card said: 1) Is this the only way to be a good mother? 2) These children have been first long enough—time for some balance. 3) Does this teach the moral/financial lesson I want to teach? Knowing her triggers, and specifically targeting the mommy traps in this way, freed Wendy to make choices, such as returning to work and setting financial limits, that made for a less stressed family overall.

Debunking the content in these mandates, the what we think, launches you in the right direction. But recall that other key element influencing most parental anxiety and guilt: how we think about parenthood. Woven all through the content of these beliefs are irrational thinking habits. If the nature of your reasoning is not reworked, realistic thinking is harder. The thinking process underlying mommy thinking traps is explained in the next chapter.

Perfectly Good Mantra:
"I can think for myself."

You don't have to buy into the guilt-inducing, anxiety-producing beliefs explained here. You can think it through.

"Why Do I Feel Like the Worst Mother Ever?"

Recognizing Mommy Thinking Traps: *How* We Think

The loudest voice running through your head is a version of "I am a terrible mother. I am the worst mother ever." This absolute certainty about your placement on the "100 worst moms of the year" list pops into your head shortly after you have a terrible secret thought, the kind of thought that you can never voice out loud at play group or around the coffeepot at work. Conversation would stop. The room would freeze. Every woman in the room would stifle a slight gasp and stare at you. (You might be lucky enough to have mother friends who refuse to honor this societal taboo. Women who do speak the truth and support each other in voicing it. Women who admit that parenting is hard and that it's even harder to feel like you are doing it well. More power to you if you have friends like this. Treasure them. If not, see Chapter 7 for ideas on building a supportive mom network.) As a psychotherapist, I hear these "terrible secrets" every day. Those in this chapter are the most common ones exposed.

When becoming parents, most women are surprised how their thoughts fail to mesh with the reality of their lives. Jillian wondered how she had craved a baby—all those years of fertility treatment—only to feel now that her life was ruined. Beth worried that she was flawed because she hated the daily grind after giving up her job—she felt her brain was turning to mush. Women like Beth and Jillian have bought into the misperceptions about parenting; these ideas seem valid and plausible, on paper. Women are expecting the family balancing act to be as easy as in the Huxtable household. Up until you actually muck through the daily grind of children, you truly don't realize the power of those pounding media images. Surprised by the day-to-day reality, many women feel like Hope Edelman in *The Bitch in the House*: "Balancing act? I was the whole damn circus, all three rings."

Terrible Mother Thoughts

The gap between how you imagined your life and how it is may span the Grand Canyon. Especially when you expect the impossible. The exhaustion sets in from trying to engineer the ideal life, and you feel like a failure with not one ounce left to give. The unspoken thoughts race in your head: *I cannot do this the right way. I am not a good mother. I am no good for this kid because I have terrible*

The Naughty 9:
Bad Mom Thoughts Exposed

In my years of experieence, here are some of the most
pervasive guilt-inducing "bad mom" thoughts. They
include:

"I hate my life."

"I can't believe I traded sleep for this."

"This kid is a brat."

"I cannot stand to play Barbies (or read *Goodnight Moon*, or
play Legos, "_____
_____ or fill
in the blank with your own personal kid plague) one
more time—or at all.

"I now understand how a parent could throw a child against
the wall."

"This kid has ruined my life/my body/my marriage."

"I just want to run away—alone."

"If that kid does not stop crying, you'll have to check me
into the funny farm."

"I'd rather be at work during busy season than with these
kids—any day."

thoughts. Women lose track of what fuels these thoughts: outside forces, now internalized and believed. They feel simply like horrid people. How can you be a good mother when you think that your life is ruined, you hate motherhood, you want to run away? You are supposed to love this job.

Why are mothers certain they are terrible for having these thoughts? Society does not just have rules about what mothers *should do.* As Pamela Redmond Satran points out in an August 2004 *Parenting* article, the world of moms has a mysterious set of expectations about what a good mother *should feel.* Rules about how mothers should feel are the most powerful trap yet. To confess to resenting motherhood is the biggest social taboo of all. You shouldn't even have these thoughts, you think. Mothers censor

"So Many Ways I've Been a Bad June:
- I have always thought that the playground is boring.
- I hate to bake.
- Barely verbal, my kids knew how to hand sign 'you drive me crazy.'
- I cry out loud when they really hurt my feelings.
- I taught them rock and roll; they know every word to 'Wooly Bully.'

There are many more June sins to list, but that short confession has done me good."

—*Colleen Kilcoyne,* I Killed June Cleaver

these thoughts, feel deficient for having them. Surely only a terrible mother allows such notions into her brain, let alone utters these heinous thoughts.

Fear of these thoughts originates in the idea that "thinking makes it so." The link from thinking like a terrible mother to acting like a terrible mother seems short. Women think, "Surely if I have these terrible mother thoughts, acting upon them is the next step." This is simply not true. As high school English teacher Caroline pointed out, the definition of character is what one does with the universal terrible thoughts that human beings have. Thinking does not make it so, or I would have won the lottery long ago.

Just as there are terrible mother thoughts, there are times when women act in ways to submarine the "mother of the year" nomination. Rare is the woman who has not suffered through appalling

Kristen van Ogtrop, in "Attila the Honey I'm Home" in *The Bitch in the House,* confesses that her children have said to her, "You're too mean to live in this house and I want you to go back to work for the rest of your life." Van Ogtrop puzzles over how she can be "an angel in the office and a horror at home." The same principle is at work that has children behaving badly at home, while earning congeniality awards at school: We unwind in a safe place, letting down our guard with those who love us.

mother moments. When I became a mother, my memorably calm mother related a time she had screamed at me and my three sisters, yelling at us to "pick up your toys," "clean up this mess," and "quit bothering" her. Clearly the guilt had been simmering for twenty years. My sister and I looked at each other blankly and shrugged off her catharsis; neither of us had any recollection of what, to her, was a dreadful event. I have had episodes like that myself, stopping the car and dumping out my teen daughter, forcing her to walk the last two blocks home. My daughter coined the phrase "troll mommy" as a result. Not a proud mother moment. Yet it doesn't make me a terrible mother overall. If I acted that way in every single interaction over her total childhood, I might deserve the terrible mother label. Perspective is required.

How Thoughts Morph into Mother Feelings

To understand how terrible mom thoughts translate into guilt, anxiety, and irritability, look at the process that affects feelings. Where do feelings come from? There are physical feelings, of course, that arise from the five senses. You feel cold when the temperature drops too low. You feel thirsty when your body signals a need for more water, its major component. You feel tired when you have chased three kids around the park.

What we commonly call feelings, or emotions, are distinct from bodily sensations like thirst or fatigue. Often emotions and bodily sensations become linked, as when a person has panic attacks or clinical depression. When that happens, it's difficult to distinguish emotions from physical feelings. If your heart is pounding, as in a panic attack, you usually interpret that as "scared." That's a gut-level feeling.

Emotions are a different beast. Many people assume that emotions arise much like bodily sensations—they just happen, with a mind of their own. Psychologists who research cognitive therapy contend that emotions arise not in our guts, but in our heads. When an event happens, all human beings have a thought—an interpretation or value placed on what just happened. If you place a positive value, and see it as a good thing, you will feel happy, proud, content. When you label the same event as negative, you feel angry, disappointed, or sad. For example, your daughter's teacher may call. Just hearing the words "This is Mrs. Carmichael" can send you instantly into feeling good or bad. Your brain may jump immediately to a negative interpretation on receiving the call. *Oh, no, what's happened now?* you think, as your heart sinks. Or you may put a positive spin on the event: *Wow, maybe Michaela won that writing contest,* you imagine and feel proud. The immediate place your brain jumps to ties directly to feeling good or bad. That's because emotions are the direct by-product of thoughts and are influenced by beliefs. These beliefs can be cultural, like those explored in Chapter 3. Or they can be very personal.

Jenny desperately wanted a baby boy. She believed she could not be a good mother to a girl, after suffering through intense mother/daughter conflict in her teen years. When she and Ted found out they were having a baby girl, Jenny felt her panic rising into a frenzy. How could she raise a girl? She would perpetuate the horrible pattern she had with her mother. *I can't do it, I can't do it* ran through her head most of each day. Ted handled the first days, getting to know baby Mia and becoming a competent daddy, while Jenny watched from the sidelines. A second constant line joined the first running through her head: *I hate being a parent. I have made a huge mistake.* Jenny felt defeated. Her belief that "I can't be a good mother to a girl" blocked the fact that this was, first and foremost, a baby. She had tons of experience with babies, from babysitting when she was young. Ted had no experience. But his belief that he could do it led him to try. Jenny's belief that she was a "loser mom" was directly tied to having a girl. After endless discussion with Ted, with his encouragement to think it through, Jenny began to see baby Mia as less foreign. By revising her thoughts, she relaxed and actually enjoyed rocking and feeding the baby. The panicked feelings disappeared. Jenny's thoughts had directly caused her feelings.

Characteristics of Illogical Thinking

Jenny's idea that she could not be a good mother to a girl reflected her individual quirky belief. It was influenced by personal experience, not by society's mandates. Jenny, completely aware of this problematic thought, voiced it repeatedly even before she became pregnant. Just as often, the thoughts that color mother self-perceptions are much more subtle. Moving through your day, you assign meaning to every event and experience: good or bad, safe or dangerous. You touch a soft fabric on a dress while shopping and think, *Ooh—feels nice.* The child who came for a playdate gives you a sour look and the thought pops into your head, *I don't like this kid.* The process of thinking and giving meaning is constant, at a level you don't perceive, until you begin to watch for it. Matthew McKay, Martha Davis, and Patrick Fanning in *Thoughts and Feelings: Taking Control of Your Moods and Your Life,* describe this process as a "waterfall of thoughts cascading down the back of your mind." These thoughts were termed *automatic thoughts* by researcher Aaron Beck. The thoughts simply pop into your head, by reflex. Also called *self-talk,* these are thoughts in your head, said to yourself alone. You are so used to this internal dialogue you rarely notice it and certainly don't stop to analyze it. Automatic thoughts just *are.* Matthew McKay and colleagues assert that events have no emotional content. It is the interpretation of events that causes feelings.

A. Event ⇒ B. Thought ⇒ C. Feeling

A is the event you react to: your child brings home a note saying children in her class have head lice. B is the thought you have, the interpretation of A: *Oh no, how yucky, people will think I am a terrible mother if they find out.* C is the feeling reaction that follows: You feel overwhelmed and depressed.

Automatic thoughts arise from all those rules about mothering described in Chapter 3 and from news media, books, entertainment, or talking around the water cooler or in play group. Much of the self-talk springing from these influences is not harmful or unrealistic. It can even be instructive: kids need education, kids need health care, kids need love and limits, kids need five fruits and veggies per day. Some patterns of automatic thinking trigger guilt and anxiety for mothers. Thoughts most likely to create bad feelings in mothers are brimming with overexaggeration and illogical thinking. This is the "how" behind mommy traps that is so seductive. This is why terrible mommy thoughts seem so horrifying. To identify thinking traps, listen for clues. Your brain runs on autopilot with these thoughts; you don't stop to think, you just act—or more importantly feel—when they kick in.

The First Clues to Illogical Thinking

The first characteristic of automatic thoughts is illogical thinking. Clues to illogical thinking can be absolutes: always, never, everybody. Another hint is polarized or black-and-white thinking: everything is great or everything sucks. You filter out important details and hear only negatives. Then you see it as all or nothing. Should, ought, must, or inflexible rules about how people act are the final clue, for example, "I should love playing Candyland." When you feel bad about the terrible mother thought *I hate my life*, your bad feelings grow right out of *I should love it*.

Most moms have illogical thinking habits, but your own automatic thoughts may be combinations. In Chapter 3, the mother shoulds that plague women were explored: Mothers should be calm, loving, quiet, affectionate, patient. Self-talk with "should" usually involves absolutes, too. The "always" is not stated but definitely is implied in any "should"—for example, you should always be calm. Moira felt she should be patient as a mother. She certainly didn't give herself credit for being patient just on Sundays. Yet for her the words *patient* and *mother* rarely went together. *Good mothers should be patient absolutely 100 percent of the time,* she thought. Hear the absolute, all-or-nothing thinking?

Shoulds don't plague mothers only about their own behavior. Shoulds apply to children, teachers, spouses, and the rest of the world. The terrible mother thought *My kid is a brat* arises from two shoulds: *She should behave,* and *I should get her to behave.* Julia thought her children should be like roommates—respecting her need for space. But kids don't understand that parents have needs. Karen thought the teacher should understand her son's sensitivity. She became incensed when the teacher insisted he follow the classroom rules. The parent calling on the cell phone in the middle of the college class felt the professor should see her child's potential. Auto thoughts spill over into each other, mixing up shoulds, all-or-nothing thinking, or absolutes.

More Clues to Irrational Thinking

The second characteristic of automatic thoughts is the tendency to "awfulize." Catastrophe, danger, and the worst that can happen are what you fear. "What if" and "I can't stand it" are key phrases, revving up your anxiety. Moira thought, *If I am not patient 100 percent of the time, it will be awful. If I yell or fuss, I'll wreck my kid's life.* Ruining your child's life is about as catastrophic as it gets. Awfulizing is piled right on top of the absolutes and all-or-nothing thinking. Moira focused utterly on her goal of patience. Only 100 percent counted. If she missed that goal, she was a bad mother—all or nothing, with no degree of success in between.

If you are stuck on "what if"—the bad that's possible—you are catastrophizing. The fear in you caused by terrible mother thoughts, discussed previously in this chapter, is linked directly to "what if." *What if I act on the thoughts?* you worry. "What if" weaves its way through many worries. Kim, a new mom, planned a much-needed break with her friends. "What if the baby cries the whole time I am gone? If the baby cries the entire time I'm at happy hour with my friends, it will be awful. The sitter will never come back. I will never have another break." She worried all afternoon. Well, it won't be fun for the sitter if the baby cries the whole time, but everyone will survive it.

The list of "what ifs" that fuels extreme parenting is endless. Gibbs recounts in her *Time* article how one family hired a college counselor to help "package" their bright, achieving, college-bound child. The counselor set to work on the admission essay with the child, asking if there was a book read outside of school that had an impact on the student. The student responded, "Why would I read a book if I didn't have to?" These anxious parents had so focused on the fear "What if he does not get into a good school?" that the child's natural curiosity was obliterated. What if she does not get the best teacher? What if he does not make the select team? Disaster is the implied answer, something along the lines of "All will be lost." In other words, failure. Anxiety or guilt for the parents. Lynn hated coloring with her daughter. *I can't stand to do this one more minute* was the refrain in her head. "I can't stand it" is a telling clue, implying "This is awful—I hate it." Guilt kicked in as she thought, *What kind of mother won't color with her daughter?* Hear the should? Then her thinking jumped to *She will be a failure at coloring, kids will make fun of her in kindergarten, she will never have friends.* Excessive exaggeration again, with disaster as the inevitable result. "Woe is me, all is lost" was Lynn's repeating theme, all because she hated coloring!

All-or-nothing thinking feeds the exaggeration of catastrophe.

Let's examine how illogical thinking rampages through Kilcoyne's "confessions" of terrible mother thoughts. "The playground is boring." Hear the should? Should you enjoy everything that four-year-olds do? "I hate to bake." Should mothers be domestic divas? How does that contribute to raising great children? "My kids hand sign 'You drive me crazy,' and I cry out loud when they really hurt my feelings." Hear the absolute, all-or-nothing thinking? Mothers should always be calm and controlled? Almost universally, illogical thinking lurks under your terrible mother thoughts. Watch for it, and wipe it out.

Reality gets squeezed out. For Ryan's eighth birthday, the party Rose planned was a triumph. Everyone went home happy and smiling; the go-carts had been a real hit. The previous year, the party was a dismal failure—at least in Rose's mind. Two kids were scared of the pony, leaving early in tears. In her all-or-nothing thinking, Rose overlooked the sixteen kids, including Ryan, who had loved the pony. She had to raise the bar on this year's party to ensure success. Awfulizing and shoulds were rampant in her thinking. She ignored the fact that a majority had fun, screening out the good about the previous year's party. She catastrophized: she might be seen as a lousy hostess; Ryan might never be invited to another party. Shoulds and absolutes lurked under this perfect hostess trap; every kid at every party should have a wonderful time.

Joni liked her house neat—at all times. When her house was picked up, she felt all was right in her world. When daughter Lily left her backpack, lunch box, jacket, and shoes in the hall, Joni went into a frenzy in her head: *The house is such a mess!* We might all be so lucky to have such small messes. In Joni's mind, the house was either clean or dirty, with clean equalling good and dirty equalling bad. This black-and-white thinking spread to her value as a mother. Good housekeeper equals good mother; bad housekeeper equals bad mother. Joni's version of black-and-white thinking involved intense tunnel vision. She ignored praise, even when it was obvious, and noticed only the bad. Joni was blind to the fact that, while the hall where Lily dumped the detritus of the school day was cluttered, other rooms were model-home perfect.

To Jessica, grades were paramount. When Hector brought home

EXAMPLES OF IRRATIONAL THINKING:

That litany in your head says:	→	And is fueled by this:
_____		_____
_____		_____
I am such a bad mother because:	→	Underlying irrational pattern(s):
_____		_____
_____		_____
I forgot the juice boxes for soccer practice.	→	**Absolute:** Good moms never forget.
I yelled at my kids.	→	**All or nothing:** I'm calm and quiet or a terrible mom—nothing in between.
I went out to lunch and left him crying with dad.	→	**Awfulizing:** His crying was dreadful.
I am sick of the playground.	→	**Should:** I should love it.
I picked a bad school.	→	**Awfulizing:** It has no strengths?
I never read to them.	→	**Absolutes:** You never have?
I took a nap instead of finishing the baby book.	→	**All or nothing:** I do for the kids all the time or I'm a loser.
I should be able to get him to stop crying.	→	**Should:** A good mother should be able to calm him.
She never gets invited to birthday parties.	→	**Awfulizing, absolutes:** 100 percent of the time? Will it really be harmful?
Everyone else makes it look easy.	→	**Absolutes:** Are you the only mom struggling?

his report card with one B, she turned into troll mommy. How could he get a B in language arts? They had worked every night on his spelling words! She ignored his As in every other subject and fumed: that he had merely eight more years until college! Her black-and-white thinking led her to conclude that Hector was a good student if he had all As and a bad student if he had anything less. A high-school guidance counselor in Gibbs's *Time* report illustrated this all-or-nothing attitude in his school—about cheating: "If you're not cheating, then you're not trying. A C means you're a loser." Rachel had her child memorize all the SAT words from the College Board list. Absolutely all—a flash card for each and every word. The teen knew them by heart, and she scored well. She was admitted to the college of her choice, receiving a full ride, only to run out of gas like an SUV in an oil embargo. She lost the scholarship at the end of her freshman year.

A rampant thinking trap is "to-do list" tunnel vision. Every night, Julie tossed and turned, stuck on what remained on her list from that day, rather than what she did accomplish. For mothers, the tunnel vision is full of value judgments about which activities are important, too. Julie chastised herself—she hadn't completed her budget report one evening and felt like a terrible employee because she read to her son for an hour instead. The should was creeping into her self-talk: *I should get it all done.* She felt better when she stopped fretting and took credit for the time she had spent with her son. Her perfectly good mantra became "Look what I did do today."

Absolutes spread like ink from that errant marker in the white laundry throughout this irrational thinking. You make a sweeping conclusion based on one bit of evidence, using words such as *all, every, none, never, always, everybody,* and *nobody.* Liz felt she would never be a good mother after her blowup at her twins. She could not imagine they would get past it. Absolutely, this one event had turned her into her mother, wiping out two years of calm interaction with her kids. Jenny fell prey to absolutes as well. She was certain having a good connection with a daughter was impossible because her relationship with her mother was so poor.

These automatic thoughts build into a crescendo of magical thinking, particularly about control. You think, *I should be in total control of my child's life. If I am, I can ensure it's perfect. I can protect my child from harm—hurt feelings, rejection, illness, or failure. If I am not able to, bad things will happen—catastrophes at every turn.* Michaela tells of one mother's fear of rabies. "This mother wouldn't let Jana play at our house because we had cats who went outside. Even though the cats had their rabies shots, they might lick the bone of an animal with rabies and give it to Jana." Jana's mother lived by the idea that "If I can just control the tiny details, my child will be immune from harm."

Through illogical thinking, mothers fall prey to this illusion of control. They buy into the truthiness: if they completely manage each and every detail they can expect a fairy-tale life.

McKay, Davis, and Fanning say

> "We often think our affairs, great or small, must be tended continuously and in detail, or our world will disintegrate, and we will lose our places in the universe. That is not true."
>
> —*Maya Angelou,* Wouldn't Take Nothing for My Journey Now

automatic thoughts seem valid and plausible, even if on close analysis they turn out to be illogical. Getting into Princeton seems like the only route for your child to have a successful and happy life. The only path to Princeton appears to be acceptance into Cheery Days Preschool. Logical analysis reveals that Princeton does indeed accept some children from other preschools in town. Happy, successful adults who graduated from schools other than those in the Ivy League are all around—or it would be a very narrow world. This illogical exaggeration is not clear in your mind. The nature of automatic thoughts is that they are accepted, natural, and widespread. You have heard them or thought them so often that they seem true. The self-talk is shorthand, flashes of single words or phrases, not fully formed thoughts or sentences. You might think *bad mother* or have a burst of feeling that everyone in the plane is judging you as your three-year-old is crying.

McKay and colleagues agree that automatic thoughts are learned. Over the years, you've watched other women, listened to family and friends, and read articles or watched TV to internalize automatic thoughts about mothering. Since these thinking traps are learned, they can be unlearned—once you tune into them. This running dialogue in your head can be unique to you, or common among many moms. Nyla's biggest parenting fear was her children's intellectual achievement. Ten points too low on the PSAT and she was refilling her Ambien prescription. Nikki's personal terror was social acceptance for her children. Watching another mother's minivan load up with every popular third-grader but hers sent shivers down her spine. Every mother has personal vulnerabilities.

Remember, there is nothing the matter with you if you fall prey to automatic mother thoughts. They are simply part of being human. You're not a bad person for thinking this way. There is an endless litany of insecurities in most mothers' heads. Watch for your own preferred modes, for deciphering your thinking traps is part of your personal quest to be a happier, more balanced person and mom. If you can hear your self-talk, you can evaluate the truth and substitute more realistic automatic thoughts.

The Connection Between Automatic Thoughts and Extreme Parenting

Automatic thoughts are part of being human. So how do we get from these glitches in thinking to extreme parenting? First, parents buy into the societal view that their children's success is a measure of their *own* worth. If you have good kids, you must be a good mom—and vice versa. Accepting that, you then control their lives perfectly—to guarantee success.

> "Mothers need to have good kids so they can be seen as good mothers."
>
> —*Andrea Buchanan,* author of Mother Shock

The next step is believing that life is getting harder and harder; only the top candidates will prosper. You need to ensure your child is tops. Finally, if your kids are not the best, you must be a bad mom. Overinvolved, over-responsible parenting becomes the way to meet this challenge. The automatic thoughts rattle on and on in this vein, telling us what to think about parenting.

When we hear these demands for parenting, they're presented as indisputable, always true, nonnegotiable. No room for adapting them to individual lives. See how the illogical thoughts about motherhood and childhood are full of shoulds, absolutes, and all-or-nothing thinking about how to act or feel? This is how we think about parenting. Mothers should be paragons of virtue, patience, control, and enlightenment absolutely 110 percent of the time. If not, total and complete catastrophe will reign. Women merge these ideal mother mandates into automatic thoughts, running in their brains like a CD on repeat. Part of your brain takes them to heart, believes them, and tries to fulfill them. You work to live up to the shoulds. You compare yourself to how others manage. But with expectations that simply aren't humanly possible, anxiety and guilt rise. How can you ever succeed?

Pressure to compete and achieve perfection, illogical thinking about parenting, and anxiety about protecting children eventually add up to extreme parenting. Mothers do ever more, controlling all the little details so intensely, grabbing that false sense of security. If you are doing all the right things, *Everything will be all right,* you think—for a fleeting moment. Anxiety and guilt lessen—at least for that second. In doing less ever so briefly, thinking perhaps you have made it, some other pressure sneaks in. The cycle begins again.

cultural ideals

automatic thoughts

anxiety and guilt

extreme parenting

We must escape this mad cycle of extreme parenting. But where to start? Discarding the cultural demands for perfection and control sounds good. Given human expectations, mothers would measure up. No more self-talk of failure making mothers miserable. This is what Warner calls for in *Perfect Madness*. This is the ideal. To wake up tomorrow, or after three years of serious political lobbying, to a society that not only expects parents to be human but supports them fully. There would be a smorgasbord of family benefits: guaranteed paid parental leave, quality child care options for all levels of work, equal division of labor in marriages. Do you have a magic wand? The current political climate in this country means programs like this won't appear in a sprinkling of fairy dust.

Meanwhile, change can come on a personal level, by stopping the anxiety that drives extreme behavior. Anxiety and guilt feed extreme parenting by calling for more, bigger, better. The thinking part of your brain realizes that "more, bigger, better, all" is a foolish course of action. There's no parenting success guarantee. But the anxiety flourishes. It eats at you like nail polish remover on a finely varnished dresser. The anxiety outshouts the logic in your head. It is reinforced by everything you see, read, and discuss with other mothers. You know you can't achieve the unattainable "perfect mother/child" goal, not with only twenty-four hours in the day. No human mother could. At the same time, you cannot stop the anxiety—you have to keep aiming to perfect, produce, or protect. If only you could locate the off switch! The only place with room to intervene is automatic thoughts. The problem lies not only in what we believe, that total control is possible in parenting. It is also how we believe, that we apply bushels of absolutes and barrels of all-or-nothing judgment to the issue. The only relief lies in bringing some reason to the madness—in a loud, clear voice. Replacing critical self-talk with a dose of realism and perspective will make you feel less anxiety and guilt. When you worry less, you can let go of unrealistic expectations. Then take the plunge into new behavior; the thinking traps loosen. Your sense of catastrophe subsides when you act in a new way. Spending less than $5,000 on a birthday party does not breed disaster. SAT scores less than perfect offer admission to many good schools. Even when you forget the juice boxes, you can still feel like a perfectly good mother.

Tackling Irrational Thinking

Automatic thoughts about "good mothers" sneak into your head faster than you can say "June Cleaver." When your behavior doesn't measure up, you feel like the worst mother ever. Sometimes a little investigative work is needed about that self-talk, so you can squash it. If you tune the thoughts out, you won't realize how they're driving you.

Detecting the Automatic Thoughts

What are your biggest shoulds? Do you get caught up in a whirlwind of "I can't stand it" and catastrophe? Are you stuck seeing a TV caricature, rather than a person? After reading the descriptions elsewhere in this chapter, the steady trickle of automatic thoughts in your head may be clear. But sometimes you have to dig deeper—beyond reading this and thinking about it in this moment. Remember: automatic thoughts are devious, flashing into your brain in small bits, catching you unaware. They seem reasonable and valid, so you believe them.

Spend a week or longer tuning in. Attention is a selective process. If you were utterly attuned to your world at all times, you could never concentrate. Like a child with attention deficit disorder, everything around you would be stimulating or distracting. It would be like driving in a minivan with seven passengers playing their own CD or DVD players at top volume. Try monitoring all the lyrics and soundtracks for appropriate content—you simply could not do it without your brain exploding. So you screen out the static in any moment. Talking on the phone, your full attention shifts to the caller. Sounds in your world fade into the background. Then alarm bells sound when your brain realizes your children are too quiet. What are they up to? Shampoo paintings on the pillows again? To hear your automatic thoughts, listen intently to what goes through your head for a while. Tune in to the always, what ifs, and black-and-white thinking. With practice, you'll hear them.

Some people find that bodily sensations and feelings are more powerful clues than words in their brains. Remember the A ➠ B ➠

Perfectly Good Mantra:
"It's no big deal."

C pattern of feelings. A is the event: in the telephone example, mom realized there was no noise. Then B: she thought "Something is wrong—too quiet!" C was the result: a brief moment of panic about what the kids were into. Tuning in to the bodily sensations alerts you before your brain catches up. The bodily sensations sneak right between A, the event, and B, the thought. Do your shoulders get tight? You catch your breath? Your teeth are clenching, stomach is churning? The self-talk has been linked with stress so often that automatic body cues occur. This link in your body is just like the cat with the can opener. My cats appear whenever I open a can—whether there is a nifty aroma, like tuna or chicken, or one they don't like, such as peaches. They have learned the sound means yummy tastes. In the same way, your body has associated automatic thoughts like *I am a such a bad mother* with a racing heart or falling mood. These bodily sensations are your personal advanced warning: *My shoulders are tight; what messages am I sending myself?*

Disputing the Automatic Thoughts

You hear the thinking glitches that send you stressing. Cut yourself some slack—challenge that self-talk. Automatic thoughts seem valid and true. "I should be able to remember that sign-up deadline." "This preschool is essential." You get sucked into that vast cultural misconception that impeccable control of childhood is possible if only parents are perfectly calm and organized. Write down the thoughts, and look for the telltale signs of irrational thinking. Is there an implied should? A hidden absolute? Catastrophe lurking? Conduct an extreme mom reality check, bringing reason to the madness. Is this really true? Do the facts support my guilt or fear? This is one event in my child's life. Is it that big a deal, or am I exaggerating? Is the outcome terrible? Give yourself permission to be human. How else can you look at this? Could good come out of it? If failure thoughts wind through your self-talk like worms in tainted meat, look at the data. Are you a failure 100 percent of the time? Think you can't do it right? Take a deep breath and tally up the small victories this week.

If you're stalled on changing your automatic thoughts, look for an alternative view. Don't zoom in on how others might feel or think. Are you mind reading: you're certain your child feels upset, or your partner is judging you? So what if your husband frowns at

Accept your human limitations, as suggested in this quote from Kristen van Ogtrop in "Attila the Honey I'm Home" in *The Bitch in the House:* "I will love my children, but my love for them will always be imperfect, damaged by my rigid personality and the demands of my work." Yes, I say—that is how it is for every mother. Every mother is fallible. In raising children to adulthood, it is impossible to protect them totally from our individual quirks. It is just what is. They will deal with it, just as you managed to grow up in spite of the chinks in your parents' armor. Welcome to the world of the perfectly good mom.

crying kids when he comes through the door. Is the frown proof you're incompetent? That's where your brain jumps. Might he be sympathetic that you've had a hard day? Maybe crying kids annoy him as much as they do you. Don't assume—you know what that makes us. Straight thinking works for your children's reactions too. Will your daughter be devastated if you forgot the snacks for her soccer game? Maybe she'll just be glad she had a good game. You yell at your son, then feel terrible—surely he thinks you are a mean old mommy. Chances are he is feeling guilty about behaving badly. Will other mothers label you a bad mom for ordering a bakery cake rather than baking it? Perhaps they'll be glad you're no Martha, like them. Think, *What else might explain that face he is making at me?* Spend your energy jumping rope, not to conclusions.

Replacing the Automatic Thoughts

Replacing the automatic thoughts that you have weeded out is the next step, once you know your self-talk. Like a four-year-old asking "Why?" over and over, themes repeat in your head—these are your personal demons to tackle. What is your biggest anxiety about parenting? Is it overperfecting, overprotecting, overproducing? Write it down. Evaluate it, then write a standard rebuttal. This new phrase makes you feel better—less stressed or guilty, more grounded. Take out the absolutes, the awfulizing. Tell yourself "It will be all right." Minimize the exaggeration. Make the phrase specific: "I give my kids good hugs" versus "I am a good mom." Recite that phrase like a daily affirmation. Write it ten times each morning. Put it on sticky notes. Place them in your wallet, on the mirror where you brush your teeth, on the current pages of your planner, on the steering wheel of your car. Saying them repeatedly begins to reprogram your thinking. Your children have to write their spelling words five times before the test. Just as repetition works for learning spelling words or multiplication tables, it's the most effective way to plant new and improved thoughts into your brain.

Your new statements need to be plausible—eventually. If you are like most women, you aren't going to buy this new self-talk the first time you say or write it. Your brain will still be in bad mommy mode: zeroing in on your goofs and tantrums rather than your calm, loving moments. You have to try them on, fake it—until they start to click. Your new thoughts will be more believable if you

Turning Failure Thoughts into Perfectly Good Mother Thoughts

"I never do anything right."	⟹	"That time-out went well."
"How could I forget that—I'm such a screw-up!"	⟹	"I'm only human."
"I am always so uptight."	⟹	"I can breathe and enjoy this moment."
"Meanest mommy ever."	⟹	"These kids will learn about real feelings."
"This has just ruined my day."	⟹	"Let's look at what went well today."

leave out absolutes and all-or-nothing thinking. To say "I can be a great mom every day" causes doubt to bubble up in your brain. It's too big a leap. Great? Every day? "I can be a pretty good mom most days" is more realistic and effective. Make your new thoughts concrete too. Saying "I can have fun playing checkers with my son each evening" is more powerful than saying "I can enjoy my son more each day."

Dismissing the Automatic Thoughts

Ferreting out and rewriting your thoughts can feel as endless as the years in diapers. Anxiety is contagious: you reword one worry, cutting yourself some slack, and another automatic thought pops

If concern about your child won't be silenced in your brain, research it. For instance, if you are worried about your son's spelling performance, do a reality check with a reliable source—like the teacher, or look at his standardized test scores. If you think your daughter is not on target with her motor skills, consult your pediatrician. Don't let your anxiety run away with you, straight to the spelling tutor or monkey-bar coach. But don't overlook a very real problem. Then trust the expert—and relax.

up to plague you, sort of like the "whack a gopher" game at Chuck E. Cheese. You have a big padded club, attached by wire to the game, and gophers keep popping their heads through holes. You have to knock them back in—up they pop, this hole, then that one over there. Two or three gophers pop up at once—you scramble. Worries do the same thing. Conquer your worry about your daughter's social acceptance, and—wham—you are fixated on your son's school performance. If this rings true for you, ignore the gophers. "That is just a gopher," you say. "No big deal." Dismiss the anxiety: "It's just worry—no big deal." Focus on where it comes from: "That is just one of those extreme mom mandates, not life or death."

Many moms need another step in letting go of the guilt and anxiety. After saying to yourself "Just worry—not real," get busy. Occupy your brain or your body in an active way. When you're turning cartwheels with your kid, zooming in on the theoretical catastrophe is impossible. Read something, do a puzzle or project that taps all of your brain. Dance, walk, or do twenty jumping jacks. Intense mental or physical activity enables your brain to switch gears.

A New Motherhood Paradigm

As you use rational, reasonable thinking to change your automatic thoughts about parenting, a new motherhood paradigm emerges: the perfectly good mother. This is not the first alternative paradigm to challenge overparenting. In reaction to the extreme mom, rebellious mothering has appeared, scoffing at any efforts at perfection. Roseanne, of the namesake sitcom, in 1988 presented a challenge to the June Cleaver/Donna Reed clones populating television. Roseanne had a job, three kids, a weight problem, and a messy house. She summed up her rebellious attitude in her quip, "If the kids are still alive by 5:00 PM, I've done my job." It was clear she loved her kids and her husband, in spite of the ever-present shouting. For the first time, TV watchers could identify with a mother character—someone flawed like them. In my office one day, Randi said, "I know I am never going to be June Cleaver—it's just not me. But I would be happy to be Roseanne; she seems real, and alive—she really knew how to enjoy her life." *Confessions of a Slacker Mom* by Muffy Mead-Ferro, *The Three-Martini Playdate* by Christie Mellor, and *Sippy Cups Are Not for Chardonnay* by Stefanie Wilder-Taylor all offer guidance for rebellious mothering, chucking the perfect parent hype in order to live your life.

Previously, mental-health experts have tried to throw out the perfect mother and replace her with the "good enough mother." English pediatrician and psychoanalyst D. W. Winnicott coined the term "good enough mother." He meant that parents do not have to be perfect; they can rear happy, healthy, and productive children in spite of normal, human mistakes. But they do need to provide certain basic commodities, like appropriate levels of love, caring, attention, and understanding, in order to produce decent children.

Efforts to ride perfection out of town on a rail are unlikely to catch on. Simply put, this culture defines "good enough" as "not good enough." Every mother I have ever offered the "good enough mother" model to looks disappointed. This is one time when the absolute is true: every single mother reacts this way. She sinks down in her chair, a defeated look on her face. As we talk, it becomes clear that "good enough" is never good enough. Again and again I have found that, for most women today, the "good enough" mother simply is seen as inadequate. Black-and-white thinking is at play, here—but it is what it is. Consider the billboard selling beer, on the freeway in Dallas, with the slogan "Never settle for good enough." A television commercial for another beer shows a man in Italy with a cartload of flowers, presumably taking them to market. He trades one bunch of flowers to the innkeeper in exchange for a sandwich. He asks for a beer, and the host refuses to give it to him for only one bouquet. At the end, the flower seller trades his entire cart of flowers for a single beer, as the screen flashes the words "Perfection has its price." And the motto of Alpha Omicron Pi sorority is "Never settle—because good enough never is."

"Hey, Even June Would Forget the Juice Box"

Enter the perfectly good mother. The perfectly good mother does a perfectly good job, most of the time. *Perfectly* is defined as "clearly, without qualification." Clearly good parenting, to the fullest extent she can accomplish. The perfectly good mother steps away from the absolutes of always and all, to a place of realism and perspective. The perfectly good mother knows that she is human. She has bad days. She excels at times, on some activities, while other activities are pretty tough for her. Perspective is her mantra. She knows that small details are just that. The perfectly good mother realizes her anxiety comes from cultural influences. She works to discount the mommy-thinking traps, to laugh in the face of the push to perfect protectionism. She talks back to the television: "Hey, June, even you would forget the juice boxes—sometimes." She tries to catch her automatic thoughts that lead to magical thinking. When she hears herself uttering a "should," or "what if," or "never," she stops and rewords it. She keeps her sense of humor. She tries on the phrases "So what?" and "No big deal." She does "whatever works." She honors the needs of everyone in the family: partner, children—even herself.

You may be worn out, buffeted by the anxiety that shifts your parenting sails to the extreme side. Extreme parenting feels bad; it's hard to go on if you never feel you're doing a good job. You aren't relaxed or confident as a parent. If McKay and colleagues say the automatic thoughts are a waterfall trickling down the back of your brain, then your waterfall is polluted. Only instead of industrial waste, your waterfall is full of doubt and self-criticism. On particularly bad days, that rebel mom picture is terribly seductive. You would love a three martini playdate—and you have never touched a drop of drink! It would be heaven to utter the words "Just go outside and play" while you read the latest bestseller. Becoming a rebel mom is too scary, too enticing. If you let yourself go into that rebel camp you might never return. You might follow in the steps of the real-life cocktail mom in Mary Jacobs's *Dallas Morning News* story, doling out "spoonfuls of a mysterious green liquid to each child" before every long car ride, giving the parents a very peaceful trip. Julia used Dimetapp in the same way: a plane trip, need a quiet afternoon, desire some one-on-one time with hubby? Dimetapp to the rescue. Simply too guilt inducing for you (not to mention potentially dangerous for the kids)? Maybe the balance and perspective of the perfectly good mother is the answer for you.

While staying reasonable and avoiding absolutes, please realize that no mother is extreme, or rebellious, or perfectly good *all* of the time. The perfectly good mother is not always patient and giving. The extreme mom is not forever a triathlete in the mom meet, constantly overdoing, on every issue. The rebel mom is not laissez-faire exclusively, either, life devoid of hugs or storytime. You're like most moms: very human, with quirky anxieties that drive you. Being a laid-back mom does not mean you are free of anxiety, guilt, or stress. Parents have worries as mixed as cat hairs on the navy sofa in a five-cat home. Remember the three categories of overdoing: perfection, protection, and production. Ginger was extremely overprotective about health issues. Carla was obsessed with giving the perfect gifts. Jill was hypersensitive about peer rejection. LouAnn couldn't care less about sports—her competitive nature got all revved up about grades. Your own personal standard need not be absolute control, or

Perfectly Good Mantra:
"No more illogical thinking about parenting."

you might strive for perfection across the board. Perhaps you dismiss perfection: "I'm no perfectionist." But protection is your bailiwick—your worst fear is not keeping your darling child from harm in the world. Some parents focus on producing the brilliant, capable child that other parents admire—in intellectual or athletic endeavors. Whether perfection, protection, or production—all parents have their moments of madness, what Elizabeth calls your "little nutty piece" that can turn you into a fanatic. That parenting touchstone you keep scrambling to achieve, such as Liz with her personal mandate to never yell. Knowing your thinking traps, the triggers that can flame your anxiety into a wildfire, is a critical factor in letting go of them. Then you can define and implement your own personalized version of a perfectly good mother.

Part Two

The Solution

Creating Your Own Version of a Perfectly Good Mother

What an enticing idea: you as a perfectly good mother. A successful parent, to the fullest extent possible. Living by what is important for your life, not by standards set by some TV maternal goddess or that catty lady next door. "Laid-back Supermom," as one client labeled it. You know that experts can offer direction and ideas, not a one-size-fits-all right answer for every family.

Want to be a perfectly good mother? You are going to have to cut yourself some slack and quit competing for mom of the century. To do this, you have to look at all those mandates about parenting, sift out the junk, and decide what works for you—given, of course, reason and certain minimum standards.

No one can impose an ideal of a relaxed mother. You have to define your own version. In Chapter 4, you identified thoughts that keep you from feeling like a good mother and looked at how to reword them in your head. For you to flourish as a mother, you have to find your own perfectly good mother, based on what you believe and what kind of life you want to have. So how does this work? If you have been feeling like a less than perfect mom, how can you feel perfectly good? By adopting rational beliefs and reasonable perspectives. This more rational thinking style is your new best friend. Throw out the unrealistic, impossible standards that filled your head from all directions. Then write a new script of automatic thoughts. A more workable, peaceful you will appear: the type of mother you want to be. This perfectly good mother is based on the idea that mothers are, first and foremost, human beings—engaged in the most difficult and demanding job yet created. What actions, in each

Wiseman and Rapoport, in *Queen Bee Moms and Kingpin Dads: Dealing with the Parents, Teachers, Coaches, and Counselors Who Can Make—or Break— Your Child's Future,* remind readers that "I hope you never assume that people who advise other people how to parent are perfect parents themselves." We are not. We may have good ideas, but you have to pick what works for you and your family, not what anyone says is the "right way."

The Perfectly Good Mother Manifesto

The rules for perfectly good mothering are pretty simple—and radical at the same time. There are six stepping stones to your version of the perfectly good mother: the Perfectly Good Mom Manifesto. The manifesto leads you in the "how to" of perfectly good mothering:

1. Be yourself—not who others think you should be.

    1a. Embrace that you are human, with unique gifts and flaws.

    1b. Accept that you will make mistakes.

2. Take care of your personal needs.

3. Have fun.

4. Encourage personal responsibility for each family member—emotionally, physically—as much as age allows.

5. Choose actively.

    5a. Let your values guide you.

6. Think rationally.

day, count toward perfectly good mothering? When you think these things through, your own version of the perfectly good mother emerges.

Rule #1: Be yourself—not who others think you should be

Countless mothers settle into my office sofa and blurt, "I don't even know who I am anymore—I am a mother, but what happened to the rest of me?" These mothers grieve that lost self: "I feel like the mother part of me drowned out the real 'me'—and I just want my old self back." A perfectly good mother doesn't have to choose. She can be herself, a mother *and* a person. No reason to freeze off the warts. This is the easier route. Mead-Ferro, in *Confessions of a Slacker Mom*, says: "Following my own instincts rather than caving in to the current cultural norms has been easier, not harder. It's been less time-consuming, not more. It costs less money, too. Oh well, I can live with that." When you act yourself, rather than playing a perfect mother, however defined, it takes less energy.

Being yourself is a core American value, right up there with "better and better," the fuel for extreme parenting. Our founding fathers declared independence. Individuality as an ideal runs on a parallel track. To

> "The thing that is really . . . amazing, is giving up on being perfect and beginning the work of becoming yourself."
>
> —*Anna Quindlen,* Being Perfect

be a perfectly good mother, you need not feel un-American. If the American ideal of achievement pushes you to extreme parenting, shift your focus to the equally solid American ideal of uniqueness. Make your own unique rules about what a good mother should do. Rules about how mothers "should" be are possible actions, not award-winning formulas. Embrace your own perfectly good mother style. No other mother can give this "one of a kind" gift to your child.

Rule #1a: Embrace that you are human, with unique gifts and flaws

Doubt that you can be a perfectly good mother, given who you are? If your most common thought is *I'm such a bad mother,* it's hard to feel like any kind of a good mother. Others in your life have loved you for who you are, so far. Your parents, your spouse, or maybe a favorite teacher? You have qualities they cherish—and that might be helpful in parenting. Have a few successes in your pocket outside of parenthood? Reconnect to those skills, affirm their value, and apply them to your parenting. Recognize how, applying who you are, with your unique assets, you already are a perfectly good person. Does that translate into a perfectly good mother?

Heather worked hard to be serene, patient, and content in her role of mother—like Tammy, her sister-in-law. Tammy had four kids, all homeschooled, which meant she stayed home all day, every day, giving to her children. Heather had never seen Tammy lose her temper. Not once. Heather, with her instant boiling point, flew into bad-mother mode often, especially when confined to the four walls of home. She just didn't get how Tammy could be satisfied staying home and perfectly maintain her patience—but she pined for that contentment. Heather's five-year-old son, Bret, was a handful: smart and sassy, constantly outwitting his parents. His arguments were truly inspired—Heather and her husband would just buckle. The more Heather tried to keep up with him at home, entertaining him through the day, the worse she felt. Before Bret, Heather was a pharmaceutical rep: energetic, always on the go, entertaining customers. When Heather looked at her assets, and gave up staying home all day like Tammy, her parenting blossomed. She took Bret on after-school outings: to a construction site, art museum, or fire station. He was challenged; and she felt secure in her parenting when she allowed herself to be the on-the-go, energetic person she was, pre-Bret.

Claim your little nutty piece. To be a perfectly good mother, it is fine for a part (or two) of parenting to show your quirks, to border

Perfectly Good Mantra:
"Being myself is perfectly good."

Are you always second-guessing? Continually doubting your choices, your value? Underneath second-guessing is never feeling good enough. Try this mantra to beat it. You are affirming that who you are—your choices, actions, or qualities—is perfectly good.

on the extreme. But just one or two. When Paula's child was a babe in arms, all the family invaded the grandparents' home. Her sister-in-law arrived with a van full of baby stuff: swing, port-a-crib, every toy known to babies. Paula brought the child. Perhaps a few diapers. She seemed to have mastered letting go—until she revealed that tucked into the diaper bag was "The Feeding Schedule." This precious piece of paper recorded every ounce that went in, and came out, of the child.

Deep down, it's hard to relax about perfection on all fronts. Maintaining a piece or two of your former madness is a reasonable accommodation for a recovering control freak. You are stretching yourself a bit—your child wore the Batman cape to preschool six times in a row. You can dress him in that seersucker suit for Sundays at Grandma's. If you must pick one or two nutty pieces to hang on to, make sure they fit these criteria: (1) *You* enjoy it; or (2) *You* have picked it, for reasons within you, not because someone else or society says you should. Amanda could not let go of concern about her son's breakfasts. Other mothers said, "They'll survive—lots of healthy choices in the pantry —at least I get them a healthy dinner each day." Amanda cooked a hot meal of bacon, pancakes, eggs—the works—*for thirteen years*. As a science teacher, she had the science of breakfast perfected: wake up, put the bacon on to setting number two while brushing teeth. Hop in the shower, four minutes, dash back to the kitchen, turn the burner to four, flip the bacon. The morning dash was more than a phrase at her house. It was important to her, and her sons quickly grew to love it. Accept that you can't do it all, and choose what's critical to you. Nothing is wrong with being a *selective* Supermom.

Rule #1b: Accept that you will make mistakes

In her career as a pharmacist, Jennifer knew that if she made a mistake, she could kill someone. Even though the thinking part of her brain knew this didn't apply directly to parenting, she held that fear deep within her. One mistake with her kids, and—boom— catastrophe. She could hardly function, so much energy was bound up in avoiding even tiny mistakes. She might give the purple cup to the baby, when her four-year-old had decreed it was his. Given the absolute way that four-year-olds think, her son exploded in a temper tantrum when she made this mistake—reinforcing her fear of errors.

Being yourself means permission to make mistakes. To accept your flaws and be human with your kids. Jennifer faced her worry by allowing a few mistakes with her children. She started small, putting the baby's shoes on the wrong feet. When her four-year-old caught it, Jennifer laughed, "Oh, silly me—people make mistakes." When you make and admit to mistakes, it's healthier for you and your child, allowing him to see a real person. Children learn best when their models don't master a task the first time. They see you cry, or rant, or fight with Dad or Grandma. Children learn good lessons living through this, as long as appropriate apologies come next. Say you are sorry—and your kids will see that you are real. As Susan Squire says in *The Bitch in the House,* "Moms, even good ones, some- times lose it a little, so as not to lose it all."

Finding the perfectly good middle ground to be yourself between perfect and your perceived human failures is like trying to make a thirteen-year-old happy on a family vacation. But it's not all or nothing. Between scowls at your children, you have given them some good hugs and had a laugh or two. Elisa Schappell said, "I mean, how crappy of a mother am I really? It isn't like they exist on a diet of Happy Meals and Ho-Hos. I don't knock them around in public or humiliate them by screaming. . . . I read them books and play pretend, I make sure they have mittens in the winter, and I insist we eat dinner together as a family. I tell them they are loved so often they sometimes roll their eyes." Sounds like a perfectly good mother to me.

Wiseman and Rapoport, co-authors of *Queen Bee Moms and Kingpin Dads,* say that "You will make mistakes. This doesn't make you a terrible parent— it makes you a parent just like everybody else. If your children see that you're doing your best to live according to your values, that you have the courage to admit your mistakes and learn from them . . . , you're golden."

Here's a fitting Perfectly Good Mantra:
"I can live with this."

Rule #2: Take care of your personal needs

Most women feel like Julie: "I am always supposed to care for my family. I never take care of myself or what I want to do." This is what society expects. There are no built-in mom breaks. If you're last on your list, there's little left to give. You give, and give, and give again, meeting others' needs, nary a minute to replenish yourself. You're running on empty; ready to explode. And you will stay in that pressure-cooker state—until you eat three meals a day, get seven or eight hours of sleep at night, rest occasionally through the day. Talk to friends, go out, and relax. Maya Angelou in *Wouldn't Take Nothing for My Journey Now* recommends a regular day away—a daylong break for oneself—to put life in perspective.

Take your vitamins. Cook and eat the foods you crave—once in awhile. So what if no one else likes them? Take a time-out where children are off-limits. Melissa took blue painter's tape and marked a kid-free zone around her favorite chair. Trespassers were shot on sight—actually, sent to their rooms. Put your children to bed, and take twenty minutes to talk kid-free with your partner. Nurture your spiritual life in a meaningful way—not necessarily running some committee. Put exercise, rest, meals, prayer, and fun on your list. Just writing items down, engraving them in stone on the daily list, means you take yourself seriously. Writing "walk thirty minutes" on your list conveys "I'm worthwhile."

I bet you've heard this before, regularly if you read women's or parenting magazines, or listen to television shows. How big a bullhorn do we need to deliver the message for you to hear it and incorporate it into your life?

The wine industry recognizes that moms need to unwind. For this path to relaxation, ask at your local wine emporium about special features for mothers: (1) "Mommy's Time-Out," a blend of 2005 Italian white wines. The label says, "We all know that being a Mommy is a difficult job. . A Mommy's Time-Out is a well-deserved break." (2) "Mad Housewife" 2004 has a pseudo fifties-era woman in pink and pearls on the label. The back reads, "Somewhere near the cool shadows of the laundry room. Past the litter box and between the plastic yard toys. This is your time. Time to enjoy a moment to yourself. A moment without the madness. The dishes can wait. Dishes be damned." As Joyce Sáenz Harris asked in the *Dallas Morning News:* "Is that a Merlot or a manifesto?" (3) During a long wait for luggage at the airport, a lively group of women relaxed nearby. They noticed my interest, and one raised a small cardboard carton in toast to me. "Have you seen these? Mommy juice boxes," she giggled, showing a single-serving box of white wine. I have looked, with no luck. Perhaps this convenience item is available in your town.

Rule #3: Have fun

The nitty-gritty of daily parenting is simply not fun. Endless diapers, carpooling, laundry, packing lunches, cleaning up vomit, waiting on hold for the pediatrician, combing lice out of hair—these are not a few of my favorite things. The day-to-day drudgery qualifies for my dad's favorite aphorism: "You don't have to like it, you just have to do it." To add "have fun" as a step to perfectly good mothering seems hugely unrealistic. A wee bit of all-or-nothing thinking inches into your interpretation of "have fun." No one can have fun all of the time. When you have choices, mixing in fun is critical.

Anna Quindlen, in a February 2005 *Newsweek* column, said, "By our actions we tell them (children) that being a mom—being their

Are anyone else's values sneaking into your perfectly good mother? If there is enough fun in your life, more power to you. Plus the fun has to be *your* version—not fun by *my* standards. Watch out—a common sentiment I hear in my office is "Picking up the house, getting it all in order, is fun for me. It really is!" To which I say, "Fine, have some housecleaning fun. But have some relaxing, non-draining fun too." It's easier to feel like a perfectly good mother if there's fun in my days. Infuse some play into the routine, or be rigorous about extracurricular amusements.

mom—is a drag, powered by fear, self-doubt and conformity, all the things we are supposed to teach them to overcome. . . . The most incandescent memories of my childhood are of making my mother laugh. My kids did the same for me. A good time is what they remember long after toddler programs and art projects are over. The rest is just scheduling."

Putting fun on the list is an extension of your self-care, so do what is fun for you. Don't be apologetic about it. When my daughters were small, I decreed playing "My Little Pony" as a mom-free activity. I'd rather scrub tar from the underside of the car on a Dallas day in July. We could go to the park, or read, or color, or dance. But no ponies. Dad might play ponies, or they could play ponies alone. The cats took the ponies and chewed on the hair—they could even play ponies with the cats. Nobody suffered much, truly, and I suffered much less. Make thoughtful choices about how to spend your flexible time, guided by "Is it fun?"

Infuse a little fun into the drudgery. Amy liked to make jokes in the car; Diana sang silly songs as she and her sons picked up the toys. Allow the kid in you to emerge. Sally had to shut down messages in her head that *Mothers don't act that way.* The serious mother voice in your head might shout, *This parenting business is serious—settle down!* Silly and lighthearted isn't illegal, if it's not hurting anyone. Do it when you are able—which won't be all the time—if it fits for you and lifts your mood. This is not a should, a mandate to sing so your kids develop musical ability. This is permission to have fun with parenting. It's a serious job. Being too outcome focused and businesslike kills the joy. As Quindlen says, the fun is what your children will treasure. When her grown son reflected on her parenting, he said, "What I remember most: having a good time." Quindlen said, "You can engrave that on my headstone right this minute."

I n "Maternal Bitch" in *The Bitch in the House*, Susan Squire said, "I struggled with the terrible, irrational child's guilt that insists, 'It's all my fault that Mommy's sad.'" Children do blame themselves for a parent's mood. Offer reassurance that your mood is not their fault, when that's true. No one can be happy all the time. With some lightheartedness, your children will prosper. If your mood is darker than regular doses of fun can lighten, consider that you may be clinically depressed. See Appendix Two: Resources for sources of help.

Rule #4: Encourage personal responsibility for each family member—emotionally, physically—as much as age allows

As your children grow, they are capable of entertaining themselves, putting themselves to sleep, making snacks, loading a backpack for the next day, and making decisions about free time—just to name a few activities you've forgotten to hand over in your quest for the perfect childhood. Physical responsibilities are the easiest to start with; even three-year-olds can clear their dishes from the table if you don't use heirloom china. Check out this Web site for ideas on involving your children in age-appropriate chores: www.parenting247.uiuc.edu.

Give very specific instruction about how you want a task done. Don't expect that a child or a husband will know unless you tell them. Kate thought her children watched how she loaded the dishes—they were always underfoot when she did. But everyone was off in their own la-la land. Kate held a mandatory dishwasher-loading class, then let each helper adapt their work style to her directions. She didn't care how the dishes got in, as long as they didn't block the water or break. She asked herself, *Is there only one way to do a chore correctly?* Distinguish between what needs to be done, and what needs to be done well. Kate made a chore chart, listing everyone's name, including hers and her husband's. She gave credit for partial completion at first, handing out stickers and ample praise. Most kids, rewarded in a meaningful yet moderate way, feel pride in household chores. Capitalize upon this natural tendency to please parents. It can lighten your load and teach responsibility.

Responsibility for your children's feelings is harder to give up. Are *you* happy all the time? Is it possible or realistic for your *child* to be happy all the time? Are you bored with parts of your life, mucking through the mundane day to day? Your kids are human, too. It's acceptable and expected they'll feel bored, lackadaisical, even unhappy at times. Revert to the "You don't have to like it, you just have to do it" truth—not truthiness—about life, for a child or an adult. Your job as a perfectly good parent is to teach responsibility, self-sufficiency, and management of feelings. This means guiding kids through tough spots, not always making it right. Even when we wish we could. Children need to learn to label, feel, and appropriately express feelings. And home—where you know you are loved, no matter what—is the best laboratory for those lessons.

Beth began with a small list that her six- and eight-year-old kids could manage on their own: hanging up backpacks and coats, putting away shoes, and amusing themselves for ten minutes while she started dinner. Rather than swooping in with attack force, Beth stopped herself from calling the mother of the child who picked on Dana on the playground one day. Beth talked with Dana about

Perfectly Good Mantra:
"Not me, not now."

Elisabeth Guthrie and Kathy Matthews, in *No More Push Parenting: How to Find Success and Balance in a Hypercompetitive World*, assert that, every now and then, this needs to be a parent's slogan. Try it once in awhile, when kids need someone to play with them or read homework to. Put your kids' demands in perspective. June never played with the Beaver; she was too busy baking and cleaning.

standing up to this bully. She asked Dana for ideas on handling it if it happened again, rather than preaching about how her daughter could protect herself. Beth and Dana practiced how to deal with the bully, acting out a sample confrontation.

In handing over responsibility, you may need to battle your own anxiety about letting go. Like chores, your family members won't do things the way you would. Your child may not amuse himself or handle feelings in a mom-approved manner. No big deal—it's a learning curve for you both. Give it time. Offer your child a choice about two after-school activities. Is one really more valuable in the long run? Is he hurting anything? Is he learning? Is his choice wrong, or does it work for him?

When stepping back from overcontrol, distinguish between losing control and letting go. Letting go feels like losing control, at first. Your worry skyrockets—catastrophic thoughts pound in your brain. Losing control feels like a disadvantage. Change perspective: letting go is a choice. It is not a loss, it is win/win. You control what you can—that feels good. You have less stress in your life when you cut yourself some slack and give up on the impossible.

Rule #5: Choose actively

While my dad may be right—there's plenty you simply have to do—you have choices. Resist the self-talk of "that's how mothers are" or "everyone is doing it." After parenting on autopilot, choices evaporate in a cloud of cultural dictates. It's hard to see what can change through the haze. You often have a choice—even if a tiny one. One or two miniscule changes in behavior are all your brain needs to reboot and install a new mothering paradigm. Search for those tiny possible changes. Control what you can. Learn to say "no." This keeps the time-suck of meaningless activities at a minimum. Tune in to what you want, and avoid snap decisions. Choose what works for you. Take steps toward perfectly good mothering that are purposeful, not automatic or haphazard.

You're not alone in wanting to take charge of your life. Take Back Your Time is an organization dedicated to helping everyone, not just parents, quit the overscheduled pace that is the norm in today's society. The Web site www.timeday.org offers excellent guidance in making changes in your life.

Rule #5a: Let your values guide you

A key perfectly good mom choice is being fully engaged: aligned with your priorities, on track emotionally with your family. The hurried lifestyle of extreme parenting, with its "do-or-die" philosophy, is as compatible with connection as siblings on a long car trip. Emotions usually aren't on the "to-do" list. You may feel better if feelings top the list. Nina practiced sitting ten minutes with each child every evening before bed. The books were put away. Nina simply listened—and hugged. Before entering each child's room, she wrote down all the "to-dos" in her head. Leaving the list on the kitchen counter freed her to concentrate on what each child was saying.

With each choice in your life, act as the mom you want to be. Forget the choices you should make, whenever possible. Choose what really matters—to you—by affirming your values. Assessing your values sounds like a lot of work—could you fit it in between 3:00 AM and 5:00 AM, perhaps? Core questions make it simple, tying behavior to beliefs. Train yourself to ask these questions, and you can replace the automatic thoughts that keep you overdoing.

Imagine your child is grown, and you are evaluating how you did as a parent. What four or five qualities do you most wish your child to have in adulthood? Jenna highly valued independence, so the

In a *Dallas Morning News* article by Sarah Kerner, life coach Kristin Taliaferro highlights the power of touch for emotional connection. When anyone returns home, she says, "Hug your husband or child for one solid minute. A minute is a long time. There's potential in there to turn the worst part of your day into the best part." The movement to reclaim dinnertime (see www.reclaimdinnertime.com) is full of great tips on reconnecting with your family over meals.

What Are Your Values?

Tune in to your values. Making perfectly good choices is easier if you're aware of your values. A value is a principle, standard, or quality considered worthwhile or desirable. The following statements can guide you to see what values are most important to you, says Leah Mullen, life coaching editor of www.bellaonline.com. Reflect on how important each item is for your children, and in your personal life:

* Spending time with family.

* Saving money rather than buying, "wants" versus "needs."

* Being physically fit.

* Creative time.

* Having good friends.

* Contributing to my community.

* Spending time on spiritual activities.

* Being honest rather than sparing someone's feelings.

* Being productive versus taking time to play.

* Emotional well-being versus achievement.

You might want to make your own list and keep it in a prominent place, allowing your values to guide your choices.

READER/CUSTOMER CARE SURVEY

We care about your opinions! Please take a moment to fill out our online Reader Survey at **http://survey.hcibooks.com.**
As a **"THANK YOU"** you will receive a **VALUABLE INSTANT COUPON** towards future book purchases as well as a **SPECIAL GIFT** available only online! Or, you may mail this card back to us and we will send you a copy of our exciting catalog with your valuable coupon inside.

(PLEASE PRINT IN ALL CAPS)

First Name _____ MI. _____ Last Name _____

Address _____ City _____

State _____ Zip _____ Email _____

1. Gender
- ☐ Female
- ☐ Male

2. Age
- ☐ 8 or younger
- ☐ 9-12
- ☐ 13-16
- ☐ 17-20
- ☐ 21-30
- ☐ 31+

3. Did you receive this book as a gift?
- ☐ Yes
- ☐ No

4. Annual Household Income
- ☐ under $25,000
- ☐ $25,000 - $34,999
- ☐ $35,000 - $49,999
- ☐ $50,000 - $74,999
- ☐ over $75,000

5. What are the ages of the children living in your house?
- ☐ 0 - 14
- ☐ 15+

6. Marital Status
- ☐ Single
- ☐ Married
- ☐ Divorced
- ☐ Widowed

7. How did you find out about the book?
(please choose one)
- ☐ Recommendation
- ☐ Store Display
- ☐ Online
- ☐ Catalog/Mailing
- ☐ Interview/Review

8. Where do you usually buy books?
(please choose one)
- ☐ Bookstore
- ☐ Online
- ☐ Book Club/Mail Order
- ☐ Price Club (Sam's Club, Costco's, etc.)
- ☐ Retail Store (Target, Wal-Mart, etc.)

9. What subject do you enjoy reading about the most?
(please choose one)
- ☐ Parenting/Family
- ☐ Relationships
- ☐ Recovery/Addictions
- ☐ Health/Nutrition
- ☐ Christianity
- ☐ Spirituality/Inspiration
- ☐ Business Self-help
- ☐ Women's Issues
- ☐ Sports

10. What attracts you most to a book?
(please choose one)
- ☐ Title
- ☐ Cover Design
- ☐ Author
- ☐ Content

TAPE IN MIDDLE; DO NOT STAPLE

FOLD HERE

Comments

pattern of nonstop play she'd gotten into with her daughter made little sense. Weaning Emily to play on her own was tough. Jenna had been Emily's favorite playmate for eight years, from horsey to Barbies. Every time Emily played on her own, she earned extra "mom time." Karen wanted her children to be compassionate. Raising socially responsible children seemed related to volunteering, and Karen found that working a monthly shift at the local food pantry as a family made an impact on her kids.

Questions to Assess Values

* Is this teaching a lesson to my child(ren) that I want to teach?

* Is this really how we want to spend this time, money, whatever?

* What kind of person does this make me? My child?

* In my heart, is that what I want?

* In my rational brain, is that the right answer for us, for now?

* Is this a need or a want?

* Is this my need or someone else's?

Rule #6: Think rationally

You have to keep chipping away at your self-talk, mastering relative, rational thinking. Being human, this is no piece of angel food. It feels at times like opening an e-mail attachment to find computer code: ÿØÿàJF H ÿáªExifM*. In spite of brain fuzz moments, you plod along, dodging "always" and "never." Mindful not to catastrophize, you listen for "what ifs" that pour gas on your anxieties. *What if the teacher hates her? What if he is wait-listed at all the colleges?* You know how those automatic thoughts can haunt you—try to spot them before you feel too badly.

Your habit is operating on gut level—feelings and preconceived notions drive you. Time to switch gears from being driven by your gut to being ruled by your head. Your brain has to be engaged to challenge your gut. The ability to think rationally is in you—guiding other decisions in your life, such as where to live, which career to pursue, what car seat to buy. Given the mundane decisions in your day, most of your behavior is driven by automatic thoughts. You just do, because your mother did or everyone around you does.

Thinking rationally means turning off autopilot. Keeping your brain engaged is so important to living your perfectly-good-mother life that you have to train your brain to think critically, rather than automatically, about how you live your life as a parent.

Become Fluent in "Perfectly Good Mom Language"

The perfectly good mother relies on a head full of coping thoughts such as *So what, No big deal, This works; it will do just fine,* instead of the unreasonable self-talk that floods her with "terrible mother" thoughts. Instead of scolding herself—"I am an awful mother because I can't stand to play Legos one more time"—she says, "I know I give to my children. But maybe a break right now is okay." These helpful phrases for challenging your automatic thoughts are standards that keep perspective. Remind yourself to "Look at the big picture" or to consider "How does this factor into the total scheme of things?" Paula found that substituting "perhaps" for "should" reminded her to keep perspective. "Perhaps Susie would like karate" carried much less weight than "I should enroll Susie in karate."

Classic children's books are full of catchy phrases to incorporate into your rational thoughts. Prone to catastrophizing? Remember Chicken Little and ask, "Will the sky fall?" Overwhelmed with a sense of dread? The refrain in your head is "I am such a bad mom, I am such a bad mom." Recall *The Little Engine that Could* saying "I think I can, I think I can." A more powerful version is "I know I can, I know I can." Your new personal mantra might be "I am a perfectly good mother," or " I can do a perfectly good job," or "This works perfectly well," or "I can live with this." Sandra had her personal slogan for letting go. Her toddler daughter struggled with socks; the seam totally devastated tiny Ava's feet. Ava would cry, "They're attacking my toes!" After too many battles, it dawned on Sandra to let her wear them wrong side out. The epiphany for Sandra was asking, "What value will it have in eternity?" End of the battle, as certainly St. Peter would not care if Ava wore her socks seam side out.

Actually writing out your version of a perfectly good mother in this new language helps it sink in. Look at the good, rather than the negative. Not just "what I don't want to be" but "what I do want to be." Claim your strengths as a mother. Validate and capitalize on them. "I am a good role model when I apologize for exploding." Or, "When I tell my kids to wait while I finish something for me, they learn their own value." Have this description reflect your values, what you really want for your children and your experience as a mother. Lisa wrote hers: "As a perfectly good mom, I can laugh with my kids at least once each day. I can get mad at them and tell them I love them anyway. I can show them that love for life is what matters, and that nothing is cast in stone. I can make choices based on what is workable, for us, for now."

Perfectly Good Mantra:
"My day is not ruined if _____."

Fill in the blank: My day is not ruined if there are dishes in the sink in the morning. My day is not ruined if my child throws a tantrum in the store. Trade the absolute for the relative.

Questions to Guide Straight Thinking

If you find yourself careening down the path to stressville, rather than discovering the perfectly good mother balance you want, you may need to stop and remember the mommy traps: irrational beliefs and expectations about how mothers should be. To bring yourself back from the mommy traps that are all around you, apply these questions to each decision, whether small (how to spend Saturday's leisure time) or large (where your child will attend school). Consider three critical areas: Is there truth guiding my decision, or is it truthiness, what we want to be fact—but isn't? Am I keeping perspective? Is this consistent with my values?

If you want a shorthand version to remind yourself, just remember three questions: What? How? Who? What are you thinking: truth or scam? How are you thinking: clearly, logically, realistically, or full of shoulds, black-and-white, catastrophic thinking? Who are you—does this reveal heartfelt values, who you want to be, the way you want to live in the world? Write out "What? How? Who?" on a three-by-five card and keep it in your wallet. You'll be reminded with every dollar spent. At any pivotal point in parenting, these questions guide you to the perfectly good mommy track.

Questions to Assess Truth

* Do the facts support the conclusion?

* Is there another explanation?

* Am I trying to control what is not controllable?

* Are there other solutions?

* Am I buying into absolutes?

* Is perfection possible here?

* Is pleasing others the most important factor?

Questions to Assess Perspective

* How are you thinking?

* Does it matter in the total scheme of our lives?

* Is it really a big deal?

* Am I exaggerating? Catastrophizing? Taking it too seriously?

* What meaning will this have for eternity?

* What has gone right today?

* Does it truly matter what anyone else says/does/thinks?

Being Your Own
"Perfectly Good Mother"

When you begin to change your perspective, it often is evident that you are already a perfectly good mother. Resist that sewer tunnel of all-or-nothing thinking, sucking you into the swirling current of absolutes. Why would you not take credit for every bit that goes well in your life as a mother? A job this hard—you deserve a medal for surviving each day! Your behavior might be perfect—at many moments—yet you still feel awful. But when you catch yourself doing lots that is right, your whole worldview shifts. Count up, and claim your successes—each and every time. Your kids show glimpses of turning into decent human beings. Significant moments of happiness pepper your life. The inevitable bad stuff is minor, infrequent—just blips on the radar screen of your life. No mammoth changes are needed when blips pop up—just subtle shifts in what you are already doing. Tell yourself you are doing a pretty good job—certainly not the worst mother ever!

Teasing Out Your Triumphs

Personalize your perfectly good mother. No one but you has the power to end the crazy extremes in your life. How can you bring some reason to the chaos of your life? What is the perfectly good mother, in your mind? Honoria thought she was "doing a good job only when no one cried." With three children under four, those days were as scarce as happy children at 5:00 PM. Dodging that cultural whammy of unrealistic expectations, she said to herself, "It is just hard right now. It is going to be hard until these kids are a bit older." She felt better when "good job" meant "crying less than 50 percent of the time," not "nobody cries." Most days, she could tell herself she was doing a "perfectly good job."

Teasing out your triumphs is not an easy task because unsolicited feedback is readily available. Judgment is all around you: frowns in the grocery store, a snide remark from your mother, a veiled comment from a teacher, even a professional-quality eye roll by your kid. Unfortunately, there are no overt, objective criteria. At

Emily kept a running list, adding to it each evening, of ways she was succeeding as a mom. "Read to Bella today." "Apologized after I screamed." "Cuddled the baby when she was crying." "Stopped 'bad mommy' litany in my head—felt perfectly good." "Tickled the baby." "Took a bubble bath with Bella." "Said 'no' to unrewarding volunteer job." "Hummed through Bella's tantrum." "Chose sleep over dishes."

Like Emily, you can try on this Perfectly Good Mantra: "This is what I did today that mattered _____

_____." Fill in the blank: what did you do today that was perfectly good? This is a powerful variation on the bedtime habit of counting your blessings.

least once you meet bare minimum standards to feed, clothe, and seat-belt your child. No national grading system or standardized achievement test to evaluate your mothering. Each woman has to find the mother she wishes to be, responding to the needs of her children, life, and moment in time. No one can judge whether you are measuring up, either—the one who holds you accountable is you. Or you and your partner. Ignore how your child may grade you, especially if she is younger than twenty-five. With all this on your shoulders, the anxiety within you may overflow like a toilet that has swallowed a teddy bear. What a mass of responsibility! Forget the absolutes, the guarantees you seek from experts. There is no right answer or foolproof formula, beyond being yourself, taking care of your needs, having fun, encouraging personal responsibility, choosing actively, and thinking rationally. You have to adapt these to your own life. Don't let the lack of rules fill you with terror: calm down, take a breath. It's not as bad as it seems. The perfectly good mother knows every effort counts. She remembers what perfectly good means: parenting in the best possible way the majority of the time. Not all of the time, not without errors.

Steps backward don't mean back to square one—they are just steps backward. Wiseman and Rapoport call for "true confessions time. If I have one single moment each week when I think I've parented well, that's a good week." Like marbles in a jar: every time you have a good life moment, imagine a marble goes into a jar. Julia's son set fire to some napkins on the kitchen counter as she talked on the phone. Smelling the matches, she turned, catching the fire in time. "I deserve ten marbles in the jar for not having to deal with a fire," she said. Another mother, not tuned into her perfectly good goals, might chastise herself for her son even striking the match. You pay a bill late, or snap "Because I said so," or talk too long to your college roommate on the phone while your daughter feeds oatmeal to the tropical fish; the marbles are not emptied out of the jar. "All or nothing" moms see the jar as empty again each time a setback occurs. The perfectly good mother sees that obstacles don't add marbles to the jar, but neither do marbles disappear. Glass does not evaporate, even under the searing temperature of a mother's anger.

Mystery writer Jill Churchill, as quoted in a 2005 *Redbook* article on "The Truth About Motherhood": "There's no way to be a perfect mother, and a million ways to be a good one."

Every parent gets attacked by those thinking glitches that steal perspective, turning you into troll mommy or stress queen. Human beings get tired, cranky, and hungry. We need sleep and breaks. When stressed, people are even more likely to lose that healthy attitude that keeps the anxiety or guilt at bay. We're fallible creatures, but capable of ongoing excellence. Give yourself some latitude on the distinction between perfection and excellence. When perfection is possible, it is only for one small task at a time. As

Vivienne said, "My perfect mothering occurred at picnics, walks, bike rides, reading goodnight books and cuddles, prayers together, catching ball, idle conversations over juice and wine. . . . Perfect motherhood was not something aspired to, it couldn't be planned or contrived. It is born out of those impromptu moments of sharing and caring." Within you is that perfectly good mother—you just have to release her. You are already a good parent, remember? Trust my judgment—poor parents don't consult books, looking for answers. There is a perfectly workable model that fits for you and your family.

Do you need to try some new behavior to feel like a perfectly good mother? Some mothers only need a different lens to view their mothering, discovering it is already perfectly good. Others want to make concrete changes each day. They wish to get through bedtime in a more relaxed manner or be more tuned in when their children are talking. Lay these out. What stops you? Detect your triggers. Are you stuck yelling, for instance, because you keep telling yourself, *I just can't do this?* Often, the behavior you detest is kindled by the self-talk you want to change. If you repeat to yourself "I am a perfectly good mother" instead of "I am the worst mother ever," you will feel better. You'll be less likely to address your children without raising your voice. Magically, new thoughts seem to allow new behavior to easily slip into place. Working with the tools in this chapter, your perfectly good mother slowly emerges.

6

Perfectly Good Mothers
in Action

Avoiding the Stumbling Blocks to
Change and Raising Great Kids

B y now, you've taken an in-depth look at the type of person and parent you want to be. You've hopefully traded in some irrational beliefs about yourself and looked for concrete evidence that you are the mom you want to be. You're headed in the right direction. You are getting a sense of your own personal perfectly good mother. A smattering of June and Martha, with maybe a healthy dose of Roseanne and that rebellious sister of yours. You know the one—if you told her the title of this book she would look at you blankly. She does not seem to have a perfectionistic or competitive bone in her body. You have an outline in your head of how you want to be, what you want to define for yourself and your family. You may have even written it out, or at least jotted down the key points.

You can banish bad-mommy days from your life—those days where you are so sucked up in stress, and the mommy traps running through your head are so loud and insistent, that you cannot be the kind of mother you want to be. Wait—alarm bells may be sounding in your head: that's all-or-nothing thinking. Everyone has bad-mommy days—some of the time. You can't oust them completely. What you can do is work to make them rare. That's the goal: to act the mother you want to be the majority of the time. One bad moment does not wipe out the perfectly good mother in you—not even fifty bad days. If you live your version of a perfectly good mom more days than not, you deserve the label.

This chapter explores how moms really incorporate their own perfectly good mother manifesto into their lives. Examples are laid out, with guidelines for applying the perfectly good mother to your parenting. Finally, stumbling blocks that trip women up as they work to make these changes in their lives are explored, to help you stay on track.

Extreme Mom Versus Perfectly Good Mom Versus Rebel Mom

Day to day, how does a perfectly good mom behave? How does she incorporate her reasonable beliefs and critical values to cut herself some slack? Is she really any different from the other mothers? Comparing the perfectly good mother to the rebel and extreme moms paints the picture more clearly.

TYPES OF MOMS

Factor	Extreme	Perfectly Good	Rebel
Philosophy	Only the best for my baby	All for one and one for all	Live and let live.
Goal	A perfect childhood	A sane and balanced life	Utter self-fulfillment
Signature Phrase	"But everyone's doing it!"	"Whatever works!"	"Go on out and play!"
Emotional Status	Frazzled	Content	Disengaged
Breakfast	Cooked every morning, organic eggs	Choice of cereal and milk	Children grab their own donut
Music lessons	Years of private lessons, regardless of interest/talent	Tries lessons for a couple of years; "We'll see how it goes."	Provides toy piano to play if child expresses interest
Sports	Private lessons weekly, never miss a practice or game, club teams from start	Signs child up if interested; miss occasional practice and usually attend games	Drags herself there if child insists on playing a sport
Clothing	Designer names, always matched perfectly	Assortment of sensible items, child chooses	Pajamas all day— they are really the sweats he slept in
Homework	Sits with child throughout, even does the work at times	Helps child plan a schedule, provides input/breaks as needed	Go do your homework! It is your homework, not mine.

TYPES OF MOMS (continued)

Television	Baby Mozart or similar DVDs–with strict limits	Set limits, child's choice from approved shows	The Cartoon Network as steady background
Leisure time	What? I don't understand the question	Plans in advance, regularly, to ensure it happens	Cocktail hour every day

The extreme mom gives her all 200 percent of the time, way more than is humanly possible. The extreme mom believes that ideal motherhood involves total absorption in her child's life. She literally lives for her child, forsaking any effort or energy for herself or her interests. The rebel mom seems much less involved—after all, they're "just kids. They'll be fine!" Between these two opposites on the continuum of parenting is the perfectly good mom, finding her own balance between her needs and those of her children.

While the extreme mom may have carefully handcrafted her children's Halloween costumes, complete with papier maché masks and hand-beaded accents, the rebel mom stops at the discount store and lets each kid choose. The perfectly good mom helps the kids pull together their own ideas using old clothes or items in the garage. She knows costumes are for the children, not her. The extreme mom plans a birthday party like Lisa did, transforming the entire first floor of the house into a princess castle. From moving boxes, Lisa spent hours drawing, cutting, and painting a castle for guests to play in. With yards and yards of pink tulle, Lisa designed a unique princess dress for each child. The rebel mom skips the party entirely—after all, the kid is only two and will never remember! The perfectly good mom sticks to the old rule—one guest for each year of child's age and invites the birthday child's best two friends for a play date and cupcakes, with a balloon each to take home.

The extreme mom sends her aspiring daughter to ballet camp for six weeks in the summer, even though the money spent could send the whole family of five to a Caribbean resort for ten days. The perfectly good mother allows her child to attend a shorter, local camp. The family can still have a fun vacation. The rebel mom says, "It's summer—you can pick up with ballet if you want in the fall." The extreme mom arrives at school for lunch with her child daily, driving thirty minutes across town to pick up the child's favorite carry-out dish. The perfectly good mom shows up at school several times a year, including for her child's birthday or the yearly "Muffins for Mom" breakfast with her child. The rebel mom says, "Lunch is to visit with your friends—not see me."

The extreme mom tucks away a hidden treat in her son's luggage for each ten days at camp. The perfectly good mom hides a note or two and sends him a postcard and a letter while he is gone. The rebel mom gives him a big hug when he comes home. The extreme mom hires an audition coach to work with her actor wannabe before each school play. The perfectly good mom signs up her child for an audition workshop offered by the local community theatre. The rebel mom offers an old bedspread as a curtain for those home-staged productions.

Being an extreme mom is not always about monetary gifts, scholastic awards, or sports overachievement, though these are the most blatant examples. It is just as often about excessive efforts at control, inordinate time spent, or supreme sacrifice of mom's own needs. The extreme mom defines success in terms of tangible accomplishments and visible trappings. In her absolute world, there is a prescribed set of behaviors for "good parents." Extreme moms, thinking irrationally, are rigid about the rules. A successful life is lived in the appointed fashion, internalizing a master list of "shoulds." This inflexibility about how to live one's life is the source of stress, anxiety, and guilt—and the possibility of diminishing those negative feelings is the impetus for perfectly good mothering.

Remember, there are hardly any mothers who are all of a type, all of the time. Practically everyone has anxiety feeding into their unique extreme momism, their personal nutty pieces, driving them to overdo. It's all a matter of degree. Every mother is a mix of extreme, perfectly good, and rebel mom moments. Balance is the key. Find a place between the extremes, from overcontrolled to laid-back, that works for you and your family. The instant that anxiety begins to churn and you start to stress, it's time to call yourself back from the extreme mom brink. No hurtling off the cliff, driven by someone else's expectations.

Even as I coach women in letting go of the stress and competitiveness that drive them, I too have been sucked up in it. One year, the YMCA Indian Princess* nation that my husband and daughters had joined sponsored a contest to create a Kachina doll. [*Sincere apologies to American Indians—this was back in the darker ages, before the name was changed to Y Princesses. Though it seems even the enlightenment of that phrasing is questionable, given the princess craze from Disney princesses to T-shirts, light switches, door signs, and bumper stickers that profess "Princess," "It's not easy being a Princess," or some other variation that insists on the special-ness of each little girl. This is just more of the "Children are fragile" philosophy, which says we have to boost their self-esteem.]

Kachina dolls are religious icons, carved and decorated to teach Hopi children about tribal mythology. Each child was to create one for a contest—with prizes! Extreme leanings confessed, my hus-band and I flitted around our daughter and set to work. He carved a body out of wood scraps, complete with working elbows and sculpted fingers. I pulled out leather and feathers to clothe it, adding tiny beads. What a masterpiece we produced! Meanwhile, our daughter lost interest and drifted away. Smiling expectantly over the finished doll, we were blown out of the workshop when, with turned-up nose, our daughter huffed, "It's not my Kachina doll." No one recalls if our psychoparent efforts won a prize. But the phrase was forever established in our family lexicon. "No, *my* Kachina doll" means parents are being pushy and need to back off. Every parent, even the perfectly good mother, has Kachina-doll moments, cues about our own cultural mythology: parents doing "more, better, all" in the guise of "helping" the child.

Perfectly Good Mothers in Action

Growing up in a large family, Josie loved socializing. She wanted that same social whirl when she had a family. Family friendships—and lots of them—seemed essential to a good life. Fast-forward twenty years: true to her childhood fantasies, Josie, her husband Jim, and kids were chest deep in social events. After the fourteenth consecutive weekend packed with commitments to birthday parties, soccer games, and neighborhood cleanup ventures, it dawned on her that her family—just the four of them—never had time together. Where had the fun gone, she wondered, as she dragged her crabby family out one more evening. This crazy social merry-go-round competed with her firmly held belief that nuclear families need to be close, as she was with her seven siblings. When she realized how far her life had veered away from her values, she took control—of what she could. She called a moratorium on off-the-cuff commitments. She memorized the words "I have to check our calendar" and used them before saying "We'll be there." These words were even written on a sticky note taped to her phone. She ran through questions in her head before saying "yes." Would an event be fun? Was it important to one of her kids? Was it critical to extended family or their immediate circle of friends? After scaling back, Josie, Jim, and the kids felt much more relaxed. Sometimes her daughter Jenna complained when she missed a party. So Josie and Jenna talked through the values behind the choice: how people can't be two places at once, that downtime is essential, that other people's feelings are important, and that we have to put ourselves first because no one else will. Josie knew that, as her kids approached the teen years, she'd have to help them make choices in the same way. Finally, she was living the life she truly wanted.

Megan had never been a morning person, yet she found herself schlepping short-order breakfast for three kids day in and day out. It made her cranky and stressed: pancakes here, sausage and eggs there, oatmeal and toast for the third. While talking through how to make her days more manageable, it became clear that this breakfast tradition had to go. Megan agreed in principle, but the automatic thoughts in her head cause her to throw out roadblocks: *But I should cook hot breakfast—it's the best start to the day—we have it as a family. They will be better equipped to learn at school. Bad mothers feed their kids toaster pastries and donuts—that would be awful!* My questioning began. Do the facts support the conclusion? For example, is a hot breakfast really the only healthy option? Does each child have to have something different each day? Did Megan even get to sit down and eat with the family, when serving as short-order cook? Would it truly be awful, affecting learning, if her kids ate cold cereal or nutritious breakfast bars instead? Did her worth as a mother come down to breakfast? Was pleasing the children the priority? She had good intentions—sitting down and enjoying the morning—but was the scenario fitting her values? Were there other solutions? Thinking rationally, Megan decided she would still cook hot breakfast—that part was important to her. But each child chose the meal one day of the week, and everyone ate that item. No more short-order cook. Megan was less stressed, and she actually sat down with the children every day.

Rae needed, financially and emotionally, to return to work since her children were now in school all day. Every mother she knew preached that if you have to work, you should find a job that's scheduled within school hours. Being bored to tears at some menial job was more socially acceptable than putting the children in after-school care. Rae hated that idea. She had loved working, for the money and the boost to her self-esteem. She was good at sales. The truthiness swirled through Rae's head: working mothers are bad for kids—on all levels. I helped Rae look at each thinking trap in turn.

Working through her thinking using questions as her guide, Rae sorted out her values. She wanted to give her daughters a model of a happy working mother; they'd need to work when they were adults. She took an upper-level sales job with some flexibility, working shorter hours two days per week. Rae picked up the children those days, taking them to dance at the same studio. After checking out the after-school program, Rae discovered her fears were unfounded. Fun classes like tumbling and karate were available on a rotating basis, with a separate quiet room for homework, staffed by college-student tutors. The transition to work was not flawless; her six-year-old cried every day for two weeks—then made a new friend in after-school care. Rae knew they all would survive, with this perfectly good set of choices, for now.

Perfectly Good Mantra:
"I can say 'no' to others."

If you're used to saying yes, no is foreign. Wayne Parker, on www.fatherhood.about.com, says we all can benefit from saying no to the unimportant. Next time you need to answer, give yourself permission to say no—even when someone else thinks it's important.

Thinking Trap	Reality Check
"I'm a bad mother if they have to ride the bus."	Most kids think riding the bus is the best part of their day: visiting with friends, being high above the cars. Is your value as a mother really tied to mode of school transport? No wonder parents drive their kids to school versus letting them ride the bus—overprotection disguised as points for the "mother of the year" award.

Thinking Trap	Reality Check
"Only the bad kids stay in the after-school program."	Are there really no honor students in that program? Are there other options for after-school care that are more desirable?

Thinking Trap	Reality Check
"Kids should come first, moms last."	Is this the message you want to send, that mothers do not matter, when your children become parents?

Thinking Trap	Reality Check
"I can't have them quit dance, or switch studios to evening classes—they would hate leaving their friends."	Are there other good dance programs? Maybe this is a chance for a new activity. Would they make new friends?

Thinking Trap	Reality Check
"It would be awful."	A bit of catastrophizing? Wouldn't everyone adjust over time?

Thinking Trap	Reality Check
"All this uproar is not fair to dump on them, in order for me to be happy."	Is this not what families do for each other—find ways to sanely balance everyone's needs? Do children need to learn that parents matter? That they can survive change? Will you be happier with work needs met—and able to give your children a less bored mom?

Raising Great Kids
with Perfectly Good Parenting

While the Perfectly Good Mother Manifesto is designed primarily to decrease the anxiety and guilt that keep you overperfecting, overprotecting, and overproducing, your stress is not the only focus. You want to make these changes because you want to raise great kids. The thinking part of your brain realizes that today's parenting focus on "doing it all" for kids not only exhausts you but may not be ideal for raising competent, emotionally stable children. All that overdoing can't be good for any of you. Children prosper emotionally when you give up overparenting—and become the great kids you want to raise.

Straight Thinking for Children

Thinking that is free of shoulds, absolutes, all-or-nothing thinking, and catastrophizing not only helps you step away from the mommy traps. It helps your children avoid perfectionism and unrealistic expectations both now and when they become parents. Teaching your children to adopt rational thinking—that is, how to see through a "perfectly good" lens—can help stress-proof them. Anxiety and depression are directly related to irrational thinking. Children naturally think in very black-and-white terms: I am a good kid or a bad kid; Callie is my friend or my enemy; the party was great or awful. When you look for the middle ground, your children copy that and temper their own thinking. Teaching kids to view the world through a "perfectly good" lens enables them to be realistic about accomplishments. If you say "Nobody's perfect," "We all make mistakes," "You are only human," when your children make a blunder, they'll learn to pick up on these mantras and go on rather than get stuck in feeling bad. They will know errors are part of life, not confirmation of failure.

Likewise, if you quit expecting total control of your universe, or theirs, everyone will have a healthier outlook. Preach "control what you can, let go of the rest." Your children will listen. Practice saying it out loud when you're frustrated. You know how kids copy every swear word that slips from your mouth. They can copy good self-talk, too. Talk your children through decision making—about social events, leisure time, structuring homework time—with this as the backdrop. Are there shoulds, about how "good kids" or "cool kids" behave? Do they fear imagined catastrophe: not making the team or being excluded from the party? Are there absolutes: "You never let me do anything!" "You always pay more attention to my sister!"? Teach them to recognize and sort out the same tangles you are learning to undo in your head. If your kids are given permission to be kids, to err and be human at an early age, imagine how free they'll feel to be themselves. This confidence will carry over to adulthood. Help your children apply the perspective of "perfectly good" to their lives, achievements, selves, and the actions of others. Emotionally healthier, less judgmental, more compassionate human beings with stronger self-esteem will appear. Isn't this why you are working so hard—for great kids?

Values and Choices in Parenting

To further apply the ideals of perfectly good parenting to your children, explore your ideas about the essential structure of your children's lives. What really matters for this family? What are the traits we want adult children to show? How do parents model these ideals, living the life they want? How can each person define "perfectly good" for himself or herself? When you look back on this time with your children, what do you most want them to remember? Focus on the fact that you are not raising a child; the child is a work in progress. You are raising an adult. Dr. Dan Myers, a Dallas psychiatrist, says a happy childhood is not the parents' job. The real responsibility of parents is to prepare children for a happy adulthood. As Wiseman and Rapoport say, "Our most important role as parents: to raise responsible, ethical kids who are well-equipped to deal with failures and disappointments."

Remember the values you listed in Chapter 5? Do you want your child to feel loved unconditionally? To be educated? To treat others kindly? To be a devout religious person, a hard worker, sensitive, financially savvy, courteous? How can you answer no to any of those questions? We want it all for each child. To be a perfectly good parent, raising a perfectly functional adult, refine your expectations. No "supers" around—you and your child are human. In fact, children are very human—they simply ooze humanity, especially standing in the stalled grocery checkout line at dinnertime. So consider who you are and the raw material you have in your kids. Pick and choose, controlling what you can. In the end, your child will do what works for him.

List the qualities you value in other adults. Do you prize trustwor-thiness, sense of humor, initiative, or organization? It is easier to feel like a perfectly good mother when you work toward inner qualities like these in your child, rather than outward criteria like being pres-ident, an athlete, or a mansion owner. Concrete goals like these prac-tically scream for overcontrol of your child's life. You are giving your child tools to survive in the world; you are not giving her the world.

Narrow your goals; pick several characteristics that are the most important to you. When you get a clear picture of qualities to instill in your child, write it down. Post it on the fridge. Read it regularly. It's your guide for the choices you need to make—about how to spend your time and treat others, young or old. Live with these goals in mind. Ponder how to lead your child in that direction. There are truckloads of books to advise you, if you're stumped about where to begin. But beware "how-to" books: the titles will trick you into thinking you have a fail-safe recipe. None exists! Books are great resources—but adapt what works for you, rather than using them as parenting bibles. The titles are infinite: just type in "raising children" in the bookstore or library catalog, and you will find endless offer-ings to fit the bill. No one could read them all! If you want specific guidance, pick one or two—no more—and use them as references. You can even take a parenting course; many religious and commu-nity organizations offer great ones. The important factor, again, is to keep perspective. No one knows your child as well as you do. No one else knows your quirks, and those of your partner. The more you can adapt recommendations to your family, the more valuable any out-side resource, including this book, will be.

Perfectly Good Outcomes

When you expect your child to be more accountable, he or she learns to take responsibility. This is true whether managing his own feelings or packing her own homework-filled backpack. Homework done by her, of course. From letting a four-month-old play on the floor for a few minutes while you dry your hair, to expecting your twelve-year-old to load the dishes so you can sit down with your husband, everyone wins. Your baby learns self-sufficiency; your twelve-year-old learns she's a valuable part of the family. When you tell your child "no," he'll step up and deal with disappointment, a critical skill for life in the big outside world. He'll learn other people have needs, which deserve respect. His future roommates, spouse, and boss will thank you. Allowing your three-year-old to make his own choices, even wearing mismatched clothes to preschool, gives him a bit of power over his world. The struggles to prove it will wane. When you are real with your five-year-old and say, "I'm angry at you—you interrupted me six times while I was on the phone," she'll see others can be angry and still love her. She learns that anger, while not fun, doesn't have to be scary or destroy people. She discovers that people make mistakes, apologize, and move on.

When you trust your eight-year-old to play over the hill out of view in a very safe park, checking in regularly, your child learns the world is not such a scary place. The child who is told, "I trust you to decide what you'd rather sign up for, soccer or baseball," develops good decision-making skills. Even if the outcome is unhappy! You have laid the groundwork for a lesson on learning to live with one's choices. Helping your child generate her own solutions to conflict with a teacher or peer teaches self-sufficiency and builds self-esteem. Rather than jumping in, solving it for her, and undermining her confidence, you convey "You can do it." You teach that a mother's job is not "making it all better"—a mother's job is giving children tools to make it right for themselves. Meanwhile, don't forget the brief lesson that "Some people are mean and we just have to deal with them." Then your child is prepared for the realities of the world.

When you say "no," even about too many friends at a party, your child learns to survive the dreaded word. You teach that hardly anything is black and white, and life isn't "ruined" by disappointments. Every time you choose in favor of your values rather than for "what everybody is doing," your children know they can safely challenge the status quo. When you explain choices according to "this family's values," your child learns that what is in her heart deserves attention. When you voice acceptance of another parent's style, saying "Everyone has to find what works for them," your child learns compassion and tolerance.

Elizabeth wanted to make sure her children grew up as generous but thrifty, sharing people. As soon as her son could toddle, she set up three piggy banks: one for saving, one for spending, and one for charity. Whenever he received cash for birthdays, it went into each bank, divided evenly. When the charity piggy was stuffed, they would make a special trip to deliver it—to the local food bank, the firefighters collecting on corners, or the animal shelter. Elizabeth felt real triumph when, on his sixth birthday, he handed her the fifty-dollar bill his grandmother sent him and said, "Feed the piggies, Mom," with a radiant smile—and no fussing.

Encourage Children to Be Themselves

Elizabeth's son was turning into a great kid. But another parent may have another definition. You may even have to reevaluate your definition of "great kid" from one child to the next. Richie and Chad were as different as two brothers could be. Victoria had always thought her sons would be great athletes, because she and her husband had met while training for a triathlon. Richie came into the world as timid as a fox; he cried when she set him at the top of the slide, preparing to whisk him down. At the same age, Chad was swinging from the monkey bars as soon as he could toddle. As the boys grew, Victoria had to accept that, while Chad was developing into a star ball player, Richie was just not wired that way. Richie gravitated toward the piano in the living room, plinking out tunes once Victoria stopped shooing him away. Both boys were great kids, with considerable talent—when Victoria accepted that they each would be themselves, and not who she thought they should be.

This is one of the most critical points in raising great kids. You need to stop and think of ways in which your kids are already great—even if they aren't fitting the model kid that you had a mind. Accept them for who they are. Determine and help them grow into their strengths. Just as to feel like a perfectly good mother you need to watch out for and take to heart the ways in which you are a perfectly good mother every day, so do you need to search out and value the ways in which your children are already wonderful human beings. Cherish them for who they are.

To raise great kids, think back to the Perfectly Good Mom

Manifesto. It applies to children too. Allow your children to be themselves, in all their muddy or shy glory. You have little control over their personalities anyway. Affirm their unique attributes: "You are a sensitive person—you feel things strongly," or "You barge into the world—sometimes you may need to slow down." Teach them to tend to their own needs: to listen when their tummies are growling, to learn about their feelings, to recognize when they've had too much play group and need to rest. This doesn't mean you don't override their preferences, though, particularly if you think bedtime should be 8:00 PM and they think it should be 1:30 AM. It's valuable to be the parent and use adult judgment when childish decisions aren't in their best interests. As soon as they're able, encourage them to meet their needs. Empower them by stocking a low shelf in the kitchen with juice and appropriate snacks, so they can help themselves. Teach them to clear their own dishes, wash their own bodies, pack their own book bags. Nurture their sense of fun and silliness by leading with your own. Encourage them to choose their activities, within limits. The ability to live by the consequences, wisely bestowed, builds self-esteem. Finally, teach your children to think rationally. Before the age of twelve, children's brains work in absolutes of good/bad, success/failure, right/wrong. But introducing the idea that some things in life are relative can help them cope with the rigors of life in the long run.

Finally, remember that raising children comes down to simple terms, in aphorisms you've heard. Love and limits. Be the person you want your child to be. Children learn best by watching models who struggle, rather than instantly triumph. Your kids see it is okay to make mistakes, admit when they are wrong or don't have the answer, if you do that too. Treat your child—and everyone around you—the way you want your child to treat others. Criticize behavior, not the person. Use natural consequences. Let your child learn by doing, not by lecture. Be consistent. These are truths about parenting; it does work this way. But you must adapt these guidelines for your parenting, for your children. In a 2004 *Psychology Today* article, Hara Estroff Marano offered "Un-Advice for Parents." Here is how to raise great kids:

How to Raise Great Kids

* Chill out! If you're not having fun, you may be pushing your kids too hard.

* Never invest more in an outcome than your child does.

* Allow children of all ages time for free play. It's a natural way to learn regulation, social, and cognitive skills.

* Be reasonable about danger: what is, and what isn't. Some risk taking is healthy.

* Don't overreact to every bad grade or encounter your child has. Sometimes discomfort is the appropriate response to a situation—and a stimulus to self-improvement.

* Don't be too willing to slap a disease label on your child at the first sign of a problem; instead, spend some time helping your child learn to deal with the problem.

* Peers are important, but kids need to spend time socializing with adults in order to know how to be adults.

* Modify your expectations about child raising in light of your child's temperament; the same actions don't work with everyone.

* Recognize that there are many paths to success. Allow your child latitude—even to take a year off before starting college.

* Don't manipulate the academic system on behalf of your child; it makes kids feel guilty and doubtful of their own ability.

* Remember that the goal of child rearing is to raise an independent adult. Encourage your children to think for themselves, to disagree (respectfully) with authority, even to incur the critical gaze of their peers.

If your life matches your goals most days, then you are living your perfectly good mother—and you're being a great model for your kids. But you're never living it perfectly—no one is. Crummy days won't vanish. Weigh it out: if your perfectly good mom days are more frequent than days when troll mommy stomps in, you are on the right track. If not, stop, admit your mistakes. Regroup, and get going again.

The Seven Stumbling Blocks to Change

Behavior change is hard for most humans. Staying stuck in your rut, of thinking or behavior, is more natural than changing. The roadblocks to action are these:

1. Habits

2. Automatic thoughts

3. Deficits in self-care

4. Others: spouse, parents, kids

5. Competing needs

6. Unrealistic expectations

7. Internal issues

Habits die long and agonizing deaths. Kids and partners want good old mom to be predictable. Finding energy to launch a change is like finding lost socks in the laundry. In true Supermom style, you overwhelm yourself, trying to change it all at speeding bullet pace. Forces outside of you pull harder in another direction, keeping you stuck. There are times when internal forces—anxiety, depression, or your unmet needs—derail you. And sometimes you are human, not very good at keeping values in sight. These are all stumbling blocks to living as a perfectly good mother. Let's keep relative, reasonable thinking handy. There's no need to judge yourself if detours appear. They're just hurdles to stride over, strengthening your parenting legs in the process. Sometimes the hurdles are closely spaced; other times, the road is clear for miles. You don't have to live the life you want all the time. It's not all or nothing. Take credit for each perfectly good moment. You deserve it.

Stumbling Block #1: Habits

How old are you? Your children? Don't expect to turn around that many years of routine in a week. Cut yourself some slack. It is simply hard for anyone to get themselves off center. Remember the Nike commercial: Just do it. Work on one change today—just one. Write it down. Say it aloud. "I will say 'no' to the next birthday party." "Rory will pack his own backpack." Change is always two steps forward and one back—for us all. To always move forward, or to change in a twinkling of fairy dust, is as likely as a tidy house after the kids are home with dad all day. Allow yourself a tortoise pace: slow and steady. Habit change takes twenty-one days, then eighteen

> "How you spend your time reveals your priorities. . . . You always have time for the things you put first."
>
> —*Taro Gold*, The Tao of Mom: Wisdom of Mothers from East to West

months before new thinking patterns are automatic. Please don't be discouraged by those figures. You won't feel badly for two years and then, in an explosion of light, be transformed. Hope for gradual improvement, scattered moments of triumph, and finally universal comfort with the new mothering model.

Another old human habit is ignoring values. Few of us keep values front and center as a guide, so we can double-check our actions against values. You can do that. Say it, write it: "We are a family that believes time together is important." "We are a family that gives back to the community." "We are a family that believes in moderation in all things." Revisit what the three to five values you want to honor are. Write them down. Match your habits to your values.

Cynthia called me, quite distressed. "I have to put myself first and say no to my kids. That's no big deal about discipline issues, but I stall when my wants conflict with theirs. I can't do it—I can't change it. I try, but I get stuck in the old way." Her daughters wanted to go to the school carnival, a hot social event, and she had already scheduled a couples weekend away. The girls would stay with Cynthia's cousin across town, who had her own children's commitments that day and could not take them to the carnival. The girls were sulking. Cynthia felt like a failure. She had conquered the first critical step—awareness. She knew, by placing her needs last, she sent her children a message that "Mothers do not matter." Awareness is necessary but not sufficient for change. You need your click moment, when you realize societal expectations for mothers aren't healthy—for kids or moms. You don't mask all the woodwork, move all the furniture, cover the carpet, and paint your dining room the same Pepto-Bismol pink that the previous owners picked. That color does not work—so you change it. The current mommy model is not workable. Once that awareness is firmly in your brain, you quit feeling that "There is something the matter with me." You accept that extreme momism doesn't teach your kids the lessons you want them to learn. Plus it wears you out. Time to change the habit. Cynthia had that weekend with her husband, and she enjoyed it so much that she began to take thirty minutes each day to read a book while her daughters played without her. A new habit was born.

Stumbling Block #2: Automatic Thoughts

That destructive self-talk is still creeping around in your head, and you just don't realize it. Thinking traps are sneaky and permeate your brain like the smell in your freshly painted house. To feel like a perfectly good mother rather than a rotten one, change them in your head. Is anxiety keeping you stuck? What automatic thoughts are trickling through your head? Take a big, deep breath, especially if you are feeling stressed, angry, or like a failure, and listen for a couple minutes each day. Are the danger words creeping into your vocabulary: should, ought, always, never, everyone, all? Are you thinking in black-and-white, all-or-nothing terms? Are the catastrophe sirens sounding? The underlying anxiety can send you for a loop to rival any carnival ride. Speak the anxiety out loud, and label it as such: "Just anxiety, not to worry." Smoke out the specific auto thoughts, write them down, and fan them away by rewording. Lynn liked to type them up and tear them to shreds. Heather recorded them on a marker board, symbolically wiping them out. She rewrote the reasonable thoughts, helping her feel like a perfectly good mother. Or distract yourself with activity. Amanda had to go for a hard walk or dance with her children. Karen found stomping up and down the stairs helpful, before she could recognize the self-talk igniting her anger.

Have you been watching television or catching up on your magazines? Maybe those glossy images reinforce the old thinking traps. Talk back to the expectations conveyed by TV and magazines, or even quit the media for a while. "What a bunch of propaganda," you can say. "That is not real!" Remind yourself that the perfect mother and the perfect childhood are *fiction*. FICTION. Heather taped reminder notes to the phone; talking to sister-in-law Tammy would no longer fire up her competitive juices! Reread Chapter 2 so you can see the sly societal pressure. Remember: It is nothing the matter with you.

Stumbling Block #3: Deficits in Self-Care

Running on empty? Then where will you get energy for change? Reread the section in Chapter 4 on self-care. No one can run on fumes—most of us need sleep, food, an invigorating jog, and mojitos on the porch with friends. If you don't take care of your own needs,

Perfectly Good Mantra:

"_____

doesn't make me a bad mom."

For example, "Losing my temper" doesn't make me a bad mom; "missing the soccer sign-up" doesn't make me a bad mom. Chances are, whatever is fueling your guilt can go in the blank—it probably doesn't make you a bad mom. Your black-and-white thinking only makes it seem so.

you can't engineer your life in a satisfying way. Karen took five minutes out of every hour for herself; she kept a magazine handy and read a few pages each hour. Nobody in the family missed her, and she felt surprisingly rejuvenated. Beth scheduled a night for sex with her husband each week. On that night, he came home a little earlier, bathed and fed the kids, and tucked them in so Beth could soak in the tub, have a glass of wine, and move her brain from mom mode to sex goddess mode. Heather tried to eat even a few crackers or a piece of fruit every time she fed her son—every two hours, it seemed, with his high energy level. This was much better for her energy than when she only ate dinner each day—revving her up enough to resume her running. Joni booked her in-laws to sit on the first Saturday of every month— cast in stone. Sometimes she took off and shopped on her own; sometimes her husband came with her to a movie and dinner.

Stumbling Block #4:
Others—Spouse, Parents, Kids

You don't parent in a vacuum. All your best-laid plans can be undermined by others. In Chapter 8, the community of women around you is explored in depth—how they can buoy you or drain you. People, your family or not, can impose subtle and blatant disapproval and disdain when you quit the perfect mother competition. Right now, those in your immediate circle are the concern. Your partner may not get it. It is easier to be a perfectly good mother if your partner understands. Elly decided that three sports were too many for their two children. Everyone was too tired and stressed from running from soccer to swimming to softball. But Dan, her husband, insisted that all were essential to building character and developing lifelong skills. He grumbled about her new agenda. Then Elly had a weekend away at a cousin's wedding. Dan stayed home and did all the running to meets, matches, and games. He usually traveled on business and rarely witnessed the kids' meltdowns caused by overcommitment. When Elly arrived home, a haggard and tired Dan was totally onboard with the plan to simplify. Bring people in your life into the loop on changes if you can, and let go if not. It's your life, after all, and you are entitled to do what works for you and your family—not for your mother-in-law or best friend.

Your children can be the biggest hurdle when you opt out of over-responsible mode. They've never picked up a sock or loaded

---

Perfectly Good Mantra:
"Enough for now."

Underlying the stress driving moms is what I call "the tyranny of one more"—one more thing to do, one more gesture. It makes you late going out the door, it reinforces the idea that you are never done. So repeat this mantra to drop some of the "to-dos" and stop—for now. More time for you is the payoff.

a dish? You check out and deliver the library books they need for that big paper? As you change, assigning them self-responsibility, mutiny can result. How would you feel if your personal maid and organizer suddenly up and quit? Angry? Stranded? As will your children if you switch gears suddenly. Eda LeShan, in an October 1992 *Parents* article, reminds that parents are an inevitable source of unhappiness for our children from the preteen or teen's point of view: "Our rules mean that they will never be popular, never be free, never be happy—ever!" Watch out for those absolutes—children get sucked up in them too. If you institute your new regime as gradually as the leaves change color in fall, resistance will be less. Require one new chore; let them suffer from forgetting their lunches a time or two. They don't have to like it, they just have to do it. And you don't have to like it, you just have to do it—if you want to have less stress in your life, more balance, and more

Mixed messages from the world around us challenge our perfectly good mother efforts. Louise described the parent orientation session when her first child went to college. One college staff member lectured parents about not being Hovercrafts, constantly calling or reminding students to do this or that. Five minutes later, another staff person instructed parents to "Remember to tell your student" X, Y, and Z. Evaluate directives like this for what fits best for your family or child, and ignore the rest.

competent, independent children. Put on your mother armor and prepare to be hated for a little while. The rewards will be plentiful—in ten or twenty years.

Your child's temperament is another roadblock. Your spirited daughter may need karate every night, even though you want to just stay home. If your son is shy, volunteering once a month at the local homeless center is painful. Perfectly good mothering means focusing on what works, not just for you, but for everyone. Lana needed more sleep to be less cranky—nine hours was her bottom line. Her three-year-old was very active, needing little sleep. Short of Dimetapp, Lana was not able to make her daughter sleep more—at least for now. Find ways to take care of yourself that are compatible with your children's quirks. Lana got a college student to play with her daughter two afternoons each week while she caught a few ZZZs. Perfectly good mothers know it's no problem to refine what works—as often as needed. The needs of children change with time. You can expect more of a twelve-year-old than a two-year-old. With no absolute definition of a perfectly good mother, there's no reason to stay stuck in stressful habits.

Stumbling Block #5:
Competing Needs

Unless you are independently wealthy with a staff of twenty, there are other demands in your life. Aging parents, work deadlines, bosses from Hades, mounting bills, and volunteer projects seem like so many octopus tentacles. Often, you can wrestle the octopus; sometimes, you feel like you're drowning. There are two key points to remember when facing external forces like these: (1) control what you can and (2) remember that perfectly good is relative.

When life pitches you a wild one, control what you can. You are powerless in the face of your favorite aunt's cancer; you want to spend every available weekend nursing her. Bad mother thoughts flare up; you can't protect your children totally, you are torn between mothering and feeling like a perfect niece. What *can* you control? Give your children a chance to discuss Auntie's illness, read books about death and dying, and arrange a fun, safe place for them to stay while you tend your aunt. Spend time with your aunt without kids, without guilt: she will not be here long. You've showered attention on your kids all their lives, banking hours that will hold them through this crisis. Think damage control—within your sphere of influence.

Always keep perspective. Perfectly good is relative—absolutely! Your boss just pitched you a huge project; you're swamped. This week, you're not the perfectly good mother you want to be. Be gentle with yourself. Perfectly good adds up over time; the marbles are not emptied out of the jar. Ever. Garrison Keillor, of *Prairie Home Companion*, says, "Nothing you do for children is ever wasted." Every act counts, even under stress—doing less than you like. In each moment, are you doing the best you can, within the constraints at hand? Not the best by standards of easy times (what would that be?) but for the current moment. Your best to the fullest extent. If not, what can give? If so, tell yourself that you're doing a perfectly good job—for now. Stress is living under siege. Just like during wartime, cut back and lower expectations. When the siege is over, whether a new baby or a work, marital, or family crisis, you can recoup. Just like a teeter-totter—up and down. The balance of perfectly good parenting over the whole of your children's lives is what matters. Don't beat yourself up about the crisis points. Everyone (yes, everyone—this absolute is fact) has stresses; most of us endure relatively unscathed.

Stumbling Block #6:
Unrealistic Expectations

Nearly every mother who walks into my office tries to change too much at once. You're only human, change is hard, and there is no magic wand—not this book, not the best therapist in the world, not winning the lottery. As Confucius said, "A journey of a thousand miles begins with a single step." It took years to build the picture of the mother you should be, watching *Leave It to Beaver, The Cosby Show,* or real-life mothers. It won't change in one night of sweet dreams. In my office, I overwhelm my clients with a zillion things to try. The perfectionists want to "do it all"—yesterday. Bring on the magic wand and the fairy godmother. The CD is on repeat again: one change at a time. Build on that, try one more. Chug along at Thomas the Tank Engine speed—you don't have to be James, the big red engine, showing off your breakneck pace. Find what works for you, revise, rework again. Bit by bit, what you do and how you feel mesh with the perfectly good mother you want to be.

Stumbling Block #7:
Internal Issues

The last stumbling block to perfectly good parenting changes lurks inside each of us. Many parents hope to fix what they hated about their own childhoods. Better and better again—than your parents. Moms give to their children in ways that they missed growing up. Kara's family never had money for dance lessons, so Kara enrolled her two-year-old in a dance studio. Liz did not want to yell, because her mother raged. When childhood hurts haunt you, preventing perfectly good mothering, taking care of your own needs is the first essential step. Distinguish between your needs and those of your children. Take their view of a situation, ask what matters to them: this is part of perfectly good mothering.

Your feelings of "not good enough" may relate to what you got, or not, growing up—rather than with what you are giving your kids. If anxiety about your child overwhelms you, look at your own issues: are you transferring concerns about your own worth to your child? Counseling is the best course of action if your anxiety and guilt don't budge with the suggestions in this book. Medications can be helpful to treat clinical levels of anxiety or depression that block your ability to be the mother you want to be. Appendix Two: Resources lists organizations to help you find a competent therapist.

In *Huck's Raft,* Steven Mintz notes a disturbing trend in extreme parents: treating "children like pint-size extensions of their parents' egos." Some high-profile and disastrous examples are these: (1) Jessica Dubrof, who died because her father wanted her to be the youngest pilot to fly across the United States; (2) JonBenet Ramsey, whose mom sought to make her a beauty queen at the tender age of six. Parents need to ask themselves, *Is this my need, or that of my child?* When aiming for adult-like accomplishments, question "Who is driving?" Can six- and eight-year-olds really aim for grown-up goals without parental prompting? If you find yourself pushing your child to overachieve in this way, please stop and think it through—and find a healthier way to meet your own needs.

Part Three

Sharing the
Solution

Safety in Numbers

No More Mommy Wars

Parenting is "the ultimate female Olympics," according to *The Mommy Myth*. Women push to control all in the quest for the perfect childhood, striving to surpass the other mothers. Julie's mom sends homemade cupcakes to school; Leeta's mom tops that with hand-shaped candy canes. Rory is going to space camp in Alabama, so Kent's mom needs to fax in that sea camp registration form as soon as she gets to work. Children get older and throw a few logs on the bonfire of this competition. When my daughter was six, she asked, "Why can't you do good stuff like the other mothers?" "Like what?" I asked, puzzled. "Play tennis, like Ali's mom, or sell cookies at the school, like Tracy's mom" was the reply.

The war is waged on the battlefield of paid work versus stay-at-home moms—by moms and children—and within each world as well. No one goes guilt free.

To keep on track with perfectly good parenting, connecting with other women is critical. You know the current standards for parenting are preposterous. Inside your own head, you're getting comfortable with that. But anxiety still trickles down: who will frown if you buck the system? Time to be upfront with other women about the monumental nature of parenting and the unrealistic drive for perfection in childhood. The competition and guilt won't end if women continue to judge each other. The collective standards can't change if women don't call them what they are: ridiculous. The elephant in the play group can no longer go unmentioned.

Anne Lamott writes about the Everest-like challenge of parenting in *Mothers Who Think: Tales of Real-Life Parenthood*. Given the frustrations and anger mothers feel, Lamott says, "While I'm not sure what the solution is, I know that what doesn't help is the terrible feeling of isolation, the fear that everyone else is doing better. . . . Good friends help. Pretending that we are doing better than we are doesn't. Shame doesn't. Being heard does." This chapter gives ideas on connecting with other women in a supportive, not competitive, manner, in order to end the mommy wars.

Supporting Each Other, Changing the Status Quo

Your hard work to live your perfectly good mother can be swept away in a flash flood after one brief moment with other moms. Missy was worn down by total devotion to her children: shuttling them here and there, filling their lives to the brim with fun and stimulation. At the park, her daughter Cara yelled, "I hate you," when Missy warned her, for the fifth time in ten minutes, to stay away from the creek. Missy burst into tears, turning to moms she knew seated on a nearby bench. "It is so hard!" she exploded "I do and do for them—do they ever say thank-you? No, they just push for more." The three women on the bench stared at her blankly. "But that's our job, as mothers," said one. "We have to give and give." Another mom looked away, while the third went to push her child on the swing. Missy froze, shocked by the biting judgment. She corralled her kids into the car, crying softly all the way home.

Missy wasn't blessed with an affirming support network or friends who would never judge. Lucky you, if you have a place where you can be honest, cry, or vent. There are ideas here for building a safety net for your perfectly good mother quest. Safety in numbers means finding like-minded women who are honest about parenting and the impossibility of perfection. Ending the mommy wars means having courage to speak openly about the day-to-day drudgery. It means supporting, not criticizing, the perfectly good choices other mothers make, even when different from ours. Finally, letting go of concern about what others think is essential.

In her landmark 1976 book, *Of Woman Born: Motherhood as Experience and Institution,* Adrienne Rich was the first to call motherhood what it is: hard physical labor paired with emotional and intellectual toil. Prior to Rich, the idea of joyous motherhood went unchallenged. In many settings, it's still taboo to voice the reality of daily parenting. In my office, Wendy lamented, "Everyone else loves motherhood, adoring their days with their kids. Am I the only one who tells the truth?" As long as women protect this secret, from themselves or the rest of the world, the mommy thinking trap of "natural, endlessly satisfying motherhood" snaps hold. To free yourself from it, call it what it is: truthiness. Perfect moments exist. But if you believe parenting is a sustained blissful breeze, you'll be blown away when hurricane moments hit—every time. Cathi Hanauer writes in *The Bitch in the House* that a "step toward solution is to talk about it. We women need to share our lives and dilemmas and frustrations, to tell the truth whenever and wherever

Connecting with Others
the Perfectly Good Mother Way

1. *Honesty is essential.*
2. *Be yourself and respect others' rights to do the same.*
3. *Straight thinking is key.*
4. *Perfectly good mothers don't judge or criticize other mothers.*
5. *Invest energy in relationships with like-minded women.*

we can. . ." If women are not forthright about the challenges, they stay stuck in "What is the matter with me?" The problem is expectations, not your abilities.

Honesty Is Essential

To live as a perfectly good mother, honesty is the foundation, with yourself and with others—mothers or not. Kate Reddy, in *I Don't Know How She Does It*, receives an e-mail from her friend Candy, saying, "Hon, U gotta cut the domestic goddess crap. Look other moms in the eye and say, I'm Busy and I'm Proud or U will be ded." In other words, exhausted by self-sacrifice. Betsy spoke up in front of her friends, challenging the entrenched notion that children always come first. A deadly silence fell on the room when Betsy said she was keeping an anniversary dinner date with her husband rather than shuttling her daughter to the third-grade end-of-year party. Most women are simply too scared to speak up as Betsy did, especially in a group. Hinting at the truth, the looks they get rival Medusa. When conversations with other women are stilted by niceties, as Rivka Solomon says in her book, *That Takes Ovaries: Bold Females and Their Brazen Acts*, it takes ovaries to be honest. The culture of motherhood is like society at large, when we ask, "How are you today?" The standard answer, "Just fine," does no good if you want to connect with others.

Truth telling ends emotional isolation. If you don't confess, you won't find other moms who feel like you do. Honesty is the first step to finding like-minded women who will support you in perfectly good mothering. Up to 80 percent of mothers of young children have negative feelings. Hiding your own frustrations about parenting could shut down four of every five women you meet. No one wants to be the trailblazer, if honesty about the mother trials makes you a harpy or a loser. But someone must speak up, breaking the ban on silence, or all moms stay stuck.

The catch-22 of honesty about parenting is like this quote from *Les Miserables:* "If I speak, I am condemned. If I stay silent, I am damned."

The Perfectly Good Mantra for this is:
"It's okay to be honest about who I am."

Mommy Traps on the Road to Honesty

Why is honesty so hard? Same old culprit: cultural expectations. The mommy thinking traps explored in Chapter 3 have another element. We buy into these unrealistic ideas to give our children the perfect, protected, productive childhood. But we also keep up appearances because we want to belong. Rosalind Wiseman and Elizabeth Rapoport in *Queen Bee Moms and Kingpins Dads* state that "Our culture makes us feel that we have to be and look a certain way so that we belong." These authors affirm that "everyone wants to belong somewhere. There's nothing weak or pathological about it." Cliques and peer pressure are not left behind in middle school; they are rampant in parent circles as well. Wiseman and Rapoport continue, "We can trick ourselves into believing that there's just one party to go to, one group to belong to, and that if we don't get in and stay in, we don't measure up."

Throwing off these thinking traps in favor of perfectly good mothering means risking rejection by peers. "Cultural rule breakers can make others extremely uncomfortable, so most people don't want them around. . . . They are rarely accepted . . . even when [others] think the rule breakers are 'right,'" say Wiseman and Rapaport. Choosing to follow your own parenting values, rather than the status quo, takes great strength. Be prepared to find a new group. Everyone won't get your new choices. Like Betsy, find the courage to stick to your values, and speak up about them honestly. Judith Newman, in a March 2005 *Ladies' Home Journal* article says, "In no other realm of life is it so hard to buck the prevailing wisdom, whatever that wisdom may be. Some of us can brave being thought of as a bad person; few will risk being thought of as a bad mother."

For fighting anxiety about how other mothers may judge or exile you if you're honest, here's a Perfectly Good Mantra:

"I need no approval but my own. I know what's best for me and my family."

Your honesty doesn't have to be flippant or cruel. Fly the honesty flag in a matter-of-fact way. Simply vow to reject the parenting madness. Don't apologize about your needs, that your children are responsible for themselves, that you value family time rather than running with the "in crowd."

Feminist therapists point out the dysfunctional expectations society has for women, just like the mommy traps. One principle of feminist change is to never go it alone. When you are bucking the societal mainstream, you always need the support of one other woman on the same upstream course. So look around and find a likely prospect.

Lynette never minced words. She committed to perfectly good parenting, meaning fewer extracurricular activities so her family could spend more time together. With her first courageous step, declining her daughter's commitment to swim team, no one blinked. By the third activity, she had calls from two friends. Lynette gave the same answer: "We are stepping out of the crazy whirl to relax more at home. The kids have one activity each from now on." Aubrey was impressed, loved the concept of doing less, and pulled her daughter from swim team too. Eve couldn't believe it. She promptly called three other moms, aghast, to rail about "Lynette ruining the teams," breaking up the close-knit group they were building.

Most of the time, as Lynette found, honesty wins a few converts for your side. Just as often, you lose a few friends. Paula took a more conservative tack. Rather than jumping into candor about parenting in her Bible study, she studied the group. Odds were someone in her circle might challenge the perfect mommy push; she thought about who was a renegade at heart. As she listened, she spotted Kate, always ready to challenge the "children first" self-sacrificing status quo. Paula didn't know her well, so she called to ask her to lunch. She planned how to begin, so they wouldn't stay stuck in pleasantries. At lunch, Paula shared her visceral reactions to the "winner-take-all, children-first" mandate most women endorse. Kate was thrilled to find "someone who thinks like me." They vowed to have lunch regularly, supporting each other in balancing their lives.

Be Yourself and Respect Others' Rights to Do the Same

Being yourself is a critical cornerstone of being a perfectly good mother, as outlined in the Perfectly Good Mom Manifesto. As you work to be honest with other women, how you communicate can convey respect for others and affirmation for yourself. Whether you

Perfectly Good Mantra:
"I can find other moms who think like me."

choose a subtle or overt style for your truth telling, consider your word choices. "I" statements, such as "I was running on empty," "I could not do it any more," are softer and more respectful of others' choices, which may not match your own. You're not coercing anyone to join you; you're simply stating your limits. You're not launching a political manifesto, raving about injustices against mothers, or judging any mother. Own your intentions and your ability to be yourself, act in less driven ways, control what you can for a more satisfying life. Focus on being frank with one or two safe people: accepting,

In *I Killed June Cleaver,* Lauren Andreano writes about "the McSecret." "This secret may shock the intelligent, socially responsible mother . . . . It's politically incorrect, crass, commercial, and downright hazardous to your health, but it can give you a precious hour of semi-peace and quiet, and keep you out of the kitchen for the night." McDonald's is the secret, and Andreano makes it sound absolutely divine: "We sat in the relative quiet. I sipped my coffee, hummed with the Muzak, and observed my kids so caught up in dunking the usually forbidden chicken chunks in ketchup . . . that they forgot to fight. 'This is good,' I sighed contentedly to myself, somewhat surprised. And it was." Mothers on the Mother's Day KERA panel elaborated: moms don't admit to shortcuts like this, fearing poor grades from other mothers about how well their kids are doing.

nonjudgmental types. Is there a specific person in your world whose acceptance you crave? Write an outline or script of how you're choosing differently and what help you need from them. With Kayla, Paula had said, "I'm tired of competing with other moms. I'm exhausted, controlling minutiae that'll take care of themselves. Instead, I'm focusing on the big picture—what is workable for us."

Withhold judgment if existing friends or family can't handle the new you. Living as a perfectly good mother is your choice—nobody else's business. Some will judge, call you selfish, negative, or bitchy. The ability to say "no" is envied in some mom circles. Onlookers feel frustrated that they can't rebel too. Some women feel threatened when friends aren't like-minded. Rita never felt secure unless her friends shared her thoughts. When friends mirrored her choices, she felt worthwhile. Cheryl Dellasega writes in *Mean Girls Grown Up: Adult Women Who Are Still Queen Bees, Middle Bees, and Afraid-to-Bees:* "Basically, any woman who challenges the status quo may become at risk for victimization." Women already doubt that they are "good enough." Others' sneers reinforce their doubts. Leora Tanenbaum, in *Catfight: Women and Competition,* says that "the majority of conflicts among women come from the need to be better than one's peers, no matter what the venue." Pearson's Kate in *I Don't Know How She Does It* compares stay-at-home moms to those working in the world. "There is an uneasy standoff between the two kinds of mother which sometimes makes it hard for us to talk to each other. . . . In order to keep going in either role, you have to convince yourself that the alternative is bad." A similar split happens between easygoing perfectly good mothers and extreme, still-harried moms. When you choose the perfectly good mother versus the driven mother, some will feel you're judging them—no matter your intentions.

Other women's reactions don't have to do with you. You made a choice for you—and only you. Is it your life, or theirs? The problem is those who criticize, not your path. One victim of female aggression that Dellasega quotes said, "I realized that the vendetta of the women involved ultimately didn't have anything to do with me. The roots of their behavior were deeper." Most women who work to perfectly control and protect their children aren't bad guys. They're simply too riddled with guilt or anxiety to see the light—yet. Do what works for you, and give others room to do the same. There are as many versions of perfectly good as genetic combinations. No one has the corner on truth—truth for your own life is all you have.

Straight Thinking Is Key

A huge hurdle to honesty with others is facing your automatic thoughts—again. The "straight thinking" of the Perfectly Good

Perfectly Good Mantra:
"So what?"

When others criticize your choices, try it on. Does it really matter what others think about your life? It's *your* life.

Mom Manifesto applies to acceptance by other women just as it affects your thinking about your child's welfare and your perform-ance as a parent. Do others think you're doing a good job? McKay, Davis, and Fanning describe the idea of personalization, an automatic thought particularly relevant to your relationships to other women.

In personalization, mothers compare themselves to other moms. In my office, Helen said, "I can't do this all. I look around at the other mothers, and they are 'doing it all.' I wonder 'what is the mat-ter with me?'" Most of us have a mental mommy block. It looks like other moms breeze through the business of parenting. The false assumptions about others' success make us clam up, hiding the true nature of our lives and leaving us feeling "less than" other moms in our own universes. From her vantage point in the dance studio window, Hannah watched her friend Gloria unload her daughters for their classes. Gloria's girls were always impeccably groomed and outfitted: wisp-free buns, snag-free tights, ballerina-motif perfectly chilled water bottles. Gloria had even managed to have her daugh-ters the right number of years apart—signing them up for classes at the same time, minimizing trips to the studio each week. Hannah sighed, eyeing her daughters' straggly ponytails, snagged tights on one girl, mismatched anklets on the other. How inadequate was she? Her two daughters were close in age, and their class schedules clashed. She had to entertain one while the other danced, or tempt the checkout-line gods with a quick run to the store for milk. Usually one girl ended up in tears before they got home for dinner. Hannah caught Gloria glancing at the hole in her daughter's tights, a mixture of pity and contempt on her face. How did Gloria do it all, when Hannah's life felt like the disaster ride at the amusement park? Mothers like Hannah compare endlessly: severity of tantrums, excitement of parties, trash level of minivan floors. In their own heads, they come up wanting, again and again. "How can I raise successful children? Will I ever fit into the world of moms?" they ruminate.

When parenting is a competition, with children's accomplishments the scorecard, not comparing yourself seems impossible. It is normal to want to belong. But falling into the personalization trap only adds to the "worst mom ever" tally in your head. You are full of false assumptions: you don't measure up, you should be a certain way, other mothers should affirm your value. If others don't approve of you, it doesn't mean you have a huge scarlet L—for loser—on your forehead.

Perfectly Good Mantra:
"Whatever works."

A basic rule of perfectly good mothering is that only *you* and your family can judge what works for you. Are you within basic legal standards of good care? Not neglecting your children? Then only your opinion matters. Not your mother's, not your neighbor's, not the Queen Bee of the PTA.

Ginger struggled to feel worthy, berating herself for her messy house, snapping at her kids too much, missing sign-ups for the "right" school programs. When I asked if Ginger judged others the way she judged herself, she stopped cold. "No—absolutely not. I never do that. What do I know about their lives?" If you fear criticism from the Glorias of your world, think of Ginger. Few perfectionists regard others as harshly, turning perfectionism only upon themselves. So be as easy on yourself as you are with other mothers. If you can cut them some slack, offer that same compassion to yourself.

I'm not naïve; the Glorias of the world do sneer at the less fortunate. Mothers criticize each other as harshly as Bree Van De Kamp on *Desperate Housewives,* rather than banding together to end the madness. Hannah may have read into the expression Gloria cast in her direction—or Gloria may have judged her. Both happen. Do you fall into the trap of thinking that "Everyone should like me, all the time—or I'm unlikable"? Watch those shoulds, all-or-nothing thinking, and absolutes. Aside from the irrational beliefs, scientifically this is simply false. When college students mingle with strangers and then rate each other, researchers find that one-third of the students like person A, one-third dislike person A, and one-third are neutral, swaying either way. You can expect this whether you are joining the church choir or the PTA board. One-third of the members will like you, one-third won't, and the other third can be recruited or ignored—it's up to you. Reverse this fact. Do you like everyone you meet? Are there any groups where you like all the members? Total acceptance from everyone *for* everyone is a myth— there are too many personalities at work.

Forget the shoulds about conforming to or competing with other mothers. Ellen flopped down in the chair in my office, bursting into tears. Through her sobs, she related how, taking a stand on the birthday party issue, she only invited four girls to her six-year-old daughter Madison's party. Tradition at her daughter's school involved slumber parties, with every girl in the class invited. Bravely, Ellen had explained to Madison that their house wasn't large enough, and Ellen not masochistic enough, to have eighteen six-year-old girls all night. Madison didn't care about the limit; she was thrilled to have her four closest friends. Standing in the carpool line, Ellen was accosted by another mother, saying, "How awful of you to exclude these poor little girls! Don't you know girls this age can never keep a secret? You should have invited them all—everyone else has bucked up and done it! Some of these girls will never get over it!" Speechless, Ellen had returned to her car and had been avoiding the other moms ever since—even the ones she liked. Examining the attack by this self-appointed arbiter of elementary school social life, Ellen deciphered the irrational thinking. Was it really awful? Did children need to learn everyone can't be included? Can girls of six never keep a secret? Last Christmas, Madison had kept the secret about her daddy's present. What was wrong with doing what worked for Ellen's family—inviting four girls—rather than what others deemed she "should"? Was a single party in first grade powerful enough to ruin a child's life? What about parents of uninvited children teaching them to deal with disappointment? Was the emotional welfare of thirteen six-year-old girls Ellen's responsibility? Ellen realized being blindsided like this might happen if she bucked the system, but she'd survive it.

In the spirit of perfectly good mothering, you're accepting your strengths and being yourself. Apply the same grace to other women. You recognize the truthiness traps; no one mother is perfect. Look for other mothers' good points, encouraging their unique perfectly good mother. When you adopt a "whatever works" philosophy, you see many relatively good paths to success. Harvard admission is no longer the only gauge of your triumph as a mom. And if there is not a single prize, then another child/mother duo with higher scores or honors won't steal your child's success. It's not a limited barrel of happiness, and you don't have to fight for your scoop.

Everybody doesn't think relatively. Irrational thinking is as common as skinned knees on the playground. Your mother-in-law, your boss, and your best friend may still have brains full of should, always, and never, and they won't hesitate to point out your mistakes. Strong opinions are a deeply ingrained part of American culture—freedom of speech, even if it's unwanted criticism. Moms like the one Ellen encountered will call you inadequate, neglectful, selfish—by their standards. When you tangle with one of these mother magistrates, think it through—are you truly making grievous errors? Is the critic applying absolutes? Have you swung the self-care pendulum too far toward Cocktail Mom? Do a self-check for piece of mind. In my experience, overachieving, overdoing moms will swing toward the middle, at best. You wouldn't be reading this book if you leaned too far toward self-indulgence; you wouldn't see the need. The strategies of perfectly good mothering can reduce anxiety and guilt, but not enough to turn you into a spoiled brat, pampering yourself at the long-term expense of your kids. It just doesn't happen, so don't let anyone convince you otherwise.

Flex your backbone and prepare to defend your new mothering style. Maya Angelou, in *Won't Take Nothing for My Journey Now*, says that if women take breaks for self-renewal and "step away for a time, we are not, as many may think and some will accuse, being irresponsible, but rather we are preparing ourselves to more ably perform our duties and discharge our obligations." Your emotional well is drained, and you will be a more effective, available, and patient mother if you fill it up again.

Focusing on their own needs is foreign to most moms. Jennifer and another mother, Liz, sat in the dance studio, talking deeply about putting themselves first. Rita walked in, asking, "What are you talking about—the kids?" Jennifer said, "No—me—we are talking about me." Rita's mouth dropped open; she turned away. Some moms are speechless if the conversation is not about kids.

Don't Judge or Criticize Other Moms

As you police your thinking, you strike out the irrational shoulds and absolutes when you see them. While making it easier to feel perfectly good as a mom, it also lets you quit competing with and criticizing other moms. We perfectly good mothers need a noncompete clause, just like in the business world, vowing to end criticism and comparisons to other mothers. In *No More Push Parenting*, Guthrie and Matthews call for a "Unilateral Push-Parenting Disarmament." Just as disarmament treaties allow all nations to stop building bombs, the treaty would let all moms stop pushing their kids in extreme fashion. Guthrie and Matthews say if we had a treaty, "we'd all stop, but as it is, if we relax, let up, cancel the tutor, our kid will miss out, fall behind, fail."

Competition is moot in raising children, if you're a perfectly good mother. Does it really matter what any other person thinks or achieves? (Besides your partner, that is. That's a real partnership, so please decide things together.) There are not a finite number of As to be assigned. No limited number of happiness molecules in the universe, for the Joneses to suck up, leaving none for you. Can't bake cookies in elaborate tiger shapes, and Jodi's mom can? So what? Is the universe tallying up the score? Yes, there are a limited number of positions on the team, slots in the preschool, or parts in the play. But is there only one worthwhile team, preschool, or class play? Endorse your own noncompete clause. Vow that "I will not compare myself to others." Unless you're an identical twin (married to an identical twin, gave birth at the same moment as your sister,

Perfectly Good Mantra:
"Parenting is not a contest."

to the same sex of child) no one else has your own unique stew of DNA and life influences. Ditto for your children. No one else's accomplishments take away from yours.

Extreme parents can be so hard to take, bragging about their child's admission to the most prestigious preschool or their latest piano piece! It can seem nearly impossible to stop those competitive juices from flowing. Andrea Buchanan, author of *Mother Shock: Loving Every (Other) Minute of It*, suggests in a 2004 blog that instead of gawking at examples of overparenting, we need to look at the underlying good intentions. Nancy McGill, a teacher, is quoted in that *Time* article by Nancy Gibbs: "The parents are not the bad guys. They're mama grizzly bears. They're going to defend that cub, no matter what, and they don't always think rationally." Recognize the motivation of extreme parents: not to show you up or knock your child out of the race, but to resolve their own anxieties about being good parents.

How to bite your tongue, when competing has been a juicy and rewarding habit? You're going to have to try a new way of connect-

Perfectly Good Mantra:
"I deserve to spend time with women who respect and support me."

Don't get stuck trying to connect with others because of confidence issues.

ing to women, to trade for put-downs and gossip. Wiseman and Rapaport offer a "Friendship Bill of Rights." Three factors—respect, honesty, and empathy—can be offered to friends. Stay in a relationship only if you get respect, honesty, and empathy back. Want others to respect your perfectly good mother path? Do the same for them. You have to look at what you get from a relationship and what it costs you when thinking about your friends. Ideally, what we put into relationships is balanced by what we get back—with no exploitation or ongoing hurt for either person. Spend time with people you enjoy, those on the same page. Limit your time with people who don't respect and support your choices as a perfectly good mother, those women who Stacy Debroff in a 2006 MSNBC article called "confidence vampires."

Invest Energy in Relationships

Hurray for you, freeing yourself from the competitive mind-set and ferreting out some like-minded souls. You've taken key steps. The next step is putting energy into those relationships, and this is key in the Perfectly Good Mom Manifesto: taking care of yourself by having fun with other women. In my office one day, Rita said, "What I need is a sponsor, like my friends have in AA." Every mom needs a group like that—"Perfectly Good Moms Anonymous" (PGMA)—where they can be honest about their struggles. PGMA could offer emotional, spiritual, social, and practical support. Build your own PGMA. Don't sit back and wait for another woman to initiate. Take the first step and invite a kindred spirit to spend some time together, with honesty about your personal parenting trials. When you are frank, you imply that "this is a place where the rules are bent—where we refuse to censor." This sets new rules, squelching the "nanny, nanny, boo boo" one-upmanship. Among friends striving to be perfectly good mothers, grow the network. If everyone invites like-minded friends along, your network mushrooms. Introduce friends to more friends. Hilary had anxiety about inviting her friend Joni along on her mom's night out. Maybe Joni would like someone else better—and Hilary would end up friendless. Just a hint of pending catastrophe in Hilary's thinking? She had to take the risk and replace her irrational self-talk. Then she remembered that she was building a whole web of connections.

You have room in your heart to love your partner and your child. Friends who are honest and compassionate have room for multiple connections too. Trust that you will not be squeezed out—remember the code of mutual respect—and that everyone can't like every person they meet. Put time aside to spend with friends, new or established—this, again, is part of taking care of yourself. Call friends routinely, or set times up for a mommy playdate. Investing energy back is a way of thanking them for what they have given to you, physically or emotionally. Giving sincere compliments is a great way to show that you value your friends. Compliments are always effective when aimed at a specific action or behavior. "You really handled that conflict with Jolie assertively" is heartfelt and shows you are paying attention. More global statements like "You are such a good mom" or "You are doing just fine" need to flow out among perfectly good moms like lawn sprinklers on a hot day too. Women supporting each other is the bedrock under the perfectly good mom path.

Open Up to Help from Others

A warning to all you stalwart Supermoms: you're going to have to ask for help if you want to connect with other moms. A hard step to take, yes. Accepting practical support seems less wimpy if you admit that parenting is hard. Women are invested in being the strong one, the helper. Black-and-white thinking again: if you ask for help, you feel like a needy slouch. We all need an emotional Red Bull at times, especially running the gauntlet of parenting.

You have to take turns in the teeter-totter of relationships. If you never ask for help, it sends the message "I am above you." And it keeps you from getting any relief. As Sara Kerner says in a 2006 *Dallas Morning News* article, "Get the help you need and don't let guilt drain your precious energy." Finally, if you want to increase your network of perfectly good moms, educate your friends. No hard-sell, Amway-style recruitment. Share this book, or others mentioned here. Copy articles that challenge the parenting status

Try this Perfectly Good Mantra if it's hard to ask for help:
"Every perfectly good mom needs help sometimes."

quo. Throw darts at the ones that don't. Catch yourself falling into the mommy traps and explain out loud, teaching friends how to do the same.

When letting go of overcontrol of your child's life, you have to link arms with like-minded mothers. Marie wanted to give her children more independence. It seemed fine to let her ten- and eight-year-old sons walk to the corner park to play. On the other hand, it felt really scary to be a pioneer; no other mothers in her neighborhood allowed this. If she let her kids go alone, what could happen? Some high school kid might offer them drugs. Or a sexual predator might be stalking the park. She was getting caught up in catastrophizing, exaggerating danger. She knew she lived in a low-crime area. When Marie heard about a new family three streets away with children the same age, she called. The new mom, Olivia, had moved from a smaller town. Her boys had played freely in the neighborhood there. Marie and Olivia decided they'd both feel better if the boys went to the park together.

Paula and Kate decided together to scale back their kids' activities. They presented a united front to the children. When Paula's son Braden wailed, "No one else has to pick just one sport!" Paula was ready. She reminded him that Kate was enforcing the same rule for her son, Ted. Ted and Braden could sympathize with each other, joining forces at their school, where everyone seemed to have six activities. The more you and your friends cooperate on changes like these, the greater the chance is that overprotective parenting can fade into the background.

What if opening yourself up to other moms is scary? Sheila

Ellison in *How Does She Do It? 101 Life Lessons from One Mother to Another* says you are allowed to keep parts of yourself secret. Choices and opinions need not be aired. No banners flying from your roof, saying you're done micromanaging your child's life. It's your decision to make, your choice to share it. "You get to decide what part of your truth to tell and what you want to keep to yourself," says Ellison. When her youngest started full-day kindergarten, Olga was euphoric about returning to work. Before her kids were born, she loved her job as a high-powered sales rep. It never occurred to her to tell less than the truth, until she announced her return to work to her close-knit group of friends. "Oh, you poor baby," said one. "Of course you'll try the school first, so you can be out when the kids are," said another. "Is your husband's job okay?" asked a third. Olga choked back her enthusiasm. A sinking feeling filled her stomach—did none of her friends know the satisfaction work brings? Or were they censoring too?

If sharing with other women firsthand feels like opening yourself up to the lions, you may feel safer seeking support in books or online. In *Confessions of a Slacker Mom,* Mead-Ferro challenges the "inevitable pressures of perfect parenting" messages, saying that our overachieving culture has pushed parents to ignore their own instincts about what is best for their children and themselves. Mead-Ferro encourages parents to reject the mommy mystique and listen to the inner voice about parenting, especially if that inner voice is recoiling against the current push to extreme parenting. In *The Three-Martini Playdate,* Mellor offers extremely useful perspective on returning your life to balance if your children have become the center of the universe. In

Sippy Cups Are Not for Chardonnay, Stefanie Wilder-Taylor reminds the reader that parenting philosophies run in cycles, like fad diets, and finding your own way as a parent involves what she calls "balanced parenting," where parents learn to trust their instincts in responding to the baby's needs. These writers present their rebellious mom dictates with wit and wisdom, knowing that they are challenging the status quo. Reading books like these can help lessen the feelings of isolation. You're not the only mom who wants to dodge the overdoing of parenting culture. Web sites are another source of support from like-minded women. Web sites that are honest about the madness that is required of motherhood are Ariel Gore's www. hipmama.com, Andrea Buchanan's www.mothershock.com/blog; The Thinking Parent at www.thinkingparent.com; "Salon Mothers Who Think" archives at www.salon.com/archives/mwt; The Imperfect Parent at www.imperfectparent.com; MotherVerse at www. motherverse.com; and Feminist Mothers at Home at www. feministmothersathome.com.

Even with the empathy and support of your own PGMA, perfectly good mothering is formidable. Kindred souls, whether around the swing set or a bottle of wine, let you see everyone's unique perfectly good mothering. Joni is a perfectly good mother because she loves to read with her kids. Elise is a perfectly good mother because she's hilarious. Fran is a perfectly good mother because she doesn't care if her kids have daily baths. Your comfort with your own quirks grows. When you share true feelings with friends, you find that your feelings are normal. You can dump the fear that "There must be something the matter with me." Watch how other women balance their lives, let go of unrealistic standards, and use their solutions to inspire your own. You'll be reminded regularly that the problem with motherhood today is the cultural expectations, not the women trying to live it. Finally, you develop trust in and closeness with other women. As George Eliot said, "What do we live for if not to make life less difficult for each other?"

The Mommy Wars and Bullying

The mommy wars explode in ways as varied as jelly been flavors. Gossip, dismissal, exclusion, open or veiled criticism, teasing, manipulation, betrayal, dishonesty, and humiliation can be aimed at moms or kids. All of these can be extremely subtle. When Anne's neighbor had her second child, Anne reached out to her, commiserating about the stress of two. The neighbor denied it completely, raving about how wonderful her life was. Later, Anne's husband was working in the yard and stopped to talk with this woman's husband. The husband talked about how overwhelmed his wife was, wanting him to not even leave the house to do the yard work. This lack of honesty about parenting is one of the primary ways women practice one-upmanship, a form of bullying.

Words, gestures, and other "seemingly innocuous behavior ... can leave you walking away wondering 'what happened?' and why you care so much," writes Dellasega. All forms of female bullying are learned in middle or high school and perpetuated in parent life. *Important:* Identify and label this behavior for what it is! When labeled as inappropriate and cruel, you let go of it more easily. Refuse to blame yourself. You're not being passive or wimpy: this is bullying. NO ONE deserves to be treated this way. Lisa grew up in a family where name-calling and derogatory teasing were as common as gulls at the beach. Not until college, living in the dorm, did she learn that all women don't tolerate such banter and can treat each other with kindness and respect.

Carol was keenly aware of the controlling women on the PTA board at her son's school. She recommended a new friend to the fund-raising committee, hoping to know the newcomer better by working with her closely. Unable to attend the nominating meeting herself, Carol was outraged the next day to hear that the president had refused to take Carol's recommendation—even though the president had agreed to the newcomer before the meeting! Instead, the president ensconced one of her cronies on the committee, a controlling know-it-all Carol had butted heads with the previous year. Kat's son Jess was loving his new soccer team. Many of the families had played together for two years, but Jess was thrilled to be on the team with many school friends. When sign-up rolled around, the "old team" families scurried around, quickly filling the roster without consulting Kat. When Kat called the team mom to check on sign-up details, the team was already full.

Bullying parent behavior includes excluding children from parties and parents from carpools, snubbing volunteers to committees, teasing about clothes or school choices, planning events without consulting all parties involved, and using relationships with teachers or school administrators to get special favors, like select programs or particular teachers. Erica was casually chatting to the board president, waiting for the theatre booster club to start. Reba walked in and sat down, gesturing to the president to join her. Erica watched aghast as the president sat down next to Reba and began to whisper in her ear, leaning around to glance at Erica every minute. Thinly veiled questions are another way that women criticize, asking "Why do you work?" or "How can you stand to stay home?" or "Doesn't that kid of hers drive you nuts?" Kendra babysat her nieces regularly for her sister-in-law Pam, who never seemed to have time to return the favor. When Kendra confronted her, saying she would not sit again until Pam reciprocated, Pam blew up with self-importance. She railed for ten minutes about how little free time she had because of her important committee work and how Kendra should support her because Kendra had "nothing else to do."

The motivation of bullying, or what Dellasega calls *relational aggression*, overlaps with the incentive to extreme parenting. Both types of parents aim for the best, whatever the price. These parents are in control every moment, without exception. While extreme parents

---

For a Perfectly Good Mantra to battle the bullies in your life, say this:

"This is bullying. I didn't bring it on—it has to do with her, not me."

If you are targeted by a bully, know that it is not your fault.

focus mostly on their children, bully parents often go beyond control of the child's life to assert power over their entire universe. Competition fuels both types of behavior. One-upmanship is the common thread, with children the ammunition of the game. Dellasega quotes one mom who says, "It's like playing a game of cards, only your kids help you win. Everyone is out to 'trump' everyone else with the [child's] accomplishments." In the bid for status and superiority, says Dellasega, motherhood and its outcome are the chips. Furthermore, relational aggression is driven by fear and anxiety, just like extreme parenting. Every parent is only acting on a "genetic, protective drive," says Dellasega, to "ensure survival of their children."

Coping with Bullying

Under the obnoxious bully surface, admitting that these parents' motivations are not too far afield from yours provides perspective. They have little nutty pieces, just like you—though some quirks are so blinding you can't spot the person's good points. These parents want to protect their children, just like you. Knowing that makes it

If you have difficulty trusting women because of bullying, try this Perfectly Good Mantra:

"There are women I can trust—and I can find them."

easier to walk away. Regardless of motive, don't tolerate bullying. The descriptions here are to increase your empathy—and to warn you. If you can see them, you can dodge the bully bullets more deftly. Call this behavior what it is: mean and inappropriate.

If you've been the target of bullying, or watched others hurt like this, don't jump into irrational thinking. All women are not out to submarine their acquaintances. Alissa had endured heinous behavior in high school after a group of girls blacklisted her. She wanted to write women off entirely; then she wouldn't be hurt again. Please don't overreact and isolate yourself like that. There are funny, smart, kind, and supportive women out there. Find them and connect with them, building your own web of perfectly good mothers. You need safety in numbers to challenge the status quo of the overachieving parent, especially against the bullies.

Wiseman and Rapoport in *Queen Bee Moms and Kingpin Dads* and Dellasega in *Mean Girls Grown Up* offer excellent advice on addressing this aggressive behavior, or stepping back from it when you're sucked in. It is not a war that can be won—refusing to play is the wisest course of action. Recommendations range from removing yourself to challenging the motives of the bully. Consult either of these books if you need more in-depth advice than offered here.

The Perfectly Good Dad/Partner

Neither Ward Nor Homer

AUTHOR'S NOTE: *This chapter provides a brief overview for dads about expectations and irrational thinking that lead to parental stress, guilt, and anxiety. Concrete guidelines for being a perfectly good dad are offered for men. Tips for both parents, to foster their relationship and their individual efforts at perfectly good parenting, conclude the chapter.*

If June Cleaver is the quintessential wife and mother, then Ward is the prototypical dad and husband. Always nattily dressed in suit and tie, Ward breezes off to the office, returning home in time for a relaxing, balanced dinner and quiet time puffing on his pipe. As a dad, Ward always has just the right wisdom—calmly spoken, of course—to teach Beaver or Wally essential life lessons. His temper never moves much past simmer; he seems to take the challenges of his rambunctious sons with the proverbial grain of salt. Fight with June? Not during the iciest day in hell. He's the perfect provider, outfitting his wife perpetually in pearls. Lord of his manor, all those in his home bow their heads, eyes downcast, with "Yes, Ward" or "Yes, Dad" as the refrain of the day. Ward is the model many fathers have in their heads for that life-altering adventure of parenthood.

Expectations of fathers today step way beyond the tidy demeanor of Ward's life. Good dads not only have to be Ward, they must go beyond—to be the entertainment, enrichment, and emotional engineering committee. Books such as *101 Secrets a Good Dad Knows* by Walter and Sue Ellin Browder up the ante. Dads not only have to be calm, wise providers, they also must know how to skip a rock, photograph lightning, tell time by the stars, find an owl, use those rare letters in Scrabble, and ninety-six other things. Good fathers are expected to be handymen, wielding screwdrivers, chain saws, tire irons, and plumbing wrenches. They change diapers, hold their hands to catch vomit, and coach soccer. Good dads play My Little Pony or wrestle hour after hour, on top of a ten-hour workday. They sort laundry, pack lunches, race to pick up at after-school care, while laughing for the fifty-third time at that lame knock-knock joke. Good dads can talk sports with the guys or rock music with the teens, especially when their own garage band is still kicking.

Good dads are in touch with their feelings. Tears trickle silently down their cheeks when watching *Field of Dreams, Rudy,* or their kindergartner singing "America the Beautiful" in the school program. They voice their anger in a reasonable way, never threatening their offspring with "the belt." Today's kids would look at them blankly. Discussion of feelings doesn't send them fleeing for the safety of the garage. Tuned in to feelings, good dads have to work even harder to make things right for their kids. They call teachers, coaches, and other parents to negotiate and coerce. Good dads balance their climb up the corporate or artistic ladder like tightrope walkers, swinging by for "Donuts for Dads" at their kids' school before that project meeting. They often work a second shift, just like moms, returning to their computers for a couple more hours after bathing the kids and patting sleepyheads to sleep.

Good Dad Stresses

Dads—just like moms—worry about the outcome for their kids and want to give their kids everything—from their time to every opportunity to learn and compete. Kevin Canty, in an essay in *The Bastard on the Couch* matter-of-factly affirms that his son and daughter always go first. "On the way out of the burning building, they go first. When we're trying to figure out where to live, how to spend the summer, when we're making the thousand large and small decisions about our lives together, their interests go first." Dads want to control it all for their kids, and it seems like giving it all—all the experiences and all the stuff—is the road to the perfect happy childhood—just like it is for moms.

In trying to "do it all," dads are easily swept up in doubts about parenting, just like the mothers of their children are. While dads may be less hard on themselves to be perfect, the stakes are still high. Anxiety plagues dads as much as moms, even though the general perception might be that dads are not worriers.

When researching fathers, guilt, and anxiety on the Internet, in Google I searched the phrase "fathers anxiety worry." The search engine corrected me, much as it does when a typographical error is inserted in the "Search" field, saying "Did you mean to search for: mothers anxiety worry?" I guess the concept of fathers and anxiety going together is simply foreign, or at least rare enough to trip up Google.

Gary Greenburg in *Brain, Child* in fall 2006 says that "The hardest part of being a parent is parsing the anxiety that it brings." Fathers in my office often turn their anxiety into control freak channels, just as mothers do. Lydia's husband constantly second-guessed her, with a continual barrage of controlling directives veiled as questions: "Shouldn't he be eating vegetables? When does he get some fruit? He should be in bed by now, shouldn't he?" Once Lydia saw the anxiety underneath his efforts at control, she reassured him. Research on expectant and new fathers shows that their anxieties— about the baby's health, the baby's caregivers, and the baby's developmental milestones—are closely parallel to the anxieties of mothers. Why would this anxiety magically evaporate as the baby grows? Sara Chatwin, a registered psychologist, states that as dads become more involved in the daily care of their children, stress and anxiety levels for men increase.

Much of the anxiety and strain that plagues fathers comes from feeling pulled between family and work. Life balance is an issue, just as it is for mothers. Fathers want to spend more time with their kids. In a study reported on www.BostonChannel.com, 54 percent of fathers would take a pay cut to spend more time with their kids. In a 1991 *Dallas Morning News* poll, 75 percent of men would rather have more time off to spend with the family than a promotion. When they can't spend this time, and miss a significant event in their child's life because of work, they feel stressed. Natalie Boizan and colleagues found that fathers who lacked flexibility at work had the highest levels of unhappiness, anxiety, and stress. In a 1999 survey by the National Center for Fathering, nearly 58 percent of respondents said that employers don't recognize the strain fathers face when balancing work and family. Research has shown that both mothers and fathers bring anxiety home from the office. Men in this study reduced their anxiety by working more, for work gave them a feeling of control, compared to the kid/family whirl. As Ken Blanchard said in a *Parents* magazine column in August 1999, "It was some primal thing . . . suddenly we had to have life insurance and a will, and I had to start socking away money for college. . . . This I could do." This author suggests that many men see work as an escape from the kid chaos at home.

Given the conventional folk wisdom that men speak about 7,000 words a day, compared to women's 20,000 words a day, it's fair to guess fathers are just as anxious and stressed as mothers—they simply report it less. Fathers claim guilt more often than anxiety. John Derbyshire, in the *National Review* in February 2003, quotes his sister, who said "Parenting equals guilt. . . . I have left undone those things which I ought to have done, and done those things which I ought not to have done." Dads judge themselves by time spent and events—"I missed the play"—rather than scattered guilt like moms: "I'm a terrible mom." In *The Bastard on the Couch* Anthony Giardina points to "the new cult of 'Presence'" in children's lives as a major source of guilt. Giardina says this insistence that parents be always present—at every athletic event, school play, or scout meeting—leaves dads torn.

John Gray in *Men Are from Mars, Women Are from Venus,* popularized the idea that men like to "fix things." Men jump feet first into "fix it" mode as often with kids as with spouses. Dads funnel anxiety and the need to make everything right into overcontrol of their children's lives, just like mothers do. Jay Coakley, in a study reported in *Leisure Studies* in 2006, says dads fall into the trap of thinking that children's achievements equal the moral worth of the parents. The women's movement called on men to be more involved with their families, and dads gravitated toward (1) a "masculine" endeavor, and, (2) what they knew: sports. And if parents are judged by their kids' outcomes, good dads had better "produce" fine athletes. That's why the sports field brews such extreme parenting. Dads attend every practice, yelling helpful tips from the sidelines and having serious talks with their budding stars on the drive home. Eager to fix things, they punch out coaches; they threaten other kids. Coakley says that dads think this is their job: to protect their kids' interests on the field or off. At one baseball game, a pitch went wild, hitting the child at bat. The batter's father went berserk, cursing out the nine-year-old pitcher!

Extreme fathers funnel their own needs into their children's accomplishments, just like moms do. James wanted his boys, twelve and ten, to love hockey as much as he did. With the popularity of the sport in their town, the boys' team ended up with 5:30 AM practice three days a week. Elaine and James endlessly fought about this crack-of-dawn routine. Elaine thought it interfered with the children's studies; James thought it would give them a strong work ethic, as he had learned in hockey. Nobody asked the boys, who were busy shuttling from school to tutoring to games.

> **"** While I admit that I would love to have my boys become superstar athletes and play professionally, I think that the most important role I play as their father is to teach them how to become great fathers. **"**
>
> —*Hogan Hilling,* The Man Who Would Be Dad

Harry always hoped, as a teen, to play pro baseball. When his son Patrick was a senior, Harry strong-armed him into a college choice where Patrick could play baseball, with a slim chance of making the major leagues, rather than picking a school based on academics. Joel Fish, Ph.D., author of *101 Ways to Be a Terrific Sports Parent,* tells how parents simply get caught up in the emotion of sports, yelling at refs or coaches. On the Web site www.enotalone.com, Fish writes about a hockey game where one boy had Wayne Gretzky's number on his shirt. "From the sideline his father shouted, 'All the time and money I put into your hockey, you should play like Gretzky.' Though the father added a 'ha, ha' and . . . appeared to be joking, it was obvious . . . with all the training, conditioning, camps, and practice . . . [the child] should be playing like a superstar and winning."

Hogan Hilling, in *The Man Who Would Be Dad,* says, "I've decided not to give in to social pressure at the expense of robbing my boys of their childhood years. Having spent the last six years watching them build their own 'field of dreams' and organizing their own games, I've discovered that my boys, along with their neighborhood friends, do a much better job at organizing games than most adults."

While competition in sports definitely sucks many dads into the extreme parenting machine, it's not the sole venue. Nancy Gibbs's *Time* article tells about a music teacher calling a father to discuss his daughter's misbehavior. The father called the teacher a "total jerk" and offered to meet the teacher "and take care of this man to man." In a local civic theatre group, Theo attended every rehearsal his daughter had scheduled, interrupting the director and pulling his daughter aside to give her tips on her character development.

Daddy Thinking Traps

Daddy thinking traps closely parallel the mommy thinking traps described in Chapters 3 and 4. The daddy shoulds take men beyond Ward, expecting them to provide, nurture, protect, and stimulate. Know any dads who can do it all?

According to a 2000 study by the National Fatherhood Initiative (NFI), one-quarter of all fathers on television are characterized negatively. TV is full of bozo dads. Dave Tarrant, writing in the *Dallas Morning News* in March 2005, says "My family loves to watch *The Simpsons,* and for me it's a guilty pleasure. It's good for the kids to see that at least one family is more dysfunctional than ours." Erica Scharrer of the University of Massachusetts has studied gender in the media, finding that TV fathers are often inept or the butt of a joke. They've gotten more foolish since the Cleaver days. Homer, Tim "The Tool Man" Taylor, even Cliff Huxtable: plenty of buffoons. In a 2005 article in the *New York Times,* John Tierney quotes Al Jean, *The Simpsons* head writer: "Homer is the father that no one will admit to being that many fathers are. He loves his kids, but there are a lot of times when he'd rather just go out for a beer." Characters like this give dads room to admit they don't love parenting, and they certainly don't have to do it perfectly. Dads look at Homer and say, "At least I'm not *that* bad—guess I am doing okay!"

Many fathers buy into the thinking trap about "moms are totally responsible for the child's development." Michael Horowitz, Ph.D., codirector of the Fatherhood Research Project, suggests that dads feel less stress because they're second in line. If mom has it covered,

Susan Reimer, in a column in the *Dallas Morning News*, describes how her husband is the perfect caretaker. "The guy is more Mr. Rogers than Mr. Rogers. . . . He once interviewed the children's television host and . . . Fred Rogers praised him for his sensitivity. . . . . He's not a gourmet cook, but he can make all the foods kids like, including pancakes in the shape of dinosaurs, snakes, or fire engines. . . . he can create custom coloring books. . . . Halloween costumes and elementary dioramas out of common household items. . . . He can still diagram sentences. . . . clean a kitchen faster than any of Martha Stewart's quaking assistants. . . . And his night-owl habits mean you can go to bed while he waits for your child to make curfew or finish the AP homework." Maybe superdad does really exist—at least in one man. Plenty of fathers don't measure up to this grand ideal of the "do-it-all" dad—but they don't care. Men are greatly invested in fathering—way more than their dads ever were. They know time given to the family is as important as financial contributions. While the father role is important to men, how they feel about themselves still comes from work—not family. Home, while important, isn't as life-defining as it is for women, whether women work or stay home.

they're off the hook. When society, and dads, believe that male influence is less critical for a child's development, this reinforces the Homer way. When dad thinks he doesn't matter, he's home less, or zoned out when home. When tuned out, he doesn't know the routine—who gets the green juice cup and which bedtime story is sacrosanct—so he becomes less capable. Even when dad is aware of the dark cloud of shoulds floating in his universe, as long as he's not a bozo he feels he's succeeding.

But fathers do buy into the thinking trap that children should always come first. Giardina in *The Bastard on the Couch* notes how, between 1979 and 1996, "a generation of parents enshrined the notion of itself as childhood worshippers, unforgivable unless we're there." Can you detect the black-and-white thinking? Children must always be the priority. *Always first* translates into children as the center of the universe—which can make for a very boring universe, according to Derbyshire in the *National Review*. Discussing his guilt as a dad, Derbyshire says, "No, the origin of my guilt is simply the awareness that I cannot be much bothered with my kids. Though they are certainly very sweet and adorable in their own way, it is a childish way, which cannot hold my attention for long. . . . Most children have a sense of humor, but it is of a primitive, undeveloped sort, and soon palls. Kids say the darnedest things, but . . . what they say is gibberish. . . . Feeling thus, I do not spend as much time with my kids as, I think, a conscientious modern parent is supposed to." Most adults, if honest with themselves, have wandered into this reality after five or six consecutive hours spent with children. Like Homer, just wanting to go out for a beer or a doughnut. In my experience, men feel freer to tell this truth than women. While they should spend time with their kids, mom is usually there as a buffer if they don't.

The guilt fathers feel by not spending every waking moment with their kids is tempered by the fact that men are better trained to care for their own needs. Nearly every mother I know has difficulty putting aside time for herself—to visit with friends, exercise, or read a juicy novel. The kids always come first. By mom's report, and dad's when he shows up at my office, it's easier for dad to sit down, put up his feet, and catch his favorite show. Mothers can't do it as well, at least in my part of the world. Carl was a very involved dad—taking his fair turn bathing kids, packing lunches, and spinning elaborate bedtime yarns. With kids tucked in, he plopped down in his chair and was done—off-duty, immovable. Sure, he was tired, complained his wife, Meg—but so was she. She envied his ability to see that the chores of the day were mostly done. Countless other moms tell the same story: dedicated husbands and fathers, able to relax at the end of the day, while mom irons out the remaining details *and* the school uniforms for the next day. These dads are only a generation or two removed from Ward, met at the door with his pipe, slippers, and paper, all cues to unwind. They've hung on to the implied permission to take care of themselves. Meanwhile, the motto "A woman's work is never done" and a scene of June scurrying to present dinner spurs women to tidy up until the wee hours. On this issue, all parents need to emulate Ward.

There's often a sizable mom-versus-dad gulf in buying into "Childhood is dangerous, children are fragile." While dads start just as anxious as moms, stereotypical parenting practices of the last fifty years give dads an edge. Little boys are told to "Be a man," "Walk it off," "Pick yourself up and brush yourself off," and "Big boys don't cry." These admonitions call upon men to tough it out. The messages turn into automatic thoughts for dads—be tough, ignore the anxiety, everything will be all right—even if the world is a dangerous place. Having been parented that way, dads slip back into that same call for toughness—especially with sons. Tough and fragile don't seem to coexist, so this parenting technique counteracts the idea that children are fragile. Maybe that's why many dads worry a bit less about the big bad world.

One automatic thought that sucks dads in as much as moms is that "more, better, all is essential for my child's success." If dad is the primary wage earner, this requirement falls squarely on his shoulders. According to Blanchard in *Parents*, one of the most stressful dad anxieties is "How are we going to pay for this?" If mom is staying at home, who pays for the preschool tutoring, the private school

"What drives us is . . . the desire to give our children every opportunity to find themselves, explore their world, take advantage of all that can help them succeed. . . . We strive to be good parents and don't want our children to miss out on anything. That can drive anyone crazy."

—*Dave Tarrant, in a* Dallas Morning News *article*

tuition, the top-of-the-line Motocross bike, the new laptop, or the SAT prep class? Dear old dad, of course. As his anxiety skyrockets, so does the pull between home and work. It's a constant seesaw: work pressure, family pressure, back and forth. When both parents work outside the home, mom and dad share this more, easing the anxiety for each on providing for the kids.

Realistic Thinking for Dads

Men are not going to be Ward on steroids—bringing home the bacon, dispensing the wisdom of the ages, building a soapbox derby car, and emoting on cue—any more than women are able to fry the bacon and vacuum in pearls à la June. Letting go of these fantasies is the first step for either parent in diminishing the anxiety and guilt. What helps is seeing that we come by these archetypes honestly. No matter how couples commit to an equal distribution of labor before children, they're shocked to be living that Ward/June pattern once children come along. Is sex of the parent the most powerful factor in who does dishes or laundry? Practice the opposite behavior from what's expected of you as a man or woman. While moms may be genetically predisposed to hear the crying children in the middle of the night, they have no biological edge in soothing them.

Remember that "fair and equitable" does not necessarily mean "equal." Couples get caught up in scorekeeping: who does more, who had the most demanding day. Parenting isn't a match between moms; it's not a contest between mom and dad, either. Both parties can work for balance, valuing their own gifts and the gifts of their partners. No one gets an easy deal; no one is right or wrong. You're both what Kristin van Ogtrop refers to in "Attila the Honey I'm Home" in *The Bitch in the House* as "partners in martyrdom."

George worked as a CPA for a big firm. Yvette had reduced her hours to part-time when their third child was born. The more George worked, the angrier Yvette became. As he approached an eighty-five hour week, she flew into a whirlwind of rage. Why would he want to come home? For endless arguments about who had the roughest life? Neither George nor Yvette had free time; nor did either feel like they were doing a good job. This is typical of couples trying to "do it all," according to Drs. Gail Saltz and Drew Pinsky on *The Today Show* in 2006. Everyone in a relationship wants to feel like number one. Not last on the list after work, children, and the dog. In the push for perfect lives and the ideal childhood, both parents feel absolutely depleted. Everyone needs a June Cleaver (or a knight in shining armor) to walk in at the end of the day, pick up the mail, draw the bath, and bake a homemade chicken pot pie for dinner. Meanwhile, give up the scorekeeping and remember you're in this together. It's hard—but it's not a tournament. Both parents can do a perfectly good job—helping each other. As Dave Tarrant says, "We need to figure out ways to make it work without killing ourselves. To be partners." Not adversaries.

Fathers don't possess the magic formula to control their children's lives, ensuring a perfect childhood, any more than mothers. You have no greater chance of protecting your child from hurt or unhappiness than ensuring that the fat kid gets picked first in kick-ball. Mark Walters addresses this father conundrum in a 2004 *Brain, Child* article, saying, "We'd all like our lives, and especially our children's lives to be clean, without shame or suffering. But because we are human, of the earth itself, it won't happen." Dads, just like moms, need to understand that total control of children's lives and behavior is futile.

Dads need to tune their ears not just to small voices, but to the thoughts about parenting that sneak through their heads. The clues are in the words: should, ought, must—aimed at you or others. When you hear those words, a demand is about to be launched like a missile.

> "Perhaps in a perfect world, he would dress just as I'd like him to, but in an imperfect one we might all be better off with the occasional superhero wandering the produce aisle."
>
> —*Mark Walters, speaking about his preschool-age son*

Henry thought his boss should understand and let him leave early for his child's performance. The coach should see how gifted your child is. Your spouse should realize how hard you work. Translate "should" into "it would be nice if" or "helpful if." The demand soft-ens; you find a way to get your point across. When a "should" isn't met, frustration or anger results. Albert Ellis, one of the founders of cognitive therapy, asked, "Should according to whom?" There's no absolute truth about what someone should do (or not), short of criminal behavior. Turning it into a request instead of a demand lessens frustration.

Dads think in absolutes just like moms do: always, never, everyone. Greg thought everyone picked on his kid. Ken's daughter always left her backpack in the doorway. Paul complained that his son never did his homework. *I am never home,* thought Raoul. This creates stress—you feel indignant about another's behavior, or guilty about your own. Think statistically instead; look at percentages, notice exceptions. The math teacher was actually kind to Greg's son. Fifty percent of the time Raoul was home before bedtime. Ken's daughter picked up the junk in her room two days

One powerful "should" I hear in my office: dads think moms should "work smarter." "She should be more organized." "She should structure her day to get more done." "She should play more with the kids." Dads who voice these concerns have the best of intentions: to help wives. Home life would be less stressful if only you could teach your wife the skills that work for you. Are you often frustrated with your partner? Listen to what fuels your frustration; is there a lurking should? You haven't been in her shoes; check your judgment at the door. Step back and ask her what kind of help she wants—don't insist on offering your answer. Answers aren't one size fits all. And often a woman who is complaining just wants a sympathetic ear, not advice or to be told what she's doing wrong according to you.

last week; he could walk in to kiss her good night. Absolute thinking ignores the positive and focuses on the negative, a surefire way to feel miserable.

Polarized thinking is another habit to trade for straight thinking. "Everything sucks with my life," said John after his boss chewed him out. Ken felt like a lousy dad because he missed his kid's concert. Filtering out important details, you see only negative. John momentarily forgot he had a job, a family who loved him, and good performance reviews overall. Ken neglected the fact that he had attended every other concert since his daughter joined choir. Straight thinking, focusing on facts rather than the presuppositions of polarized thinking, can help you keep perspective on your life.

Catastrophizing is the final thinking trap that can snare dads just like moms. Catastrophizing is tuning into danger, "the worst that can happen." Rich couldn't leave the house without thinking about the security of his home; the possibility of a break-in and the need to keep his family safe were ever present. Awfulizing is a slightly tempered version: how awful will an outcome be? It might not be dangerous, but it sure will be unbearable. Frank regularly flew into high anxiety about "how awful that those kids treated Gillian that way." Overexaggerating the negative is another way to feel miserable and out of control in your world. Clues to awfulizing and catastrophizing are phrases such as "what if" and "I can't stand it." "What if Tom does not get into the gifted program?" "I can't stand listening to that kid whine one more minute." To deal with this type of thinking, deep breaths and straight thinking are required. Yes, it might be unpleasant listening to a child whine—

but it never killed anybody. A dad might feel really badly if his daughter has been picked on—but he can help her survive it, rather than get hurt or violated himself. Outrage and overemphasis on negatives help no one move forward.

Dads can benefit from Perfectly Good Mantras just like moms. Repeat to yourself any of the mantras scattered throughout this book, for help in changing persistent negative thinking that feeds anxiety and guilt. Key popular mantras that help anyone let go of irrational thinking are:

* "So what?"
* "No big deal."
* "What difference does this make in the total scheme of things?"
* "I can live with this."
* "Whatever works."
* "I can be a perfectly good person."

The Perfectly Good Dad/Partner

Balanced somewhere between SuperWard and Homer is the perfectly good dad. The perfectly good dad is only human. He knows that "Superdad" is shelved in the same section as "Supermom": fiction. He's not master of the universe, but he controls what he can. As Mark Walters said in *Brain, Child*, "The parent's quickest route to a coronary is to believe and behave as if he or she can control the child like an additional limb." As a perfectly good dad, you can direct, steer, and cajole, but ultimately everyone in your life has a mind of their own. Wouldn't you rather deal with real people than Stepford children, or a wife who says "Yes, Dear" in automaton tones?

The perfectly good dad supports his family in a reasonable way. He may be a financial partner with his spouse, or he might be the sole wage earner, or he may have chosen the "slow lane" of stay-at-home dad. Financial comfort is key. But he also knows that spending, like glue, can be "too much of a good thing," as Browder and Browder say in *101 Secrets a Good Dad Knows*. Perfectly good dads know giving to their children is important, and one way to show love. But it's not the only way. Perfectly good dads know what years of research on fatherhood confirms: that fathers are just as important as mothers, and that kids value dads who spend time with them. Perfectly good fathers know it's acceptable, even valuable, to say no. Even when the kids whine for the latest video game and stampeding through his head is the thought that "Good dads give kids everything they want." Forget launching into a "tromping uphill twenty miles to school in the snow" rant. The answer can just be "no," softened with the gift of your time.

The perfectly good dad knows that he's not "Answer Man," even though some expect him to be. Gary Greenburg describes this honesty with his seven-year-old son in *Brain, Child* in fall 2006. His son wanted to stop and sled down an icy hill on the way home, pestering, "Why not?" Greenburg responded, "'It's just no, okay? I don't really know why not. I'm making this up as I go along.' Silence. 'I mean, I've never been the father of a seven-year-old boy before. I'm flying by the seat of my pants.'" Greenburg says he had not thought about the "stakes of confessing my cluelessness" but certainly it would be better for his son's character in the long run. This is how a perfectly good dad is honest and human with his kids—sometimes enraging them and sometimes endearing them.

Role models for "the new dad" are few, and most men are hammering it out, fine-tuning whatever works as they go along. Perfectly good dads have the confidence, as Greenburg says, that "all those doctors don't know any better than you do how to be a parent for this child." Kevin Canty says in *The Bastard on the Couch* that, in the wake of the feminist shake-up of mother/father roles, "we all find ourselves scrambling . . . to find new roles that seem to make sense . . . and haunting the whole process is the knowledge that we are actually making all of this up, that none of these new roles are blessed by anything other than our own convictions." Perfectly good dads tune into those convictions and build their lives based on what matters most, to them. Not to society, not to the grandparents. There are just as many varieties of kids, and routes as good fathers, as car models on the used car lot. Perfectly good dads make mistakes, lose track of what's important, and wish they could just chuck it all and go out for a beer. Devotion to your family keeps the balance. Step up to the plate, and step back when you need a break. Perfectly good dads juggle nicely, scrambling to work and home again, tossing in a night of overtime like a handful of bacon in the omelet—as needed. In the end, the teeter-totter of life shifts daily, balancing only in the big picture.

Defining Perfectly Good Dad Values

Perfectly good dads/partners know that life is sweet when tied to your values. There are no right and wrong answers. There is only what matters to you, two parents working together. Perfectly good dads consider their mission for this family, in consultation with perfectly good moms. When these children are twenty-five, what do you most want them to remember? What characteristics will launch them into adulthood? Manners? Love of knowledge? A marketable skill? Financial savvy? Spirituality? Overzealous parents easily spew out forty-six criteria for their children. Define three to five qualities that you and your partner most wish to see in your adult children.

The book *101 Secrets a Good Dad Knows* offers this: "Good Dad Wisdom: Forget what 'everybody else' is doing. God made you to be an original." This applies not just to your kids, but to you as a perfectly good dad.

Write them down, and heed them in making choices for your family. Plan your time to support these values. Andrew felt strongly about his children developing and maintaining fitness as adults, so he woke up thirty minutes earlier each day to run. Chris wanted his children to be compassionate, but his criticism of every driver on the street, not to mention his sons, was not modeling this trait. He sought counseling to handle his stress and be less demanding of his sons, so he could act in a compassionate way toward them and others. Regular performance evaluations are important for your family in staying on track, just as at work. Are revisions necessary? What works? How best can you accept each individual's strengths and flaws?

Questions to Assess Values

* Is this teaching a lesson to my child(ren) that I want to teach?

* Is this really how we want to spend this time or money?

* What kind of person does this make me? My child?

* In my heart, is that what I want?

* In my rational brain, is that the right answer for us, for now?

* Is this a need or a want?

* Is this my need or that of someone else?

Perfectly good dads can follow the Perfectly Good Manifesto—the same as moms do. Perfectly good dads work to be themselves—not who others think they should be. "Others" include spouse, children, parents, boss, or big brother. Perfectly good dads take care of personal needs. Just like moms, they have to replenish themselves with sleep, exercise, sex, and fun to have energy for work and family. They know their limits, and they negotiate time off when needed. Perfectly good dads try to have fun with parenting. That big kid inside can come out freely. Perfectly good dads encourage personal responsibility for each family member—emotionally, physically—as age allows. Kids can be given chores; you can demonstrate that you have to contribute to the upkeep of the home too. Even if you'd rather watch football or read a new mystery. Perfectly good dads choose actively—speaking up about how this family works. You know your contribution to the family ranks right up there with that of mom and kids, and you claim your responsibility in making life work with the choices you make.

Perfectly Good Dad Thinking

Perfectly good dads think rationally—when possible. They watch out for absolutes, all-or-nothing thinking, and shoulds that lead them to overdo. Since there's no one "right way" to be a parent or a family, recycle the question of "What works for us?" Scale back exaggerations and keep catastrophes in perspective. Balance comes with finding that gray area between winning and losing, success or failure. To detect thinking traps, perfectly good dads ask themselves questions such as those learned by perfectly good moms in Chapter 5, to get at truth, perspective, and values.

When perfectly good dads get frustrated, they admit their struggles. Maintaining perfectly good dad behavior is a huge challenge. If you're stuck, seek out information to cope, ask for advice from an

Questions to Assess Truth and Perspective

* Do the facts support the conclusion?
* Is there another explanation?
* Am I trying to control what is not controllable?
* Are there other solutions?
* Am I buying into absolutes?
* Is perfection possible here?
* Is pleasing others the most important factor?
* Does it matter in the total scheme of our lives?
* Is it really such a big deal?
* Am I exaggerating? Catastrophizing? Taking it too seriously?
* What meaning will this have for eternity?
* What has gone right today?
* Does it really matter what anyone else says/does/thinks?

experienced dad, or seek counseling. If getting caught up in kids' sports is hard for you, please see the excellent advice of Joel Fish in *101 Ways to Be a Terrific Sports Parent.*

Perfectly Good Parents Together

Perfectly good parents have to support each other. Saying "We're in this together" helps. Jenny and Rich committed to be equal partners in parenting before little Hayden was born. Rich was already good at the nitty-gritty around the house, like scrubbing the toilets. They vowed to avoid the housework battles their parents had waged. But in Hayden's first three months of life, Jenny got madder and madder as Rich worked overtime to supplement the income lost by her maternity leave. Jenny began to complain about how he cleaned the toilets and how he roughhoused with Hayden. A constant argument raged: who was more tired, who was the better parent, who had the harder life? Like most couples, Jenny and Rich thought they could rise above habitual roles of "nurturer and provider." Jeannette Crenshaw, president-elect of Lamaze International, likes to remind new parents that, given different biology, "fair and equitable" in parenting doesn't mean "equal." Every night Rich worked late was like gasoline on Jenny's anger. The madder she was, the less he wanted to be home.

Rich and Jenny had to recognize that neither had a life of ease. They dropped the contest of right or wrong, good parent or bad. When both spouses get in the habit of seeing what's perfectly good in themselves, they can see perfectly good in their partner too. Jenny and Rich mapped out what was most important to them: a peaceful, loving household, where everyone was treated with respect. Fat chance of this if they divorced! They found a sitter who could give Jenny breaks during the week, so she would be less stressed, plus one weekend evening so they could go out together. When they had fun, Jenny and Rich were more affectionate, so Hayden could feel he was living in the midst of love.

Perfectly good dads need to detect the ways their partners are perfectly good, and vice versa. Share your hurdles; offer help to your partner when you see him or her stuck in the old overparenting. Monitor, support, and applaud each other for triumphs in perfectly good parenting. Celebrate your triumphs—give each other a medal or an evening out. Perfectly good parents shift the center of the universe away from the children. Building your relationship means enjoying each other. Effort and money that used to go into "giving it all" to the kids can go toward the two of you as a couple. Treat each other with respect and kindness, giving hugs and kisses every time you leave the house or return home. Take turns planning dates—and go on them. Take a class together. Set aside time each evening to collapse on the couch together. Renew your sex life. (See helpful titles in Appendix Two.) What a gift to give your kids: the message that relationships are important and take work. When you feel better because you are loving and enjoying each other, stress melts away like ice cream in a hot convertible.

A Final Word—
Fostering Perfectly Good Dads and Moms

Besides making time for yourselves as a couple, moms and dads can help their partners with perfectly good parenting. Gregory Keer, columnist and parenting coach, makes some recommendations for "Tapping Dad's Potential" at the Web site http://fatherhood.about. com. Apply these guidelines for both parents. To begin, both parents need to ditch the old stereotypes. This is the essence of perfectly good parenting—each doing what he or she is best at, while managing the flaws. Dads have no corner on discipline or block towers. Moms are not the only soft shoulders to cry on. Negotiate your parenting and household duties based on time available and tolerance for the task—not on male versus female anatomy. Becky had very sensitive ears and simply could not hold Justin, their baby, when he headed into his eardrum-splitting scream. Curtis simply had to take over.

If fathers have been seduced into thinking they're less important, moms sometimes need to invite him in. Encourage each parent to claim one nightly kid chore as his or her own. Plan outings that everyone will enjoy. Involving your partner sends the message "We are both critical for our children." Jody loved to take the kids to the park, and she planned that nearly every weekend, weather permitting. Peter had bad allergies and simply suffered through it. When they compromised and discovered a family museum, everyone had more fun. As Keer says, the sooner dad is involved, the better for the family. Matt knew nothing about babies, and Linda loved that stage, so she gladly took on most of the baby care. She missed baby Gaia all day at work, and she was hungry for her dose of her daughter. For almost eighteen months, Matt continued about his regular routine each evening and weekend, as if his life had not changed. When Gaia was nearly two, Linda's schedule change required her to work two nights a week. Involving Matt then was extremely difficult, for he hadn't learned his daughter's preferences. And Gaia had not figured out what to make of her daddy.

While most moms have good intentions, anxiety about tasks being done in the "right" way causes them to block dad's involvement. Countless mothers in my office report that the well-meaning husband would do more around the house, but she would rather do it her way. Husbands too complain that mom's "rules"—from playing with the children to making the bed—simply stop him cold. Many men report, "I get chewed out if I don't do it, and I get chewed out if I do." Is control of how it's done really that critical? Is there a big fat should hidden here? Can misfolded towels really be more important than having time for a bubble bath? Time for "perfectly good" perspective. If moms want dads involved, they need to think about what really matters. Say "So what" in your own head if he or she does it "wrong." Translated, that's "not how I would do it." Different isn't wrong—for parenting or housekeeping—it's only different. It's good for kids to see multiple ways to do something. You don't wrestle with your daughter, but having rambunctious playtime with dad may be the high point of her day. Dad's unique contributions benefit kids, just like mom's do. He's doing a lot that's valuable, like that fantasy storytelling that the kids love each night. Appreciate that your partner is doing a perfectly good job, even if it's not your way. The benefit of his parenting or housekeeping is well-deserved relief for you.

Men can be just as critical of women's housekeeping or parenting. It's no one-way street. In "perfectly good" philosophy, there are endless ways to approach a task, from making beds to bathing children. Call a moratorium on the shoulds. Your partner is not you, and they could bring creative ideas to the daily drudgery. Negotiate. If you can't sleep if those dishes are loaded backwards then put that on your list. Lydia didn't grow up in a family that preached "Yes, ma'am" and "No, sir." She and her siblings learned to say please and thank you, but her parents weren't manners police. Lydia married Jeff, whose parents were etiquette fanatics, ranting about elbows on the dinner table. When their first child reached trainable age, Lydia didn't understand Jeff's angry insistence that she turn into Emily Post. "You are raising them to be heathens," he barked. After talking it out, Jeff took on the manners training because it was so important to him. Lydia didn't undercut him, but she didn't have to monitor it at every meal, either. Respect each other's contributions. Remember that this is the benefit of two parents—you each have unique gifts to apply to your life as a family.

Keer recommends that women applaud the efforts of their partners, whether in parenting or household chores. Catch each other doing something right. Maybe no one is jumping up and down when you unload the dishwasher—but everyone thrives on praise and appreciation. Is that not the goal? You both need thanks for your accomplishments—day in and day out. Tell yourself that you are a perfectly good parent—point it out, applaud each other. That's the foundation of building a perfectly good life for your family.

9

The Big Picture: Spreading the Perfectly Good Paradigm

Josie brought her schedule in line with her wish for family togetherness by being selective about her family's social commitments, saying no to invitations that seemed obligatory rather than heartfelt. Instead of eating in her office, she made a point to join her coworkers in the cafeteria, reinforcing her connections with other adults. Michelle pounded away at the beliefs in her head that made her feel like a failure every time she served packaged cookies or snapped at her kids, repeating, "My name is not June, my name is not June." Jenny and Rich revamped the family chore list, abandoning some tasks, hiring out another, and reciting "Our housekeeping is perfectly acceptable." Elaine and James looked hard at their commitment to hockey, with its early morning practice, and the benefit for their sons. Once they considered who enjoyed it more—James or the boys—it became clear this was Dad's need and the boys could quit. With more sleep, more homework was finished. The tutoring their kids had needed no longer seemed necessary. Each couple changed the extreme parenting tendencies that had driven them to madness in their family lives, and they took a serious look at a more relative, workable model for a "perfectly good life."

Challenged to look at the big picture, Josie, Jenny, Elaine, and Michelle applied their new "perfectly good" philosophy in different ways. Josie began two women's groups, one at work and one in her neighborhood. They met monthly, talking about the obstacles to perfectly good parenting. Michelle quickly had her husband and children mimicking her "perfectly good" chant when angry or frustrated with homework. No one in her home feels like a failure anymore, and their acceptance of "being human" is spreading to friends and relatives. Elaine and James so enjoyed catching up on their sleep. For the first time in years, they had energy and free time—so they decided to take ballroom dance for a regular couple's night out. Jenny revved up her interest in political action, dormant since college, and began an e-mail campaign urging friends and family to write letters to members of Congress whenever an issue important to family support comes up, such as day care, early childhood education, and family leave.

Adopting the perfectly good mother paradigm in your life can be powerful. The core issue of extreme parenting, parents pushing to control their children's lives to perfect ends, continues to rampage through this culture. Maintaining lasting change can be as hard as keeping the fridge stocked for teenage boys. This chapter briefly explores ways to spread this new view of parenthood and end the current madness. We all can work toward societal and cultural changes, applying and reinforcing "perfectly good" parenting at the same time.

Social change happens at many levels: (1) parenting differently, (2) teaching children to view the world and themselves through a "perfectly good" lens, dropping standards of perfection, and (3) social and political action. All these facets of change are critical. But individual women can make changes at their own comfort level. If you're motivated to affect the "big picture," strategies for working toward new programs and services to support mothers in the local community are available. Avenues for change in the country at large—voting, letter writing—complete the picture of moving toward social change, and there are some resources listed here for that too. I think we'll all feel better when extreme parenting becomes the minority view in U.S. culture. Each perfectly good mom can play a part that feels right to her.

Realistic Steps Forward

The switch in your mind from mommy thinking traps to embracing the perfectly good mother is a journey of small steps. Progress is even slower than those wild days when your baby went from inching along the couch edge to tottering across the room to running breakneck down the driveway. Change like this is remarkably hard for an individual: step by step, automatic thought by automatic thought, choice by choice. Imagine the infinitesimal pace for change on a larger scale. Gradually the change in you will be obvious to your friend, sister, or coworker. When you model a perfectly good acceptance of yourself, and talk about it in the network of straight-thinking mothers that you're assembling, the idea spreads. It's taken twenty years for our reigning ideas about parenting to swing toward extremes. It's not going to snap back to a reasonable, balanced place overnight. Be patient, yet persistent, keeping expectations in line with reality. The path is circuitous—you make some mistakes, you get sucked into anxiety or guilt about how your child, or your life, will turn out. Then you take a few deep breaths, say a few comforting words in your head, dispute those crazy ideas about control. You redefine what really matters and make some healthier choices. Each step moves you forward along the path.

With constant media and societal pressures, it's going to feel like a battle to maintain perfectly good mothering. Perfectly good parents need to have extra-powerful antennae to scope out the crazy-making around them. The superparent push to deliver a perfect childhood hasn't relented. There are examples everywhere I look. A cake-mix ad showed a boy licking the icing spatula, with the phrase "Making his day is a piece of cake." In just one month, a parenting magazine featured stories on (1) raising bilingual children "requiring serious commitment, but . . . well worth the effort," (2) planning a "fairy-tale vacation" to the castles of Scotland, and (3) how one mom transformed her wooded backyard for an enchanted forest birthday party. *Wow, that sounds wonderful,* you think, stuck in automatic mode, *I could do that.* No, no, no—please stop! You have to be able to detect these images as they hurtle through the pages or airwaves at you, before they embed themselves in your trusting brain and egg you back into extreme parenting.

Name it everywhere you see it; challenge these messages as often as you can. These expectations are preposterous, unattainable, and unhealthy. Say to yourself: *Uh, oh—truthiness—I might wish it were true, to feel more in control—but it's not!* What an unrealistic expectation—even June and Ward reincarnated could not achieve that! Talk back to the commercials, the headlines, the neighbors and friends, the anxiety in your own brain. You have to know the warning signs in your own head, remembering "Oh, that's right—that knot in my stomach—that feeling of failure—that bad mommy thought popping into my head—means I just stumbled into a thinking trap." Remember, the problem is with what we expect of parents, not your ability to carry it out. You're doing a perfectly good job. Search out the external whammy that knocked you into feeling bad again. Recognize it, step back, regain perspective, retune your antennae. The trend is shifting in the direction of perspective and reason, but ever so slowly. When I first began talking about postpartum depression and mothering issues nearly twenty years ago, the idea of mothers having emotional, physical, and social needs was novel. And we were nowhere near encouraging mothers to meet those needs. Now the idea of self-care is generally accepted, even while women struggle to live it. At least we're moving in a healthier direction.

Parenting as Perfectly Good
Mother Propaganda

The way you move through parenting, dodging the mommy thinking traps, is the most powerful means to sow perfectly good parenting. When you refuse to sacrifice your fun and your well-being, others see that parenting doesn't have to be synonymous with self-sacrifice. Each time you have a night out, or make the kids relinquish the television for your favorite show, or invite only four kids to the party is proof that madness need not rule. Keep all the shoulds in perspective. Use facts, and your values, to chart multiple routes to raising your child to be a successful adult. When you makes choices that enrich rather than deplete you, other parents see that they can do that too. Have more fun and satisfaction in family life. You'll stress less, and the next generation sees that parenting isn't about years of misery.

Refuse to tally parent points. This means less flaunting of your child's latest accomplishment. What a tough one—but closely tied to taking care of yourself. You'll have less need to brag about your kid when you save some pieces in the pie of your life for yourself. You'll have more energy, too—all that competition is draining. Set some realistic boundaries with your children—about their responsibility for themselves, about material goods, about time. When we watch another parent say no, we gain courage to do the same. Every time you affirm your worth as a parent by practicing self-care, every mother who watches is strengthened a tiny bit. Every mother who joins you is invigorated and inspired to do more.

Sharing the Perfectly Good Paradigm with Your Social Network

Others around you can learn a great deal about perfectly good parenting just by watching you. But you can make your efforts with other moms more overt too. Connecting with other women—being honest, sharing goals to stress less—is uplifting. It's practically impossible to challenge the status quo without a few close allies in the war on extreme parenting. The benefit—for you—of connecting to other women was discussed in Chapter 7. You can inspire other women to adopt this more realistic view of mothering. You can support and mentor them. You can become a spokesmom, either on an individual or larger level, for the perfectly good way of life. Do other women a favor—challenge the momism and madness out loud. You can be the trailblazer, setting new standards for your immediate social circle.

Meredith Berlin, former editor of *Seventeen* magazine, wrote a letter to the *Newsweek* editor after Andrea Yates drowned her children, saying, "Unless we start admitting to ourselves and each other that it's not always a walk in the park, our guilt, anger, fear and depression will continue to go underground . . . not a healthy place for them to be."

Consciousness-raising is this simple. Be open and honest about the pressures on women to control all aspects of our children's lives, with a perfect outcome. That's all consciousness-raising is—admitting to the truths that impale mothers upon the stake of self-sacrifice. In words from *The Tao of Mom*, "Reject social currents that value the valueless." Consciousness-raising is casting aside the current standard for mothering. Sure, these shoulds exist. But does that mean they're inescapable—or right—or possible? Just because everyone else in your world is diving headfirst into extreme parenting doesn't mean you have to jump off the bridge too. As Margaret Mead said, "Never doubt that a small group of thoughtful, committed citizens can change the world.® Indeed, it is the only thing that ever has."

Be a standard-bearer for perfectly good mothering, where everything turns out pretty well. Admit that sometimes we mess up—and we handle it. Speak up honestly, calling the current expectations for parenting what they are: impossible, unrealistic, bad for children and mothers. That is all there is to consciousness-raising—being conscious of mommy thinking traps, sidestepping them as you make choices in your life, and sharing your growing insight with those around you. Susan B. Anthony, in the battle for women's right to vote, said, "Cautious, careful people always casting about to preserve their reputation can never effect a reform." You simply cannot stay focused on perfectly good mothering in your own life without living it, and if you live it, others will see. You will feel good. When you choose to share it with mothers you know, you are raising their conscious awareness—that is, consciousness-raising.

Calling it consciousness-raising may scare you a bit—all those women's lib overtones. If you're engaging in consciousness-raising, are you a feminist? Will you have to speak in whispered tones at PTA or "Mommy and Me" to avoid being branded an antifamily man hater? Though on some terrible mommy days, when the dog has barfed on the baby's play mat, your children break your favorite lamp by hurtling stuffed animals at each other, there is no milk in the fridge, and your husband just called to say he has to work late, you have to admit that antifamily, husband hating is how you feel, deep down, at least for an hour or so. Forget the bra-burning, militaristic vendettas—who would be the target, anyway?

Relax on this whole feminism issue. Feminism is not an F-word. Feminists believe in equal rights for men and women, equal pay for equal work. "Women's liberation is the liberation of the feminine in

In a 1998 article in the *Yale Herald*, student Amanda Poppei challenged myths about feminism. Poppei said, "Feminists need not fit the stereotype of male-bashing, belligerent, overly aggressive women who scorn all men's views and alienate themselves from society. Feminists can wear pink . . . they can have a great weakness for ball-gowns . . . and they can be men. . . . What unites these people is their belief that women are just as good as men. Not better, not more deserving—but simply equal."

the man and the masculine in the woman," says Corita Kent, U.S. muralist and printmaker, in *The Tao of Mom*. In an article at www. newsobserver.com, Marcy Smith Rice quotes Laura Jent, a women's rights activist. "Feminism is not a bad word," Jent says. "It"s a word for social change. . . . If you're alive and you're a woman and you feel like you should be treated equally, then you're a feminist."

Barb Ritter in *The Feminist Psychologist* defines feminists as those who "didn't just accept society's expectations for them; they examined the issues and created their own destiny." Ritter continues, "Feminists can indeed be feminine and may occasionally succumb to craziness by shaving their legs! . . . The important point is that feminists, more so than other women, examine the issues and choose to shave their legs of their own free will rather than just because they should."

If you're trying to be a perfectly good mother, this is what you are doing. You're examining the cultural formula for being a good parent and finding that it does not fit you. You are creating your life according to what works for you and your family, not just how you should. At heart, that means you're a feminist. Never fear—no need to add feminist bumper stickers to your car or subversive buttons to your lapel to be a perfectly good mother. For many women, this is an issue to keep to yourself. You might have friends and family who don't understand going against the grain—in this or anything.

But don't be afraid to call yourself a feminist, either. We all owe thanks to the women's movement. The revolution in fatherhood that has dads changing diapers, packing lunches, carving Kachina dolls, and staying home—with sick kids or day after day—began when the women's movement questioned the assumption that women were the only capable parents. Mothers took this to heart, thrusting crying children into dad's arms, and fathers stepped up, with surprising skill. According to the Family and Work Institute, fathers now spend only 25 percent less time than mothers on child care and housework. This is an improvement from 70 percent less in 1977. Thank the women's movement. Living as a perfectly good mother, sticking to your values, means you take another step for gender equality. You challenge assumptions about how mothers parent as well.

On the Web page "Feminist Mothers at Home," Ann Allen writes about "Being a Mother at Home: My Feminist Choice." "I am a feminist mother at home. No, it is not an oxymoron. It is a way of life that is as natural as breathing. . . . A part of me that I won't turn off. . . . A feminist may work outside the home or choose to stay at home and raise the children. A feminist can come in any color, race or creed. . . . You probably know someone that cringes at the word 'feminist.' They associate it with the fringe element. Man-hating, bra-burning, radical left wing wackos. . . . The more people see 'just plain folks' calling themselves feminists the less fear the word will evoke."

If the perfectly good mother works for you, and you want to spread the word, talk to your friends and acquaintances. Just share, don't preach. Encourage them to broadcast the word to their friends. Pull together a group of like-minded women and start your own group—coffee klatch, book group, Mom's night or morning out, for social support and increased awareness. Sponsor each other, like Rita suggested. Point out new assumptions that pop up. When you question the "pressing need" for the latest enrichment lesson, toy, or boy/girl sleepover, it's easier to keep your senses. Perfectly good parenting groups can be sponsored by your women's organization or religious group.

Groups have sprung up around the country to connect parents who want a saner family life. In Boulder, Colorado, the Parent Engagement Network (PEN) was begun in 2001 as a call to action by Superintendent George Garcia of the Boulder Valley School District. Originally, the group focused on prevention of substance abuse problems, which mushroomed when parents wouldn't "say no" to their kids. Since the group's founding, however, its mission has broadened to include parent education on all topics. According to the group's Web site, parents need to join forces in order "to help parents be parents, rather than the child's best friend." Sounds like this group is responding to a few of the mommy traps named in Chapter 3, such as "children should always come first" and "more, better, all is essential for my child's success." This group allows parents to join forces, setting reasonable limits on their kids in an age of excess.

Putting Family First was founded in Wayzata, Minnesota, as a grassroots movement devoted to making a priority of family time and activities, "in a world that pulls families apart." Parents who began the movement were concerned with overscheduled kids, increased demands on the family because of kids' activities, and the loss of family togetherness and balance. The organization has sponsored events such as family nights, when families put nothing on the calendar except time together to play games or talk. Putting Family First recently joined forces with the Take Back Your Time movement to increase sanity in daily lives. According to the Web site, Take Back Your Time is a major U.S./Canadian initiative to "challenge the epidemic of overwork, overscheduling and time famine that now threatens our health, our families and relationships, our communities, and our environment." Together, Putting Family First and Take Back Your Time partnered with Panera Bread to reclaim dinnertime, declaring October 24, 2006, as a day for families to have dinner together. It is hard for families to resist social pressures to do "more, better, all" for their children. Groups like these can give your family a boost in making perfectly good choices for your lives and connecting with other families who share your values.

Define what will work for you and your network—revise it as you see fit. Carry the torch of perfectly good mothering in any way that

Putting Families First lists good ideas for changing your own family, as well as starting a group in your area, at www.puttingfamilyfirst.org.

works for you. Continue the dialogue. Build your network; mentor other women. Most important, perhaps, is staying tuned into the messages the culture throws in the direction of mothers. And remember to tell other mothers "You are doing a good job."

Moving into Political Action

Not every perfectly good mother wants to take it to the next level: political action. Judith Warner in *Perfect Madness: Motherhood in the Age of Anxiety* calls for social change through government policies. Warner found, while living in France, a much different attitude toward mothers. "The needs of the mother were considered every bit as central to family happiness as the needs of the child." Social programs like quality affordable preschool, flexible day care, and access to health care supported mothers. Warner said there's much to be learned from the psychology of the French system "that if you support mothers materially, you support them emotionally, and this support translates into a much lower level of anxiety."

If you are interested in social change, where to start? In fall 2005, editor Stephanie Wilkinson explored this question in a *Brain, Child* article on a mothers' movement. Wilkinson agrees with one premise underlying perfectly good mothering: "Motherhood is great, but it isn't all hearts and flowers; it's hard work and we shouldn't have to pretend that it isn't. . . . Maybe it's harder than it needs to be; maybe we should ask for some changes." The various players in a motherhood movement that could work for mothers have slightly different agendas and varied angles on how best to build a better world for mothers. Wilkinson lays out the major players. The Motherhood Project focuses on how mothers in this culture are not valued, and it seeks to increase support for mothers. The National Alliance of Mothers' Centers (NAMC) has begun an initiative called Mothers Ought to Have Equal Rights (MOTHERS)

If you want to explore political action more fully: Stephanie Wilkinson lists information about all the groups mentioned in her article at the magazine's Web site, www.brainchildmag.com. Subscribe to *Brain, Child: The Magazine for Thinking Mothers* for excellent ongoing coverage of motherhood issues, as well as some of the best writing around that challenges the status quo about mothering. An important book about the state of America's working mothers and their families is *The Motherhood Manifesto*. Coauthors Joan Blades, cofounder of www.MoveOn.org, and Kristin Rowe-Finkbeiner, author of *The "F" Word*, call for action and lay out a blueprint for change. In *Perfect Madness*, Judith Warner has a great chapter on addressing political change. Other Web sites that are talking back to the madness that is required of motherhood were listed in Chapter 7 as ways to connect with other mothers. See these on page 216.

that is focused on an economic empowerment agenda. This agenda would address issues such as paid family leave, refundable caregiver tax credits, an end to the marriage tax penalty, and evaluation of Social Security for mothers. The Mothers Movement Online (MMO) seeks to bring principles of the women's movement to bear on poor, disadvantaged, underserved mothers, calling for government support for parenting. Mothers & More has served primarily as a way for mothers to connect and share support about mothering, but could move into an advocacy role. All the women Wilkinson interviewed agreed that tiny steps are being achieved, allowing women to be more honest with each other. This frankness is about two issues: the ways society does mothers a disservice, either emotionally or financially, and the fact that the job of parenting is hard. Wilkinson said, "Every single person I talked to about a mothers' movement talked about the need for mothers to have their consciousness raised. For a movement to go anywhere, enough mothers have to start to believe that: 1) it's okay to want help caring for your children and family; and 2) it doesn't have to be a personal solution, like asking your friends or parents or your church." Wilkinson reports that Linda Juergens, NAMC director, says that "Mothers are opening their mouths. The culture is shifting." Wilkinson concludes with a quote from her interview with Ann Crittenden, author of *The Price of Motherhood: Why the Most Important Job in the World Is Still the Least Valued*, about the motherhood movement: "Social change is incremental and under the surface. The real revolution will happen in people's minds. When their minds are changed, structures change."

Changing Minds

As Crittenden says in *Brain, Child,* the real change occurs in people's minds. The transformation from control-focused, perfection-driven, extreme parenting happens in a parent's mind—one mind at a time. It is an attitude shift: forsaking constant worry, guilt, and second-guessing that you are not good enough as a parent. It means accepting that your child can turn out great—with a hundred paths to a dozen different versions of a perfectly functional adult. It is letting go of trivia that feed the truthiness about control of your child's world, and guarantees for successful outcomes. It is embracing your values, what really matters to you in parenting. It is remembering that you are a human being, prone to overexaggeration, absolutes, and all-or-nothing thinking, and that these thought patterns obscure the perfectly good job you are doing. You can ditch these old thinking traps, adopting reasoning that frees you to be yourself, not a Stepford script. It is realizing children can turn into great adults even when their parents have fun and lose their tempers occasionally. The change of mind to embrace is that you are a perfectly good parent—most days of your child's life. And even when terrible days happen, as they will, everyone will grow stronger and more emotionally aware as a result.

Appendix One

Historical Influences on Extreme Parenting— The United States: Progress Defined

The United States as a nation has always stood for betterment. Improved prosperity and the chance to control one's destiny were the driving forces that built this country. The founding fathers and mothers arrived on these shores seeking a better life, whether they came seeking religious or political freedom, economic opportunity, or just a preferable way to serve out a prison sentence than in a damp and dingy English cell. Indeed, immigrants today still consider the United States of America a symbol of an improved life. No one wants to lose ground—that is failure defined.

Over history, the definition of a better life continues to evolve. Your parents or grandparents, growing up during the Great Depression or World War II, had to focus on survival. There was little time, energy, or money for much beyond that. But that was success for them: putting food on the table, and cleaning that plate! As technological advances have offered greater leisure time and perceived wealth, families raised their criteria for a "successful life." When

Granny could afford a washing machine and no longer had to wring clothes out by hand, she felt that she had "made it." Each generation raises the bar. In the 1950s, one car, a home, and a high school education were the pinnacle for many. By the millenium, the standard had become at least two cars, a larger home and education at the level of college or beyond. Today's parents expect even more for their children.

The Challenge of Shrinking Resources

Even though we want more for our children, just as previous generations of American parents did, that task seems harder and harder. The population continues to swell. When the U.S. population hit 300 million in October 2006, headlines shouted about dwindling resources, from nature to the supply of physicians to care for all those people. Natural resources such as available oil and land, scenic or not, continue to shrink because everyone wants a piece of success—defined as an SUV or a new house in the suburbs. Financial opportunities seem less abundant than for our parents, and monetary success is harder to achieve because of inflation. Everything costs double or triple what it did when our parents were starting out. For example, an average house in 1970 required about three times the amount of a family's median income. In 2006, an average home in the United States cost nearly four and a half times the usual yearly income. Our economy requires that we must work more, and harder, to maintain. Forget getting ahead, as we all wish to do. In a world of diminishing resources, whether natural or financial, it's logical that the push for a better life translates into extreme parenting. If your child is going to be the next CEO of IBM, getting into MIT is critical. Getting into MIT means seven after school activities and top SAT scores, which means more carpools in the SUV. Back it up further and this drive for advancement translates into math tutoring at six or Baby Einstein coaching at six months. A better life means no false starts out of the blocks, from pregnancy on. Any stumbling and you have surely lost what tiny edge you had managed to carve out with your superparent efforts.

It is simply un-American to reject this cultural bias toward betterment. Therefore, parents feel trapped. But this push to always be better is not the sole factor fueling extreme parenting. The current generation of parents has been shaped by popular parenting philosophies, media pressures that reflect cultural biases, and the expectations of the women's movement. Extreme parenting is born.

Changes in Views of Children

Before the industrial revolution, children were valued for what they could give back to the family. Boys, in particular, contributed to the family's advancement by working the farm. Girls were hopefully married off, so their food and shelter weren't a burden their whole lives. Ideally, daughters "married up," snagging a wealthy guy who provided for Mom and Pop in their old age, compensating for what daughters lacked in earning potential. Even with the onset of industry and the growth of cities, the earning potential of offspring stayed critical to the family's well-being.

Medical advances contributed to the switch from seeing children as adding to the family's finances versus draining the family bank. In *Anxious Parents: A History of Modern Childrearing in America*, Peter Stearns points out how the role of children in the family has changed. In the nineteenth century, childhood diseases and infant mortality were commonplace. Infant or child death was a grim fact of life. Parents could not count on their children reaching adulthood. They protected themselves, expecting loss. Medical advances such as vaccinations, prenatal care, and birth control methods raised the value of children. Children could be expected to live to adulthood. With reliable birth control, families would have fewer children—fewer to spare, and therefore each more intrinsically precious. Given our good old American tendency to make things "better and better, every day in every way" the standard for children's well-being was raised. Not only were kids living long enough to grow up, they had to be happy, healthy, successful: the American dream. They were entitled to freedom from child labor, to free quality education, even to their own rooms, which in the early part of the twentieth century was pushed as a way to promote better physical health.

How were the wee ones going to achieve these advances? Parents, of course. A parallel shift in the cultural view of children from the nineteenth to twentieth centuries, says Stearns, involved how kids were perceived emotionally as well as financially. In the nineteenth century, even if children were at risk of early mortality, emotionally they were seen as naturally sturdy, able to grow up well with minimal parental involvement. By the twentieth century, however, kids were viewed as more vulnerable and fragile psychologically, requiring special handling. Parental anxieties blossomed as the standards soared. If your children could expect so much more from life than their grandparents, implicitly it was parental intervention that would get them there. And if parents could make this happen, parents could also screw it up. Jay Coakley, author of *Sports in Society: Issues and Controversies,* describes this change in perception of parental control over the years. When he was a child, Coakley said, parents were said to be "lucky" when a child was successful at sports. When his now-adult children were young, parents were "proud" if their offspring showed skill in sports. Now, when a child is a notable athlete, like Tiger Woods, others ask the parents "How did you do it?" This over-responsibility for the outcome of the child falls on parents in more realms than sports: academics, character, financial success.

The Influence of Parenting Practices

New moms by the droves are overwhelmed by their babies' crying—the very first event they fail to control, leaving them feeling powerless, especially when crying has no identifiable cause or remedy. As Tracy Hogg says in *Secrets of the Baby Whisperer,* one of the greatest and most damaging misconceptions new parents have is that "a crying baby equals bad parenting." Even when new parents have read or been constantly reassured by grandma or their pediatrician that this is not true, this fear seems to be imprinted on their brains. Book titles such as *The Happiest Baby on the Block: The New Way to Calm Crying and Help Your Baby Sleep Longer* (by Harvey Karp, M.D.) and *The No-Cry Sleep Solution* (by Elizabeth Pantley) imply that whether your baby cries a lot and sleeps well is indeed under your control. You just have to respond the "right way" to those cries and sleep needs. When I had my first daughter, some friends made me a T-shirt that said, "Yes, she sleeps through the night," to save me from the hassle of repeatedly answering *the* most common question to mothers of newborns. It stopped those pesky old ladies in the grocery store from quizzing me continually. Wearing it was like a badge of honor: I was a good mommy, because my baby slept through the night at an early age. It is a societal given: good sleep = good baby; happy baby (translate: minimal crying) = good parent.

You might think that the popular parenting philosophies are as different as chips and tofu: schedule your baby or let your baby schedule you. The common ground in all the popular parenting philosophies is this unrealistic expectation: if you can control your child's crying in infancy, you lay the groundwork for ultimately governing all your child's feelings. Sears and Sears in *The Attachment Parenting Book* teach that how you respond to your baby's cries can teach baby to cry less, and in a less disturbing manner. More than one parent, listening to the baby head into the third hour of crying for the day, jumps to the conclusion that since this kid is crying more, not less, "it must be my fault." In *On Becoming Babywise*, Ezzo and Bucknam suggest that parents can learn to recognize a baby's different cries. After listening to and analyzing the cry, allegedly the parent knows how to respond with confident action. If you cannot figure out your crying baby's intent, or everything you try only worsens the crying, once again you circle around to blaming yourself. The reality is explained by Harvey Karp, M.D. in *The Happiest Baby on the Block*. Dr. Karp says that forty years of studies by leading colic researchers have found that the advice "Just listen, you will learn your baby's cries" is a big fat lie. Parents (and experienced baby nurses) were found to be right about the meaning of their child's cry from 25 to 50 percent of the time. Odds less than chance. Flip a coin; sometimes a strategy works and sometimes it doesn't.

In *Raising America,* Ann Hulbert tells how parenting standards evolved again and again, as knowledge about children grew. Hulbert points out that two competing schools of thought on raising children always have existed, led by the experts of the day. These polar opposites, over the whole twentieth century, compared the "soft" manner of parenting on one hand to the "firm" model on the other. This continues today, with the "soft" orientation of the attachment parenting school versus the "firm" orientation of *Babywise* proponents. Each side has always thought their way is "The Answer" to the ills of the world. The bottom line is that parents and children are too diverse for a single answer to exist.

When you have two schools of thought, as Steven Mintz says in *Huck's Raft,* there's no end to debates about the "right way." In the 1960s, parenting experts cautioned mothers about overbearing involvement with their children: the precursor to extreme parenting. Theodore Dreikurs in *Children: the Challenge* encouraged parents to foster competence and independence in their kids, because "unrestricted freedom has made tyrants of children and slaves of the parents." How often do you feel like a slave to your own tiny tyrant? In 1968, Dr. Spock spoke out against "the morally and socially corrosive effects of 'today's child-centered viewpoint.'" This was a few short years after he had laid the groundwork for mothers to expend massive amounts of time devoted to their children, entertaining, motivating, and allowing them to vent their feelings! Even the experts can't make up their minds. And when the experts don't have "The Answer" to guarantee the happiness, success, and competitiveness of your child in this world, how can you do anything but overcontrol, overproduce, overprotect, and overperfect? You see no other answer. Extreme parenting is born.

Appendix Two

Perfectly Good Mother Mantras . . .
for Your Dashboard or Your Daytimer

Feel free to copy any of the mantras on the following page that reasonate with you: Don't be afraid to tape them to your vehicle dashboard, your family calendar, or your refrigerator. Let them help you stay focused and refreshed on your journey to being your own Perfectly Good Mother

To Stop Overperfecting

* Parenting is not a contest.
* There are no perfect mothers.
* Taking care of me means more to give to my kids.
* I can live with this.
* So what?
* Many factors affect my child—I don't have to blame myself.
* My day is not ruined if _____.

To Stop Overprotecting

* Children are more resilient than society assumes.
* Children are more capable than society assumes.
* Children are more adaptable than society assumes.
* What are the odds?
* Control what you can; let go of the rest.

To Stop Overproducing

* Parenting is not a contest.
* Less is more.
* Enough for now.
* I need no approval but my own. I know what's best for me and my family.

To Stop Bad Mom Thoughts

* Love the kid, hate the job.
* Parenting is the hardest job I'll ever do—but the rewards will come.
* Being myself is perfectly good.
* I can think for myself.
* No more illogical thinking about parenting.
* _____ doesn't make me a bad mom.
* It's okay to be honest about who I am.
* Every perfectly good mom needs help sometimes.
* I deserve to spend time with women who respect and support me.
* There is nothing the matter with me.

Appendix Three

Resources

Great Books About Real Moms (and Dads)

Borchard, Therese, ed., *The Imperfect Mom: Candid Confessions of Mothers Living in the Real World,* New York: Broadway, 2006.

Buchanan, Andrea, *Mother Shock: Loving Every (Other) Minute of It,* Emeryville, CA: Seal Press, 2003.

Buchanan, Andrea, and Amy Hudock, eds., *Literary Mama: Reading for the Maternally Inclined,* Emeryville, CA: Seal Press, 2005.

Gore, Ariel, ed. *The Essential Hip Mama: Writing from the Cutting Edge of Parenting,* Emeryville, CA: Seal Press, 2004.

Gore, Ariel, *The Mother Trip: Hip Mama's Guide to Staying Sane in the Chaos of Motherhood,* Emeryville, CA: Seal Press, 2000.

Hanauer, Cathi, ed., *The Bitch in the House,* New York: Perennial, 2002.

Jones, Daniel, ed., *The Bastard on the Couch,* New York: Perennial Currents, 2004.

Lamott, Anne, *Operating Instructions: A Journal of My Son's First Year,* New York: Anchor, 2005.

Laskas, Jeanne Marie, *Growing Girls: The Mother of All Adventures,* New York: Bantam, 2006.

Mead-Ferro, Muffy, *Confessions of a Slacker Mom*, Cambridge, MA: Da Capo Lifelong Books, 2004.

Mellor, Christie, *The Three-Martini Playdate: A Practical Guide to Happy Parenting*, San Francisco: Chronicle Books, 2004.

Peri, Camille, and Kate Moses, eds., *Mothers Who Think*, New York: Villard, 1999.

Peri, Camille, and Kate Moses, eds., *Because I Said So*, New York: HarperCollins, 2005.

Shelton, Sandi Kahn, *Preschool Confidential*, New York: St. Martin's Press, 2001.

Shelton, Sandi Kahn, *Sleeping Through the Night and Other Lies*, New York: St. Martin's Press, 2000.

Shelton, Sandi Kahn, *You Might as Well Laugh Because Crying Will Only Smear Your Mascara*, New York: St. Martin's Press, 1999.

Wilder-Taylor, Stefanie, *Sippy Cups Are Not for Chardonnay and Other Things I Had to Learn as a New Mom*, New York: Simon Spotlight Entertainment, 2006.

Books About Reviving Your Sex Life

Raskin, Valerie Davis, *Great Sex for Moms: Ten Steps to Nurturing Passion While Raising Kids*, New York: Fireside, 2002.

Raykeil, Heidi, *Confessions of a Naughty Mommy: How I Found My Lost Libido*, Emeryville, CA: Seal Press, 2006.

Winks, Cathy, and Anne Semans, *Sexy Mamas: Keeping Your Sex Life Alive While Raising Kids*, San Francisco: Inner Ocean Publishing, 2004.

Books About Coping with Other Women

Dellasega, Cheryl, *Mean Girls Grown Up: Adult Women Who Are Still Queen Bees, Middle Bees, and Afraid-to-Bees*, New York: John Wiley and Sons, 2005.

Pryor, Liz, *What Did I Do Wrong: When Women Don't Tell Each Other the Friendship Is Over*, New York: Free Press, 2006.

Wiseman, Rosalind, and Elizabeth Rapoport, *Queen Bee Moms and Kingpin Dads: Dealing with the Parents, Teachers, Coaches, and Counselors Who Can Make—or Break—Your Child's Future,* New York: Three Rivers Press, 2003.

Yager, Jan, *When Friendship Hurts: How to Deal with Friends Who Betray, Abandon, or Wound You,* New York: Fireside Books, 2002.

Helping Professionals: Types and Sources

Psychiatrists

Psychiatrists are physicians (M.D. or D.O.) who have completed additional training in mental health issues. Many psychiatrists see medication as the first option in treatment and may put less emphasis on "talk" or cognitive therapy.

American Psychiatric Association
1000 Wilson Boulevard, Suite 1825
Arlington, VA 22209-3901
(703) 907-7300
www.psych.org

Psychologists

In most states, psychologists are required to have a doctoral degree and to pass a standardized exam for licensure. Some states license master's-level psychologists. Clinical and counseling psychologists have special training in psychotherapy, but in almost all states are not able to administer medication. Many psychologists, however, work in close consultation with a physician who can prescribe medications.

American Psychological Association
750 First Street NE
Washington, DC 20002-4242
(800) 374-2721
www.apa.org

National Register of Health Service Providers in Psychology
1120 G Street NW, Ste 330
Washington DC 20005
(202) 783-7663
www.nationalregister.org

Other Therapists and Counselors

Many helping professionals have a master's degree in social work (M.S.W.) or a master's degree in marriage and family counseling (M.S. or M.A.). Many states require clinical social workers to be licensed; investigate the requirements in your state. There is a wide range of training, background, and credentials among persons who call themselves therapists or counselors, usually with a minimum of a master's degree in counseling, education, psychology, or a related field. Marriage and family counselors have training primarily in relationship, rather than individual, issues. Pastoral counselors often place special emphasis on religious issues in therapy and may be ordained clergy as well.

American Association for Marriage and Family Therapy
112 South Alfred Street
Alexandria, VA 22314-3061
(703) 838-9808
www.aamft.org

American Association of Pastoral Counselors

9504A Lee Highway

Fairfax, VA 22031

(703) 385-6967

www.aapc.org

National Association of Social Workers

750 First Street NE, Suite 700

Washington, DC 20002

(800) 638-8799

www.socialworkers.org

References

Chapter 1

Douglas, Susan J., and Meredith W. Michaels, *The Mommy Myth: The Idealization of Motherhood and How It Has Undermined All Women* (New York: Free Press, 2005).

Kasen, Stephanie, Patricia Cohen, Henian Chen, and Dorothy Castille, "Depression in Adult Women: Age Changes and Cohort Effects," *American Journal of Public Health,* vol. 93, no. 12, 2003.

Pearson, Allison, *I Don't Know How She Does It* (New York: Random House, 2002).

Schappell, Elissa, "Crossing the Line in the Sand: How Mad Can Mother Get?" in *The Bitch in the House: 26 Women Tell the Truth About Sex, Solitude, Work, Motherhood, and Marriage,* ed. Cathi Hanauer (New York: Perennial, 2002).

Van Ogtrop, Kristin, "Attila the Honey I'm Home," in *The Bitch in the House: 26 Women Tell the Truth About Sex, Solitude, Work, Motherhood, and Marriage,* ed. Cathi Hanauer (New York: Perennial, 2002).

Warner, Judith, *Perfect Madness: Motherhood in the Age of Anxiety* (New York: Riverhead Books, 2005).

Chapter 2

Barry, Dave, *Dave Barry's Money Secrets: Like, Why Is There a Giant Eyeball on the Dollar?* (New York: Crown Publishers, 2006).

Belkin, Lisa, "The Mother of All Conflicts," *O/The Oprah Magazine*, May 2006.

Bolotin, Susan, "The Disciples of Discipline," *New York Times Magazine*, February 14, 1999.

Bowlby, John, *Attachment and Loss* (New York, Basic Books, 1969).

Buchanan, Andrea, quoted in Victoria Clayton, "Overparenting: When Good Intentions Go Too Far, Kids Can Suffer," MSNBC.com, December 7, 2004. Retrieved January 16, 2007, at http://www.mothershock.com/blog/archives/2004/12/overparenting.html.

Chief Learning Officer, "Survey: Fewer Executives and Managers Working Long Hours," *Industry News*. Retrieved April 12, 2006, at http://www.clomedia.com/common/newscenter/newsdisplay.cfm?id=5065.

Clayton, Victoria, "Overparenting: When Good Intentions Go Too Far, Kids Can Suffer." Retrieved January 16, 2007, at http://www.mothershock.com/blog/archives/2004/12/overparenting.html.

"Daddy's Boy," *House, M.D.*, Season 2, Episode 5, Fox Television, 2006.

Douglas, Susan J., and Meredith W. Michaels, *The Mommy Myth: The Idealization of Motherhood and How It Has Undermined All Women* (New York: Free Press, 2005).

Marano, Hara Estroff, "A Nation of Wimps," *Psychology Today*, November/December 2004.

Evanson, Ranae, and Robin Simon, "Clarifying the Relationship Between Parenthood and Depression," *Journal of Health and Social Behavior*, vol. 46, no. 4, 2005.

Friedan, Betty, *The Feminine Mystique* (New York, W. W. Norton, 1963).

Furstenberg, Frank, "The Sociology of Adolescence and Youth in the 1990s: A Critical Commentary," *Journal of Marriage and the Family*, vol. 62, no. 4.

Hays, Sharon, *The Cultural Contradictions of Motherhood* (New Haven, CT: Yale University Press, 1998).

Hulbert, Ann, *Raising America: Experts, Parents, and a Century of Advice About Children* (New York: Knopf, 2003).

Kahneman, Daniel, Alan B. Krueger, David A. Schkade, Norbert Schwarz, and Arthur A. Stone, "A Survey Method for Characterizing Daily Life Experience: The Day Reconstruction Method," *Science*, vol. 306, no. 5702, 2004.

Kasen, Stephanie, Patricia Cohen, Henian Chen, and Dorothy Castille, "Depression in Adult Women: Age Changes and Cohort Effects," *American Journal of Public Health*, vol. 93, no. 12, 2003.

Mead-Ferro, Muffy, *Confessions of a Slacker Mom* (Cambridge, MA: De Capo Life Long Books, 2004), 134.

Opinion Research Corporation, poll, April 8–11, 2006, reported in *Dallas Morning News*, May 4, 2006.

Orenstein, Peggy, *Flux: Women on Sex, Work, Love, Kids, and Life in a Half-Changed World* (New York: Anchor Books, 2001).

Pearson, Allison, *I Don't Know How She Does It* (New York: Random House, 2002).

Quindlen, Anna, "The Good Enough Mother," *Newsweek*, February 21, 2005.

Robinson, Linda. "Antidepressant Trends Among Children Diagnosed with Depression, 1990–2001." Paper presented at the 2004 annual meeting of the American Psychiatric Association, New York.

Spock, Benjamin, *Baby and Child Care* (New York: Pocket Books, 1968).

Stearns, Peter, *Anxious Parents: A History of Modern Childrearing in America* (New York: New York University Press, 2003).

"Survey of Motherhood," *Redbook*, March 2006. Retrieved January 16, 2007, at http://www.98pxy.com/Detail.aspx?dct=17&id=2073&mid=216.

Warner, Judith, *Perfect Madness: Motherhood in the Age of Anxiety* (New York: Riverhead Books, 2005).

Washington, Shirley, and Ann Dunnewold, *The Motherhood Club* (Deerfield Beach, FL: Health Communications, Inc., 2003).

Chapter 3

American Academy of Pediatrics, "Media Guidelines for Parents." Retrieved January 16, 2007, at http://www.aap.org/pubed/ZZZGVL4PQ7C.htm?&sub_cat=17.

Billingsley, Barbara, interview by Karen Herman, July 14, 2000, Archives of American Television, Academy of Television Arts and Sciences Foundation. Retrieved January 16, 2007, at www.emmystv.com.

Bodden, Alonzo, *Last Comic Standing,* NBC, August 9, 2006.

Bordessa, Kris, "Are Today's Kids Overpraised? Yes!" *Brain, Child,* Summer 2004.

Colbert, Stephen, interview by Morley Safer, *Sixty Minutes,* CBS, April 30, 2006.

Cottle, Michelle, "This Essay Will Help Your Kid Get Ahead," *Time,* September 4, 2006.

Culbreth, Judson, "The Perfect Childhood: Why It's Bad For Kids," *Reader's Digest,* September 2005.

The Early Show, "Outsourcing Messier Parts of Parenting." CBS News. Retrieved January 16, 2007, at http://www.cbsnews.com/stories/2006/04/17/earlyshow/living/parenting/main1502329.shtml.

Failure to Launch, Paramount Pictures, 2006.

"Fathers Influence Child Language Development More than Mothers," *Science Daily,* November 1, 2006. Retrieved January 16, 2007, at http://www.sciencedaily.com/releases/2006/10/061030183039.htm.

Floyd, Jacquielynn, "Parents, It's Time to Lose Your Cool," *Dallas Morning News,* October 2, 2004.

Fulmer, Melinda, "Kids' Parties at Spare-No-Expense Prices," *MSN Money.* Retrieved January 16, 2007, at http://articles.moneycentral.msn.com/College AndFamily/RaiseKids/KidsPartiesatSpareNoExpensePrices.aspx.

Gibbs, Nancy, "Parents Behaving Badly," *Time,* February 21, 2005.

"How to Be a Cool Parent," *Overflow.* Retrieved January 16, 2007, at http://cross impact.net/archives/2005/10/31/how-to-be-a-cool-parent.

Interview with panel of mothers, KERA 90FM, May 8, 2005.

Jacobs, Mary, "Avoiding the Madness: Cocktail Mom," *Dallas Morning News*, March 23, 2005.

Kilcoyne, Colleen, "I Killed June Cleaver," in *I Killed June Cleaver: Modern Moms Shatter the Myth of Perfect Parenting*, ed. Deborah Werksman (Naperville, IL: Sourcebooks, Inc., 1999).

Klaus, Marshall, and John Kennell, *Parent-Infant Bonding* (St. Louis, MO: Mosby, 1982).

Knudsen, Eric I., James J. Heckman, Judy L. Cameron, and Jack P. Shonkoff, "Economic, Neurobiological, and Behavioral Perspectives on Building America's Future Workforce," *Proceedings of National Academy of Sciences*, vol. 103, no. 27, 2006.

Kohn, Alfie, *Punished by Rewards: The Trouble with Gold Stars, Incentive Plans, A's, Praise, and Other Bribes* (New York: Houghton Mifflin, 1993).

Lamott, Anne, "Mother Anger: Theory and Practice," in *Mothers Who Think*, ed. Camille Peri and Kate Moses (New York: Villard, 1999).

Laskas, Jeanne Marie, "A Reality Check from a Mom," *Dallas Morning News*, August 21, 2006.

Mean Girls, Paramount Pictures, 2004.

Mintz, Steven, *Huck's Raft: A History of American Childhood* (Cambridge, MA: The Belknap Press of Harvard University Press, 2004).

Neal, Nicole, "How Dangerous Is Childhood?" *Palm Beach Post*, August 13, 2006.

Pearson, Allison, *I Don't Know How She Does It* (New York: Random House, 2002).

Pierpont, Ian, Synovate vice president, quoted in Jacquielynn Floyd, "Parents, It's Time to Lose Your Cool," *Dallas Morning News*, October 2, 2004.

Quart, Alissa, *Hothouse Kids: The Dilemma of the Gifted Child* (New York: Penguin, 2006).

Quindlen, Anna, "The Good Enough Mother," *Newsweek*, February 21, 2005.

Smith, Holly, "Apgar Prep," *Brain, Child*, Summer 2003.

Twenge, Jean, interview by Katie Couric, *Today Show*, NBC, April 20, 2006.

Chapter 4

Alpha omicron pi, definitions. Retrieved January 16, 2007, at http://www.urbandictionary.com/define.php?term=alpha+omicron+pi.

Angelou, Maya, *Wouldn't Take Nothing for My Journey Now* (New York: Random House, 1993).

Buchanan, Andrea, quoted in Victoria Clayton, "Overparenting: When Good Intentions Go Too Far, Kids Can Suffer," MSNBC.com, December 7, 2004. Retrieved January 16, 2007, at http://www.mothershock.com/blog/archives/2004/12/overparenting.html.

Edelman, Hope, "The Myth of Co-Parenting," in *The Bitch in the House: 26 Women Tell the Truth About Sex, Solitude, Work, Motherhood, and Marriage,* ed. Cathi Hanauer (New York: Perennial, 2002).

Gibbs, Nancy, "Parents Behaving Badly," *Time,* February 21, 2005.

Jacobs, Mary, "Avoiding the Madness: Cocktail Mom," *Dallas Morning News,* March 23, 2005.

Kilcoyne, Colleen, "I Killed June Cleaver," in *I Killed June Cleaver: Modern Moms Shatter the Myth of Perfect Parenting,* ed. Deborah Werksman (Naperville, IL: Sourcebooks, Inc., 1999).

McKay, Matthew, Martha Davis, and Patrick Fanning, in *Thoughts and Feelings: Taking Control of Your Moods and Your Life* (Oakland, CA: New Harbinger, 1998), excerpted in *Family Guide to Emotional Wellness,* eds. Patrick Fanning and Matthew McKay (Oakland, CA: New Harbinger, 2000).

Satran, Pamela Redmond, "The Secrets Moms Keep," *Parenting,* August 2004.

Stella Artois advertisement.

Van Ogtrop, Kristin, "Attila the Honey I'm Home," in *The Bitch in the House: 26 Women Tell the Truth About Sex, Solitude, Work, Motherhood, and Marriage,* ed. Cathi Hanauer (New York: Perennial, 2002).

Warner, Judith, *Perfect Madness: Motherhood in the Age of Anxiety* (New York: Riverhead Books, 2005).

Winnicott, D. W., "Transitional Objects and Transitional Phenomena—A Study of the First Not-Me Possession," *International Journal of Psychoanalysis* (1953), 34.

Chapter 5

Angelou, Maya, *Wouldn't Take Nothing for My Journey Now* (New York: Random House, 1993).

Churchill, Jill, quoted in "The Truth About Motherhood," *Redbook,* May 2005.

Guthrie, Elisabeth, and Kathy Matthews, *No More Push Parenting: How to Find Success and Balance in a Hypercompetitive World* (New York: Broadway Books, 2002).

Harris, Joyce Sáenz, "Toasting (Toasted?) Motherhood," *Dallas Morning News,* July 26, 2006.

Kerner, Sarah, "Straddling Two Worlds," *Dallas Morning News,* May 15, 2006.

Mead-Ferro, Muffy, *Confessions of a Slacker Mom* (Cambridge, MA: De Capo Life Long Books, 2004).

Quindlen, Anna, "The Good Enough Mother," *Newsweek,* February 21, 2005.

———, *Being Perfect* (New York: Random House, 2005).

Schappell, Elissa, "Crossing the Line in the Sand: How Mad Can Mother Get?" in *The Bitch in the House: 26 Women Tell the Truth About Sex, Solitude, Work, Motherhood, and Marriage,* ed. Cathi Hanauer (New York: Perennial, 2002).

Squire, Susan, "Maternal Bitch," in *The Bitch in the House: 26 Women Tell the Truth About Sex, Solitude, Work, Motherhood, and Marriage,* ed. Cathi Hanauer (New York: Perennial, 2002).

Wiseman, Rosalind, and Elizabeth Rapoport, *Queen Bee Moms and Kingpin Dads: Dealing with the Parents, Teachers, Coaches, and Counselors Who Can Make—or Break—Your Child's Future* (New York: Three Rivers Press, 2003).

Chapter 6

Gold, Taro, *Tao of Mom: Wisdom of Mothers from East to West* (Kansas City: Andrews McMeel, 2004).

Keillor, Garrison, host of *Prairie Home Companion,* American Public Media, http://prairiehome.publicradio.org.

LeShan, Eda, "When You Can't Make It 'All Better,'" *Parents,* October 1992.

Marano, Hara Estroff, "A Nation of Wimps," *Psychology Today,* November/ December 2004.

Mintz, Steven, *Huck's Raft: A History of American Childhood* (Cambridge, MA: The Belknap Press of Harvard University Press, 2004).

Parker, Wayne, "Top 10 Ways to Balance Life and Work." Retrieved January 16, 2007, at fatherhood.about.com/od/workingfathers/tp/balance_ideas.htm.

Wiseman, Rosalind, and Elizabeth Rapoport, *Queen Bee Moms and Kingpin Dads: Dealing with the Parents, Teachers, Coaches, and Counselors Who Can Make—or Break—Your Child's Future* (New York: Three Rivers Press, 2003).

Chapter 7

Andreano, Lauren, "The McSecret," in *I Killed June Cleaver: Modern Moms Shatter The Myth of Perfect Parenting,* ed. Deborah Werksman (Naperville, IL: Sourcebooks, Inc., 1999).

Angelou, Maya, *Wouldn't Take Nothing for My Journey Now* (New York: Random House, 1993).

Buchanan, Andrea, quoted in Victoria Clayton, "Overparenting: When Good Intentions Go Too Far, Kids Can Suffer," MSNBC.com, December 7, 2004. Retrieved January 16, 2007, at http://www.mothershock.com/blog/archives/ 2004/12/overparenting.html.

Debroff, Stacy, "Tips to Help You Boost Your Mommy Confidence," July 24, 2006, MSNBC. Retrieved January 16, 2007, at http://www.msnbc.msn.com/id/ 14008697.

Dellasega, Cheryl, *Mean Girls Grown Up: Adult Women Who Are Still Queen Bees, Middle Bees, and Afraid-to-Bees* (New York: Wiley, 2005).

Douglas, Susan J., and Meredith W. Michaels, *The Mommy Myth: The Idealization of Motherhood and How It Has Undermined All Women* (New York: Free Press, 2005).

Ellison, Sheila, *How Does She Do It? 101 Life Lessons from One Mother to Another* (San Francisco: Harper Collins, 2004).

Gibbs, Nancy, "Parents Behaving Badly," *Time,* February 21, 2005.

Guthrie, Elisabeth, and Kathy Matthews, *No More Push Parenting: How to Find Success and Balance in a Hypercompetitive World* (New York: Broadway Books, 2002).

Hanauer, Cathi, ed., *The Bitch in the House:26 Women Tell the Truth About Sex, Solitude, Work, Motherhood, and Marriage* (New York: Perennial, 2002).

Interview with panel of mothers, KERA 90FM, May 8, 2005.

Kerner, Sarah, "Straddling Two Worlds," *Dallas Morning News,* May 15, 2006.

Lamott, Anne, "Mother Anger: Theory and Practice," in *Mothers Who Think,* ed. Camille Peri and Kate Moses (New York: Villard, 1999).

McKay, Matthew, Martha Davis, and Patrick Fanning, in *Thoughts and Feelings: Taking Control of Your Moods and Your Life* (Oakland, CA: New Harbinger, 1998), excerpted in *Family Guide to Emotional Wellness,* eds. Patrick Fanning and Matthew McKay (Oakland, CA: New Harbinger, 2000).

Mead-Ferro, Muffy, *Confessions of a Slacker Mom* (Cambridge, MA: De Capo Life Long Books, 2004).

Mellor, Christie, *The Three-Martini Playdate: A Practical Guide to Happy Parenting* (San Francisco: Chronicle Books, 2004).

Newman, Judith, "Be Your Own Woman," *Ladies' Home Journal,* March 2005.

Pearson, Allison, *I Don't Know How She Does It* (New York: Random House, 2002).

Rich, Adrienne, *Of Woman Born* (New York: W. W. Norton, 1976, 1995).

Solomon, Rivka, ed., *That Takes Ovaries: Bold Females and Their Brazen Acts* (New York: Three Rivers Press, 2002).

Tanenbaum, Leora, *Catfight: Women and Competition* (New York: Seven Stories Press, 2002).

Wilder-Taylor, Stefanie, *Sippy Cups Are Not for Chardonnay and Other Things I Had to Learn as a New Mom* (New York: Simon Spotlight Entertainment, 2006).

Wiseman, Rosalind, and Elizabeth Rapoport, *Queen Bee Moms and Kingpin Dads: Dealing with the Parents, Teachers, Coaches, and Counselors Who Can Make—or Break—Your Child's Future* (New York: Three Rivers Press, 2003).

Chapter 8

Blanchard, Ken, "Dad Anxiety," *Parents,* August 1999.

Boizan, Natalie, Fran Gale, Michael Dudley, "Time to Father," *Social Work in HealthCare,* vol. 39, no. 1–2, 2004.

Browder, Walter, and Sue Ellin Browder, *101 Secrets a Good Dad Knows* (Nashville, TN: Rutledge Hill Press, 2000).

Canty, Kevin, "The Dog in Me," in *The Bastard on the Couch,* ed. Daniel Jones (New York: Perennial Currents, 2004).

Chatwin, Sara, "Stress and Anxiety," Littlies for Practical Parenting. Retrieved January 16, 2007, at http://www.littlies.co.nz/page.asp?id=229&level=2.

Coakley, Jay, "The Good Father: Parental Expectations and Youth Sports," *Leisure Studies,* vol. 25, no. 2, 2006.

————————, personal communication, October 2006.

Condon, J., P. Boyce, C. Corkindale, "The First-Time Fathers Study: A Prospective Study of the Mental Health and Wellbeing of Men During the Transition to Parenthood," *Australia/New Zealand Journal of Psychiatry,* vol. 38, no.1–2, 2004.

Crenshaw, Jeannette, personal communication.

Derbyshire, John, "The Straggler: Dads and Cads: Child-raising Guilt," *National Review,* February 24, 2003.

Fish, Joel, and Susan Magee, "101 Ways to Be a Terrific Sports Parent." Retrieved January 16, 2007, at http://www.enotalone.com/article/5442.html.

Giardina, Anthony, "A Brief History of the (Over)involved Father," in *The Bastard on the Couch,* ed. Daniel Jones (New York: Perennial Currents, 2004).

Gibbs, Nancy, "Parents Behaving Badly," *Time,* February 21, 2005.

Gray, John, *Men Are from Mars, Women Are from Venus: A Practical Guide for Improving Communication and Getting What You Want in Your Relationships* (New York: HarperCollins, 1992).

Greenburg, Gary, "Gravity Sucks," *Brain, Child,* Fall 2006.

Hilling, Hogan, *The Man Who Would Be Dad* (Herndon, VA: Capital Books, 2002).

Horowitz, Michael, Ph.D., codirector of the Fatherhood Research Project, personal communication, November 2, 2006.

Keer, Gregory, "Tapping Dad's Potential." Retrieved January 16, 2007, at http://fatherhood.about.com/od/newdadsresources/a/dads_potential.htm.

Liberman, Mark, "Sex-Linked Lexical Budgets." Retrieved January 16, 2007, at http://itre.cis.upenn.edu/~myl/languagelog/archives/003420.html.

Matjasko, Jennifer, and Amy Feldman, "Bringing Work Home: The Emotional Experience of Mothers and Fathers," *Journal of Family Psychology*, vol. 20, no. 1, 2006.

The National Fatherhood Initiative, "Fatherhood and TV: An Evaluation Report," Gaithersburg, Maryland. Retrieved May 22, 2001, at http://www.father hood.org.

Reimer, Susan, "Manny from Heaven," *Dallas Morning News*, October 16, 2006.

Saltz, Gail, and Drew Pinsky, interview with Meredith Vieira, *The Today Show*, NBC, September 28, 2006.

Scharrer, Erica, personal communication, October 2006.

"Survey: Many Dads Willing to Stay Home: Almost Half of Fathers Would Take Pay Cut to Spend More Time with Kids." Retrieved January 16, 2007, at http://www.thebostonchannel.com/asseenon5/9373551/detail.html.

"Tapping Dad's Potential," *Dallas Morning News* poll, quoted by Gregory Keer. Retrieved January 16, 2007, at http://fatherhood.about.com/od/newdadsre-sources/a/dads_potential.htm.

"Tensions Faced by Working Fathers," 1999 National Center for Fathering. Retrieved January 16, 2007, at http://www.fathers.com/research/fatherbalance. html.

Tarrant, Dave, "Avoiding the Madness: Why Are Dads Always Left Out of the Discussion?" *Dallas Morning News*, March 23, 2005.

Tierney, John, "The Doofus Dad," *New York Times*, June 18, 2005.

Van Ogtrop, Kristin, "Attila the Honey I'm Home," in *The Bitch in the House: 26 Women Tell the Truth About Sex, Solitude, Work, Motherhood, and Marriage*, ed. Cathi Hanauer (New York: Perennial, 2002).

Walters, Mark, "Control: The Problem with Jumping in Puddles," *Brain, Child,* Spring 2004.

Chapter 9

Allen, Ann, "Being A Mother at Home: My Feminist Choice," *Feminist Mothers at Home.* Retrieved January 16, 2007, at http://homepages.rootsweb.com/~home spun/mdstories4.html.

Blades, Joan, and Kristin Rowe-Finkbeiner, *The Motherhood Manifesto: What America's Moms Want—and What to Do About It* (New York: Nation Press, 2006).

Brainchildmag.com. For information about *Brain, Child, The Magazine for Thinking Mothers,* visit the Web site at http://www.brainchildmag.com.

Cookie, October/November, 2006.

Crittenden, Ann, *The Price of Motherhood: Why the Most Important Job in The World Is Still the Least Valued* (Metropolitan Books, 2002).

Duncan Hines ad, *Dallas Morning News,* November 5, 2006.

Family and Work Institute, "National Study of the Changing Workforce Reveals Significant Changes in Work and Family Lives of U.S. Employes." Retrieved January 16, 2007, at http://www.familiesandwork.org/press/NSCW2002 release.html.

Gold, Taro, *Tao of Mom: Wisdom of Mothers from East to West* (Kansas City: Andrews McMeel, 2004).

"Mail Call: Our Readers on the Tragedy of Andrea Yates and the Toll of Post-partum Depression," *Newsweek,* July 23, 2001.

Margaret Mead quote used courtesy of The Institute for Intercultural Studies, Inc., New York.

Poppei, Amanda, "Shattering the Myth: Feminism Is not a Dirty Word," *Yale Herald.* Retrieved January 16, 2007, at http://www.yaleherald.com/archive/xxvi/ 10.9.98/opinion/feminism.html.

Rice, Marcy Smith, "It's Not a Dirty Word." Retrieved January 16, 2007, at http:// www.newsobserver.com/105/story/488830.html.

Ritter, Barb, "Five Myths About Feminists," *The Feminist Psychologist,* Winter 2005.

Warner, Judith, *Perfect Madness: Motherhood in the Age of Anxiety* (New York: Riverhead Books, 2005).

Wilkinson, Stephanie, "Say You Want a Revolution," *Brain, Child,* Fall 2005.

Appendix One

Coakley, Jay, personal communication, October 2006.

Dreikurs, Rudolf, with Vicki Stolz, *Children: The Challenge* (New York: Plume, 1964).

Ezzo, Gary, and Robert Bucknam, *On Becoming Babywise* (Sisters, OR: Multnomah Books, 1995).

Hogg, Tracy, *Secrets of the Baby Whisperer: How to Calm, Connect, and Communicate with Your Baby* (New York: Ballantine Books, 2001).

Hulbert, Ann, *Raising America: Experts, Parents, and a Century of Advice About Children* (New York: Knopf, 2003).

Karp, Harvey, *The Happiest Baby on the Block: The New Way to Calm Crying and Help Your Baby Sleep Longer* (New York: Bantam Books, 2002).

Mintz, Steven, *Huck's Raft: A History of American Childhood* (Cambridge, MA: The Belknap Press of Harvard University Press, 2004).

Pantley, Elizabeth, *The No-Cry Sleep Solution: Gentle Ways to Help Your Baby Sleep Through the Night* (New York: McGraw-Hill, 2002).

Sears, Martha, and William Sears, *The Attachment Parenting Book: A No-Nonsense Guide to Understanding and Nurturing Your Baby* (Boston: Little, Brown, 2001).

Spock, Benjamin, *Baby and Child Care,* (New York: Pocket Books, 1968).

Stearns, Peter, *Anxious Parents: A History of Modern Childrearing in America* (New York: New York University Press, 2003).

http://www.1970sflashback.com/1970/Economy.asp

Index

About the Author

Ann Dunnewold, Ph.D., is a licensed psychologist and a nationally recognized expert on postpartum depression and anxiety. She has appeared as an expert on the *Today Show* and has been quoted in *Fit Pregnancy*, *Parents*, and *Dallas Child* magazines. She also has appeared in two videos, which air in many hospital systems through the Lamaze Channel. She is the coauthor of *Postpartum Survival Guide* and *The Motherhood Club*.

Dr. Dunnewold has raised two daughters—both great kids. Reach her at: adunnewold@yahoo.com.